DESIGN, MAKE, PLAY

"The case for the urgent need to inspire more young people to pursue college and career in science, technology, engineering, and mathematics is irrefutable. Our leadership abroad and quality of life at home depend upon it. Now comes this delightful, thoughtful, and practical book that tells us how to move forward. Using real-world examples, it shows us how to ignite passion, stimulate learning, and equip a diverse generation of innovators and makers. If you care about the future of our country, you should read this book and then put its lessons to work. Few things are as important."
　　　　　—Ursula Burns, Chairwoman and CEO, Xerox Corporation

"In our digitally interconnected world, it is possible to forget the importance of children touching and making things as a key element of enhancing their learning. Touching and making sparks their imaginations and excites them about science and engineering. The idea of time together to design, and actually touch and make things, as part of play, is important to enhancing our children's education. This book elucidates the important role of extracurricular learning that takes place outside of the formal school setting. Design, Make, Play is a book that every individual interested in STEM education and our children's overall educational progress should read."
　　　　　—Shirley Ann Jackson, Ph.D., President, Rensselaer
　　　　　Polytechnic Institute

"Margaret Honey and David Kanter have created a thought-provoking volume on one of contemporary education's most pressing challenges: how to ensure—and further, enhance—engaging STEM learning at America's schools in the 21st century. Universities, facing the prospect of a dwindling pipeline of STEM-qualified students, have a direct stake in the outcomes. By showcasing cutting-edge methods, the contributors argue convincingly for the power of creative, hands-on instructional play in fostering the love of learning critical for success in school, college, and far beyond."
　　　　　—John Sexton, President, New York University

"Design, Make, Play is a wonderful and useful book. (In fact, any book with a chapter entitled "No Bored Kids" is bound to be helpful.) Through multiple case studies, it shows in concrete ways how to initiate, integrate, and promote the learning and joy of science through discovery and doing. Many pay lip service to discovery-based learning, but this book presents the real thing. This book accomplishes something else very important—it has discovered the T and E in STEM through its cogent presentations about tinkering and about the Maker movement and its philosophy. This is a great read and guide to those interested in retooling STEM education for early learners."

—Charles Vest, President, National Academy of Engineering;
President Emeritus, Massachusetts Institute of Technology

Design, Make, Play: Growing the Next Generation of STEM Innovators is a resource for practitioners, policymakers, researchers, and program developers that illuminates creative, cutting edge ways to inspire and motivate young people about science and technology learning. The book is aligned with the National Research Council's new Framework for Science Education, which includes an explicit focus on engineering and design content, as well as integration across disciplines. Extensive case studies explore real-world examples of innovative programs that take place in a variety of settings, including schools, museums, community centers, and virtual spaces. Design, Make, and Play are each presented as learning methodologies that have the power to rekindle children's intrinsic motivation and innate curiosity about STEM (science, technology, engineering, and mathematics) fields. A companion website (dmp.nysci.org) showcases rich multimedia that brings the stories and successes of each program—and the students who learn there—to life.

Dr. Margaret Honey is President and CEO of the New York Hall of Science.

Dr. David E. Kanter is Director of the Sara Lee Schupf Family Center for Play, Science, and Technology Learning at the New York Hall of Science.

DESIGN, MAKE, PLAY
GROWING THE NEXT GENERATION
OF STEM INNOVATORS

EDITED BY
MARGARET HONEY
DAVID E. KANTER

Routledge
Taylor & Francis Group

NEW YORK AND LONDON

First published 2013
by Routledge
711 Third Avenue, New York, NY 10017

Simultaneously published in the UK
by Routledge
2 Park Square, Milton Park, Abingdon, Oxon OX14 4RN

Routledge is an imprint of the Taylor & Francis Group, an informa business

Library of Congress Cataloging in Publication Data
    Design, make, play: growing the next generation of STEM innovators /
    edited by Margaret Honey and David E. Kanter.
    p. cm.
    Includes bibliographical references and index.
    1. Science—Study and teaching—Activity programs.
    2. Technology—Study and teaching—Activity programs.
    3. Mathematics—Study and teaching—Activity programs.
    I. Honey, Margaret. II. Kanter, David (David E.)
    Q181.D369 2013
    500.1—dc23
    2012029542

ISBN: 978-0-415-53916-6 (hbk)
ISBN: 978-0-415-53920-3 (pbk)
ISBN: 978-0-203-10835-2 (ebk)

Typeset in Minion
by Florence Production Ltd, Stoodleigh, Devon, UK

CONTENTS

CONTRIBUTORS

Philip Bell pursues a cognitive and cultural program of research across diverse environments focused on how people learn about STEM in ways that are personally consequential to them. He is an Associate Professor of the Learning Sciences at the University of Washington, Seattle, where he directs the Institute for Science and Math Education and co-directs the NSF-funded Learning in Informal and Formal Environments (LIFE) center. He was a member of the committee that authored the National Research Council "Framework for K-12 Science Education."

Dorothy Bennett is Director of Design-Based Learning in Schools at the New York Hall of Science (NYSCI). She has over 25 years of experience researching and developing educational media, curricula, and teacher enhancement programs in science, mathematics, and technology. She has collaborated with a broad range of institutions to investigate and develop programs that explore how design can serve as a powerful pathway into science and technology for children, including the American Museum of Natural History, the Australian Children's Television Foundation, IBM, CUNY Schools of Engineering, and K-12 school districts across the country. She was also a formative researcher for five years with the Children's Television Workshop's award-winning mathematics series, *Square One TV*. She holds a master's of science in Education from Bank Street College of Education.

Bronwyn Bevan is Associate Director of Program at San Francisco's Exploratorium, where she has worked since 1991. Bevan serves as Principal or Co-Principal Investigator on several projects, including the

NSF AYS Research & Evaluation Center; the *California Informal Science Education Makers Network*; and the *Relating Research to Practice* project. Bevan's work in both research and professional development focuses on how different institutional settings shape opportunities for learning. She is an editor of the Science Learning in Everyday Life section of the journal *Science Education.*

Lisa Brahms is Director of Learning and Research, and Research Fellow at Children's Museum of Pittsburgh. She has been a facilitator and designer of formal and informal learning experiences and environments for over a decade, working in schools, and at many museums including Brooklyn Children's Museum, American Museum of Natural History, New Museum of Contemporary Art, and the Center for Architecture Foundation. Lisa holds a master's degree in Museum Education and Childhood Education from Bank Street School of Education. She is currently pursuing her Ph.D. in learning sciences and policy at the University of Pittsburgh, where she is a member of the University of Pittsburgh Center for Learning in Out of School Environments (UPCLOSE) at the Learning Research and Development Center (LRDC). As the Children's Museum's Director of Learning and Research Fellow, Lisa's research considers the design of informal learning environments for meaningful participation in creative processes with digital and physical media.

Greg Brown joined the executive team of RAFT, Resource Area For Teaching, in 2008 and today is its Director of Education. Earlier in his career, he served as a manager at the FMC Corporate Technology Center, where he directed leading-edge work in robotics, simulation, human factors, video, and design. Following FMC, Greg was a member of the start-up team at the Tech Museum of Innovation. As the Tech's Vice President of Content Development, Greg worked with teachers and technologists to define the mission and content for the museum. He led the development of over 200 hands-on exhibits and educational programs and set up programs to recruit and train gallery specialists and volunteers. Greg launched the Tech Challenge, a design-based learning competition now in its 25th year. Greg has taught at both San Jose State and Stanford University, and has served on nonprofit boards, including the International Science and Engineering Fair and the Third Street Community Center. Greg is a registered professional engineer and holds a master's of science in Engineering from Stanford University.

Ruth Diones is a Research Fellow at the Sara Lee Schupf Family Center for Play, Science, and Technology Learning (SciPlay) at NYSCI. She graduated from CUNY Graduate Center with a Ph.D. in Educational Psychology (Quantitative Methods and Research Design).

Dale Dougherty is the co-founder of O'Reilly Media based in Sebastopol, California. He is the founding editor and publisher of *Make* magazine and the co-creator of Maker Faire. *Make* magazine started in 2005, followed by the first Maker Faire, in the Bay Area, in 2006. In 2011, Maker Faire was held in the Bay Area to over 100,000 guests, and also at a smaller scale in Detroit and New York City. Dale was a lecturer at the UC Berkeley School of Information from 1997 to 2002. Prior to *Make*, he was the developer of Global Network Navigator (GNN), the first commercial website, launched in 1993 and sold to America Online in 1995. He was also developer and publisher of *Web Review*, the online magazine for web designers from 1995 to 1999. Dale was publisher of the O'Reilly Network and developed the Hacks series of books. He is passionate about fostering a new generation of "makers" who are creative, innovative, and curious. On February 19, 2012, he was featured on CNN's "The Next List," and interviewed by Sanjay Gupta at *Make* headquarters in Sebastopol. On November 3, 2011, the White House recognized Dale as one of the "Champions of Change: Make It in America," for his work in helping to create high-quality jobs in the United States. In May 2012, Dale led the launch of the Maker Education Initiative, a nonprofit dedicated to creating opportunities for young people to make.

Adiel Fernandez is project manager and lead instructional designer for the Sara Lee Schupf Family Center for Play, Science, and Technology Learning (SciPlay) at NYSCI. He has a B.S. in Physics with a specialization in Science Education from City College, CUNY, and will soon begin graduate studies in Design and Technology at Parsons The New School for Design.

Kelly Fisher, Ph.D., is an SRCD/AAAS Executive Branch Fellow and the co-founder of Global Abilities Foundation. Her research examines how playful learning influences children's early learning, development, and creative problem-solving. She also examines the impact of educational interventions on learning and development of children and adults with diverse backgrounds and abilities. In addition to her research, Kelly is deeply invested in translating science to practice. She provides consultation and presentations to educators, parents, museum staff, health professionals, researchers, and federal agencies.

Roberta Michnick Golinkoff, Ph.D., H. Rodney Sharp Professor of Education at the University of Delaware, has won the John Simon Guggenheim Fellowship, the James McKeen Cattell prize, the American Psychological Association's Award for Distinguished Service to Psychological Science, and the Urie Bronfenbrenner Lifetime Achievement

Award. She recently won the Francis Alison Award, the highest honor at her university. Having written over 150 articles and 12 books, including *A Mandate for Playful Learning in Preschool* (Oxford), she is an expert on language development and playful learning. Passionate about dissemination, she co-founded the Ultimate Block Party movement to celebrate the science behind play.

Kathy Hirsh-Pasek is the Stanley and Debra Lefkowitz Fellow in the Department of Psychology at Temple University, where she serves as Director of the Infant Language Laboratory and Co-Founder of CiRCLE (The Center for Re-Imagining Children's Learning and Education). Kathy received her bachelor's degree from the University of Pittsburgh and her Ph.D. at the University of Pennsylvania. Her research in the areas of early language development, literacy, and infant cognition has been funded by the National Science Foundation, the National Institutes of Health and Human Development, and the Department of Education (IES), resulting in 11 books and over 150 publications. With her long-time collaborator Roberta Golinkoff, she is a recipient of the APA Bronfenbrenner Award for lifetime contribution to the science of developmental psychology in the service of science and society and the APA Award for Distinguished Service to Psychological Science. She also received Temple University's Great Teacher Award and the Paul Eberman Research Award. She is a Fellow of the American Psychological Association and the American Psychological Society, served as the Associate Editor of *Child Development*, and Treasurer of the International Association for Infant Studies. Her book, *Einstein Never Used Flashcards: How Children Really Learn and Why They Need to Play More and Memorize Less* (Rodale Books), won the prestigious Books for Better Life Award as the best psychology book in 2003. Kathy is deeply invested in bridging the gap between research and practice. To that end, she was a researcher on the NICHD Study of Early Child Care and Youth Development, co-developed the language and literacy preschool curricula for the State of California, and was the co-founder of the Ultimate Block Party (www.ultimateblockparty.com) and L-rn (www. L-rn.com), the Learning Resource Network. She serves on the advisory boards of Disney Junior, Fred Rogers Center, Jumpstart, the New York Hall of Science, and the Dupage Children's Museum.

Margaret Honey, Ph.D., is President and CEO of the New York Hall of Science. She is widely recognized for her work using digital technologies to support children's learning across science, technology, engineering, and math. Since coming to NYSCI in 2008, she has launched a number of initiatives that use the informal environment of a science museum as a laboratory to innovate new models for science teaching and learning, both in and out of the classroom.

Sameer Honwad's research interests focus on how people use science to make decisions in their everyday lives. He was a Research Fellow at the Sara Lee Schupf Family Center for Play, Science, and Technology Learning (SciPlay) at NYSCI when the SciPlay chapter was written. He is to be a National Academy of Education/Spencer Postdoctoral Fellow studying the role of indigenous knowledge systems on environmental decision-making processes in Himalayan villages. He holds a Ph.D. from Pennsylvania State University in Learning and Performance Systems.

Thomas Kalil is the Deputy Director of the White House Office of Science and Technology Policy. He has previously served as Special Assistant to the Chancellor for Science and Technology at UC Berkeley, the Chair of the Global Health Working Group of the Clinton Global Initiative, and Deputy Assistant to President Clinton for Technology and Economic Policy.

David E. Kanter is the inaugural Director of the Sara Lee Schupf Family Center for Play, Science, and Technology Learning (SciPlay), an applied research and development center within the New York Hall of Science (NYSCI) that focuses on designing, building, and studying technology-enhanced learning environments that harness the potential of play for deeper engagement and science learning. Kanter has taught science education as an assistant professor at Temple University, and conducted research in the learning sciences at Northwestern University. Kanter holds a B.S. in Engineering and in Economics from the University of Pennsylvania, and a Ph.D. in Biomedical Engineering from the Johns Hopkins School of Medicine. His most recent work focuses on new ways to productively bridge informal and formal science learning environments.

Charles Mojkowski has worked as a consultant to education and business organizations for over 30 years. He works primarily in the areas of school, program, and curriculum design; leadership and organizational development; and innovative applications of technology in these areas. He has authored numerous articles on unconventional designs for schools and schooling.

He is a former English teacher, elementary school assistant principal, and administrator in the Rhode Island Department of Education. He was also an Associate Professor in the Doctoral Program in Educational Leadership at Johnson & Wales University. He currently serves as a Senior Associate at Big Picture Learning.

Peggy Monahan is Exhibit Projects Creative Director at the New York Hall of Science. According to Peggy, "I am an educator, and my medium is exhibition." She has more than two decades of experience in museums such as the Boston Children's Museum and San Francisco's Exploratorium, and has created and directed exhibitions on topics ranging from genetics to creativity. She strives to create deeply interactive social exhibits that get visitors of all ages involved for extended periods. Currently, she is leading the creative development of the Design Lab exhibition.

Mike Petrich: As Director of the Making Collaborative at the Exploratorium, Mike is curious about how people develop personal and unique understandings of the world for themselves. With a background in fine arts, filmmaking, and photography, he applies the act of careful observation to much of his work as an educator and facilitator. Mike has been working at this for 20 years, with audiences as diverse as museum visitors, primary school students, Tibetan monks, prison inmates, and graduate school researchers.

Helen Quinn is a Professor Emerita of Physics at the SLAC National Accelerator Laboratory and was the chair of the committee that developed *A Framework for K-12 Science Education.*

Mitchel Resnick, Professor of Learning Research at the MIT Media Lab, develops new technologies and activities to engage people in creative learning experiences. His Lifelong Kindergarten research group developed ideas and technologies underlying the LEGO Mindstorms robotics kits and Scratch programming software, used by millions of young people around the world. He also co-founded the Computer Clubhouse project, an international network of 100 afterschool learning centers for youth from low-income communities. Resnick earned a B.S. in Physics from Princeton, and an M.S. and Ph.D. in Computer Science from MIT. In 2011, he was awarded the McGraw Prize in Education and the World Technology Award in Education.

Eric Rosenbaum is a doctoral student in the Lifelong Kindergarten group at MIT Media Lab, where he creates new technologies at the intersection of music, improvisation, play, and learning. His projects include the MaKey MaKey invention kit, Singing Fingers software for finger painting with sound, the Glowdoodle system for painting with light, MmmTsss software for improvising with looping sounds, and a Scratch-like language for creating interactive behaviors in the virtual world of Second Life. Eric holds a bachelor's degree in Psychology and a master's degree in Technology in Education from Harvard University. He also holds a master's degree in Media Arts and Sciences from MIT Media Lab, for which he developed Jots, a system to support reflective learning in the Scratch programming environment.

Mary Simon is Executive Director and Founder of RAFT, Resource Area For Teaching. Before that, she was an elementary school teacher specializing in hands-on math and science education. Wanting to make a bigger impact, she created RAFT, a special place for teachers that provides support and resources for hands-on education. Over the past 18 years, Mary has served as the Executive Director. RAFT has grown to be a $3 million organization, serving over 10,000 educators reaching over 800,000 children each year. Mary holds a certificate in Nonprofit Leadership from the Stanford Graduate School of Business and is a Senior Fellow in American Leadership Forum—Silicon Valley. Mary has been recognized with the Tribute to American Women (TWIN) Award for exemplifying excellence in executive leadership and the Woman of Achievement Award for Community Service with commendation by the City of San Jose.

AnnMarie Thomas is the Executive Director of the Maker Education Initiative. Previously, she was an engineering professor at the University of St. Thomas, in St. Paul, Minnesota. She earned an S.B. in Ocean Engineering from MIT, and M.S./Ph.D. degrees in Mechanical Engineering from Caltech.

Elliot Washor is the co-founder and co-director of The Big Picture Learning in Providence, Rhode Island, and San Diego, California. He is also the co-founder of The Met Center in Providence.

Elliot has been involved in school reform for more than 35 years as a teacher, principal, administrator, video producer, and writer. He has taught and is interested in all levels of school from kindergarten through college, in urban and rural settings, across all disciplines. His work has spanned across school design, pedagogy, learning environments, and education reform. He is supporting others doing similar work throughout the world. Elliot's interests lie in the field of how schools can connect with communities to understand tacit and disciplinary learning both in and outside of school.

His professional development programs won an "Innovations in State and Local Government Award" from the Ford Foundation and the Kennedy School of Government at Harvard University. He has been selected as the educator to watch in Rhode Island and has been selected as one of the Daring Dozen — The Twelve Most Daring Educators by the George Lucas Education Foundation.

Jane Werner's 30 years of museum experience includes 22 years at the Children's Museum of Pittsburgh, where she has served as Program Director, Deputy Director, and Executive Director. Werner is responsible for all aspects of the museum's mission and vision, exhibits, public programming, funding, and operations. Among many achievements under her direction, the museum received the 2006 American Institute of Architects National Award and 2006 National Trust for Historic Preservation Award for its expansion, received the 2009 National Medal from the Institute of Museum and Library Services for its work in the community, and was named one of the top 10 children's museums in the country by *Parents* magazine in 2011. Jane received the 2007 ASTC Roy Schaeffer Leading Edge Award for Experienced Leadership in the Field, and is currently the President of the Association of Children's Museums. She sits on the advisory boards of the Forbes Fund, Kids and Creativity Working Group, the Fred Rogers' Center, and the Maker Education Initiative.

Karen Wilkinson: As Director of the Learning Studio, Karen sees her role at the Exploratorium as an advocate for making as a way of knowing. She believes deeply in studio pedagogy, and the ability we all have to think with our hands. As an undergrad working in environmental design, she came to see museums as places that recognize this approach. Karen started her museum career as a volunteer at the Science Museum of Minnesota, soon met people from the Exploratorium and other institutions, and quickly realized how deeply a museum philosophy resonated with her own. Now, years later, after pursuing graduate studies in education and technology, she is even more committed to the idea that constructionism is an incredibly powerful way of learning, and that aesthetics matter a great deal. These two ideas are often overlooked in more formal education settings, outside of kindergarten or graduate school. Informal learning spaces for making and tinkering offer people a chance to connect to their own learning in a deeply personal way, which is why she is thrilled to be able to work with such a delightfully quirky group of people in the Tinkering Studio.

Steven Zipkes is the founding Principal of the national-award-winning Manor New Technology High School in Manor, Texas. His peers call him a principal who "walks his talk," practicing what he preaches: project-based learning, integrated STEM, and 21st-century skills. The success of MNTH's students and teachers has inspired many other districts and schools around the country to reorganize their practices to prepare the learners of today to be leaders for tomorrow.

Jennifer M. Zosh, Ph.D., is an Assistant Professor of Human Development and Family Studies at Pennsylvania State University, Brandywine Campus. She is the Director of the Brandywine Child Development Lab, where she involves undergraduate researchers in the study of developmental cognition. She recently won the Distinguished Teacher Award at her university and has authored chapters and articles in the areas of working memory, mathematical cognition, language acquisition, and playful learning. She engages the community as a social media consultant for the Ultimate Block Party, where she also serves as an advisory board member.

ACKNOWLEDGMENTS

As is true with any undertaking, many people have played a role in bringing the ideas contained in this book to life. First and foremost, we thank the authors whose work and writing this book features: Philip Bell, Dorothy Bennett, Bronwyn Bevan, Lisa Brahms, Greg Brown, Dale Dougherty, Kelly Fisher, Roberta Michnick Golinkoff, Kathy Hirsh-Pasek, Thomas Kalil, Peggy Monahan, Charles Mojkowski, Mike Petrich, Helen Quinn, Mitchel Resnick, Eric Rosenbaum, Mary Simon, AnnMarie Thomas, Elliot Washor, Jane Werner, Karen Wilkinson, Jennifer Zosh, and Steve Zipkes.

These individuals are leaders in the creation of deeply engaging models of science, technology, engineering, and mathematics learning; they are involved in creating new and powerful frameworks for shaping how science is taught in schools; they are at the forefront of catalyzing and shaping the Maker Movement; they are advocates for the power of playful learning; and they have pioneered design projects that generate both delight and deep knowledge.

We also extend our deepest gratitude to Carol Shookhoff, who worked tirelessly to provide thoughtful editorial guidance to all of the authors.

This publication was made possible with generous support from our lead sponsor, Time Warner Cable, and with funding from our program sponsors: the National Science Foundation, the Carnegie Corporation, and the Kauffman Foundation of Entrepreneurship. We are grateful to each of you for your willingness to embrace new and creative approaches to science learning. The statements made and views expressed in this publication are, however, solely the responsibility of the authors.

We are so very grateful to our editor at Routledge, Alex Masulis, for embracing this project from its inception. And we are grateful as well to Madeleine Hamlin for her always-gracious patience and organization in helping to put this book together.

And finally, we thank our NYSCI colleagues. You are a continuous source of inspiration and joy.

Margaret Honey and David E. Kanter

DESIGN, MAKE, PLAY
Growing the Next Generation of Science Innovators

MARGARET HONEY AND DAVID E. KANTER

> I want us all to think about new and creative ways to engage young people in science and engineering, whether it's science festivals, robotics competitions, fairs that encourage young people to create and build and invent—to be makers of things, not just consumers of things.
> President Barack Obama at the National Academies of Science
> (April 27, 2009)

We seek to inspire opportunities through which today's young people can become inspired and passionate science and technology learners. Toward that end, we hope this book, illustrating real-world examples of innovative programs for science and technology learning, will serve as a resource for policymakers, practitioners, researchers, and program developers. We use the *design-make-play* triad (DMP) to illuminate methodologies of engagement that foster motivation and learning.

THE RATIONALE

The winners of Google's 2011 international science competition were three young women. Their projects manifested not only clear aspirations to use science to solve problems of consequence, but also their deployment of resources from their entire community, beyond simply their schooling, to engage these challenges. Curiosity about science had been instilled in these young women at an early age. They had taken advanced science courses, attended enriching science camps, participated in numerous science competitions, been supported by family members and other caring adults who have nurtured their success, and had been rewarded and recognized for their accomplishments. As they prepared for college, and ultimately to enter the workforce, they had exceedingly high expectations for themselves, expecting to pursue Ph.D. research programs after college.

They each had fallen in love with science when they discovered that science is a way of looking at the world that equipped them to solve problems and address challenges that have a direct human impact. Most important, they had succeeded at marrying their convictions and enthusiasms with opportunities to advance. As one of our colleagues noted: "It's funny how girls have that uncanny ability to find problems worth solving."

We know it is possible to enable young people to fall in love with science and technology by presenting science as a creative, hands-on, and passionate endeavor.

The stories featured here stand in sharp contrast to what we know about science education in our nation's schools, how it is delivered by teachers and texts, and how it is received by students. Today, science, at the elementary level, is taught for less than three hours a week. There is a growing body of evidence indicating that grade-level, high-stakes testing is heavily biasing the curriculum toward the teaching of tested subjects and away from less-frequently tested subjects such as science. Further, when science is given time during the school week, students are much more likely to be memorizing information presented in textbooks and answering questions at the end of the chapter than engaging in the kind of real-world problem-solving that is key to building young people's passions for science learning.

The future can—and must—be different.

We know what can work to motivate children. Perhaps the greatest asset is to leverage children's innate curiosity about the world around them. Children are born curious and come equipped with a desire to learn that rivals that of even the most determined scientist. Early in school, however, this spark—what psychologists have dubbed intrinsic motivation—is all-too-frequently extinguished by the extrinsic goals and expectations of school.

Fortunately, there is research-based evidence that says it is possible to rekindle this natural motivation to learn by designing environments that are supportive, that engage learners in meaningful activities, that lessen a student's anxiety and fear, and that provide a level of challenge matched to students' skills.

The Carnegie Corporation's Institute for Advanced Study Commission on Mathematics and Science Education argues that for such a trans-formation to occur, we must move away from the current system of "telling" students about science to helping students gain critical problem-solving and inquiry skills in the context of relevant, real-world, interdisciplinary problems. While it is clear from the Commission's research that young people care deeply about contemporary science- and engineering-related problems and are motivated to solve them (e.g., health and global warming), we need to develop learning practices that can stimulate students' passions for science and teaching methodologies that motivate students and support deeper learning.

FRAMING THE WORK

The newly released *Framework for K-12 Science Education* published by the National Research Council lays the foundation upon which a new generation of science standards will be developed. Recognizing that science is the key to solving the world's most pressing challenges, the Framework seeks to ensure that:

> by the end of 12th grade all students have some appreciation for the beauty and wonder of science; possess sufficient knowledge of science and engineering to engage in public discussions on related issues; are careful consumers of scientific and technological information related to their everyday lives; are able to continue to learn about science outside school; and have the skills to enter careers of their choice, including (but not limited to) careers in science, engineering, and technology.

The framework charts a new and important pathway for science learning by recognizing that science content learning must be intimately coupled with the practices of doing science and engineering, and must build students' understandings and appreciation of the scientific enterprise over multiple years.

We see our emphasis on *design-make-play* learning methodologies as illustrative of the new *Framework for K-12 Science Education*. These are methodologies that have the potential to foster young people's scientific imaginations.

Design—the iterative selection and arrangement of elements to form a whole by which people create artifacts, systems, and tools intended to solve a range of problems, large and small. A process central to engineering and technology, design is a powerful vehicle for teaching science, technology, engineering, and math (STEM) content in an integrated and inspiring way. Through the design process, one learns how to identify a problem or need, how to consider options and constraints, and how to plan, model, test, and iterate solutions, rendering higher-order thinking skills, tangible and visible.

Design-based learning engages students as critical thinkers and problem-solvers and presents science and technology as powerful tools to use in solving some of the world's most pressing challenges.

Make—to build or adapt objects by hand, for the simple personal pleasure of figuring out how things work. Long before the rules of science were written down, people engaged with scientific disciplines by making things; things to help us do what we need to do, or things that are just fun. A quiet revolution is unfolding in communities across the country that is deeply rooted in this defining characteristic of our species and that has the potential to transform science learning. Known as the *Maker Movement*, and spurred largely by the success of *Make* magazine (http://makezine.com) and Maker Faires (http://makerfaire.com), makers are drawn together by a shared delight in the magic of tinkering, hacking, creating, and reusing materials and technology. The essential characteristics of the maker sensibility—deep engagement with content, experimentation, exploration, problem-solving, collaboration, and learning to learn—are the very ingredients that make for inspired and passionate STEM learners.

Play—a fun, voluntary activity that often involves make-believe, invention, and innovation. There are strong analogies between the learning of science and children's natural inclinations to play, invent, and explore. Both are motivated by curiosity, investigation, and discovery, and at the core of both is creativity. Play encourages a diverse ecology of different engagement strategies, from kinetic to contemplative, from experiential to instructional. The thread through all of these strategies is unpressured exploration and invention, the very characteristics that can lead to creative thought and innovation for science learning.

THE CONTRIBUTIONS

We are pleased to have assembled here a wide span of pre-eminent researchers, theoreticians, and practitioners of DMP. These include the founder of both *Make* magazine and Maker Faire, the director of the MIT's Lifelong Kindergarten group, the principal of an award-winning high school, museum educators, and more. We hope you will find the chapters enlightening, provocative, and fun.

Dale Dougherty, *Maker Mindset*: Making is an important source of innovation as well as personally satisfying to the maker. The Maker Movement is growing across the country, stimulated by the introduction of new, inexpensive technologies, and has great potential to catalyze innovative science learning in both formal and informal contexts.

Thomas Kalil, *Have Fun—Learn Something, Do Something, Make Something*: President Obama wants young people "to be makers of things, not just consumers of things," and he has endorsed the spirit and practices of the Maker Movement in support of STEM education. Makers design and make things for the sheer pleasure of figuring out how things work and repurposing those things at will. The Maker Movement is a naturally powerful vehicle that can help get kids excited about science and technology. Several federal agencies are now promoting making, but the efforts of private and public organizations are needed as well.

Helen Quinn and Philip Bell, *How Designing, Making, and Playing Relate to the Goals of K-12 Science Education*: The NRC's new Framework for next-generation science standards broadens the idea of K-12 science learning goals to include engineering practices. These practices share many approaches with informal science-related learning that is often associated with design- make-play activities. Together, the formal and informal approaches support the common goals of effective engagement of students in science and engineering learning.

THE CASES

Dorothy Bennett and Peggy Monahan, *NYSCI Design Lab: No Bored Kids*: Design-based learning has the potential to engage reluctant learners when design challenges can be quickly understood and allow for multiple points of entry into STEM.

Mike Petrich, Karen Wilkinson, and Bronwyn Bevan, *It Looks Like Fun, But Are They Learning?* Carefully designed tinkering activities can support engagement, intentionality, innovation, and solidarity that can provide accessible opportunities for learners to engage in scientific and engineering practices that are both epistemologically and ontologically meaningful.

Lisa Brahms and Jane Warner, *Designing Makerspaces for Family Learning in Museums and Science Centers*: At *MAKESHOP*, children and families engage in authentic making experiences with *real stuff*—materials, tools, processes, and ideas. It is the culmination of a process of collaborative and iterative development with careful attention to the essential design features that support visitors' making as a dynamic, shared learning process.

Jennifer Zosh, Kelly Fisher, Roberta Michnick Golinkoff, and Kathy Hirsh-Pasek, *The Ultimate Block Party: Bridging the Science of Learning and the Importance of Play*: At the first Ultimate Block Party event, held in New York City's Central Park, leading experts helped spread the message that playful learning is not only fun, but crucial for children's development. Over 50,000 people participated in dozens of activities that helped showcase the power of play.

AnnMarie Thomas, *Squishy Circuits*: Squishy circuits uses conductive and non-conductive homemade play dough in place of wires to create and explore simple electrical circuits. If you do not like the circuit you have made, you can simply squish it up and start over. This project has been used in a variety of settings, from homes to classrooms to museums.

Mary Simon and Greg Brown, *RAFT: A Maker Palace for Educators*: This innovative nonprofit focuses on hands-on learning by offering a warehouse full of industrial discards (cardboard tubes, countertop laminate samples, outdated corporate letterhead) to teachers, along with idea sheets, activity kits, and professional development.

Mitchel Resnick and Eric Rosenbaum, *Designing for Tinkerability*: Tinkering is a playful, experimental, iterative style of engagement, in which people are continually reassessing their goals, exploring new paths, and imagining new possibilities. Technologies can be designed to encourage and support tinkering, as illustrated by two computational construction kits, Scratch and MaKey MaKey, designed explicitly to engage young people in tinkering.

David E. Kanter, Sameer Honwad, Ruth Diones, and Adiel Fernandez, *SciGames: Guided Play Games that Enhance Both Student Engagement and Learning in Tandem*: Playground games can be guided to support students' learning of science content while also harnessing the inherent power of play to bolster behavioral, emotional, and cognitive engagement. Future work will focus on guided play games that pass data automatically from the playground games back to the science classroom for scientific inquiry and even deeper science content learning.

Elliot Washor and Charles Mojkowski, *Making Their Way in the World: Creating a Generation of Tinkerer-Scientists*: Schools need to prepare all students to be tinkerer-scientists; that is, citizens who are competent and comfortable using science, math, and technology tools and processes to address real-world challenges they discover in their lives and careers.

Steven Zipkes, *Manor New Technology High School*: A Texas high school with a heterogeneous student population organizes the entire curriculum around project-based learning. The outcomes have been stunning. Attendance rates have soared, with a 97% rate over the past five years. In 2009/10, Manor New Tech graduated its first class, with a 100% senior class completion rate and a 0% dropout rate. Every one of the seniors was accepted into college, 84% into four-year colleges and universities. The following year, 2010/11, MNTH graduated its second class, and again 100% of the seniors completed high school with a 0% dropout rate. Of these, 97% were accepted into college, 80% into four-year colleges and universities.

CHAPTER 1

THE MAKER MINDSET

DALE DOUGHERTY

The Maker Movement continues to gain momentum. We can see the growth of maker communities online as well as the development of physical community workspaces, called makerspaces, and the spread of Maker Faire around the world. The Maker Movement is spurred by the introduction of new technologies such as 3D printing and the Arduino microcontroller; new opportunities created by faster prototyping and fabrication tools as well as easier sourcing of parts and direct distribution of physical products online; and the increasing participation of all kinds of people in interconnected communities, defined by interests and skills online as well as hyper-local efforts to convene those who share common goals.

Yet the origin of the Maker Movement is found in something quite personal: what I might call "experimental play." When I started *Make* magazine, I recognized that makers were enthusiasts who played with technology to learn about it. A new technology presented an invitation to play, and makers regard this kind of play as highly satisfying. Makers give it a try; they take things apart; and they try to do things that even the manufacturer did not think of doing. Whether it is figuring out what you can do with a 3D printer or an autonomous drone aircraft, makers are exploring what these things can do and they are learning as well. Out of that process emerge new ideas, which may lead to real-world applications or new business ventures. Making is a source of innovation.

While technology has been the spark of the Maker Movement, it has also become a social movement that includes all kinds of making and all kinds of makers, connecting to the past as well as changing how we look at the future. Indeed, the Maker Movement seems to be a renewal of some deeply held cultural values, a recognition rooted in our history and culture that making comes to define us. As Frank Bidart has written in his poem "Advice to the Players": "We are creatures who need to make."

All together, makers are seeking an alternative to being regarded as consumers, rejecting the idea that you are defined by what you buy. Instead, makers have a sense of what they can do and what they can learn to do. Like artists, they are motivated by internal goals, not extrinsic rewards. They are inspired by the work of others. Most importantly, they do not wait until the future to create and make. They feel an urgency to do something now— or lose the opportunity to do it at all.

Making is no longer, however, a mainstream activity or aspiration, although it once was a core attribute of the American middle class. Today, making lives on the margins of society, but it is thriving nonetheless. Makers are likely to see themselves as outsiders, like some artists and writers, who do not follow the traditional paths. They create their own paths, which is what innovative and creative people do. Quite simply, we need to encourage more young people to explore, create, discover, and make their own way.

The biggest challenge and the biggest opportunity for the Maker Movement is to transform education. My hope is that the agents of change will be the students themselves. Increasingly, technology has given students more control over their lives, and even the simplest cellphone can change a person's sense of agency. Students are seeking to direct their own education lives, looking to engage in creative and stimulating experiences. Many understand the difference between the *pain* of education and the *pleasure* of real learning. Unfortunately, they are forced to seek opportunities outside of school to express themselves and to demonstrate what they can do.

Formal education has become such a serious business, defined as success at abstract thinking and high-stakes testing, that there is no time and no context for play. If play is what students do outside school, then that is where the real learning will take place and that is where innovation and creativity will be found.

The rigid academic system is short-changing all students, even though an elite few seem to do well by academic standards. However, there is increasing skepticism that even those who succeed academically are not the kind of creative, innovative thinkers and doers that we need.

Dr. Stuart Brown's book, *Play: How It Shapes the Brain, Opens the Imagination, and Invigorates the Soul*, tells the story of how the Jet Propulsion Laboratory realized that although they were hiring the best and brightest college graduates, they were hiring the wrong kind of people. Something had changed in the kind of people that came to work at JPL:

> The JPL managers went back to look at their own retiring engineers and
> . . . found that in their youth, their older, problem-solving employees had

taken apart clocks to see how they worked, or made soapbox derby racers, or built hi-fi stereos, or fixed appliances. The young engineering school graduates who had also done these things, who had played with their hands, were adept at the kinds of problem solving that management sought.

Those who hadn't, generally were not. From that point on, JPL made questions about applicants "youthful projects and play" a standard part of job interviews. Through research the JPL managers discovered that there is a kind of magic in play.

We must try to bring this kind of magic into schools, hard as it may be. I have been focusing on the importance of creating a space where kids have the opportunity to make—a place where some tools, materials, and enough expertise can get them started. These places, called makerspaces, share some aspects of the shop class, home economics class, the art studio, and science labs. In effect, a makerspace is a physical mash-up of different places that allows makers and projects to integrate these different kinds of skills.

We can create a workshop or makerspace, and we can acquire tools and materials, but we will not have succeeded at creating innovative thinkers and doers unless we are able to foster a maker mindset.

Carol Dweck, a Stanford psychology professor, has written a book called *Mindset* that distinguishes between fixed and growth mindsets. People with a fixed mindset tend to believe that their capabilities are set, as though these abilities were out of their control. People with a growth mindset tend to believe that capabilities can be developed, improved, and expanded. A growth mindset tolerates risk and failure, while a fixed mindset avoids risk and its accompanying frustration. It is obvious which mindset helps someone adapt to and contribute to a world that is constantly changing. Dweck points out that many who excel academically have a fixed mindset, which limits them to exploring only the areas they were told they were good at. Conversely, many who do poorly in school have taken too seriously the judgment of others about their ability in subjects such as math or science. In both cases, such limiting views of oneself are self-defeating and can hold people back from exploring new areas and developing unknown capabilities. Making is about developing one's full potential.

Dweck's growth mindset maps very well to the maker mindset, which is a can-do attitude that can be summarized as "what can you do with what you know?" It is an invitation to take ideas and turn them into various kinds of reality. It is the process of iterating over a project to improve it. It is a chance to participate in communities of makers of all ages by sharing your work and expertise. Making can be a compelling social experience, built around relationships.

Fostering the maker mindset through education is a fundamentally human project—to support the growth and development of another person not just physically, but mentally and emotionally. Learning should focus on the whole person because any truly creative enterprise requires all of us, not just some part. It should also be rooted in the kind of sharing of knowledge and skills that humans do best face to face.

One might reasonably fear that making will be reduced to another failed approach at education reform. Making can be described as "project-based learning" or "hands-on learning," yet doing projects or working with your hands is only what making looks like, not what it is. In his book on education, *To Understand Is to Invent*, Jean Piaget wrote that educators should "lead the child to construct for himself the tools that will transform him from the inside—that is, in a real sense, and not just on the surface." It is the difference between a child who is directed to perform a task and one who is self-directed to figure out what to do. That kind of transformation, that kind of personal and social change, is what making is about.

Here are some thoughts for bringing the Maker Movement to education:

- to create a context that develops the maker mindset, a growth mindset that encourages students to believe they can learn to do anything;
- to build a new body of practice in teaching making and develop a corps of practitioners;
- to design and develop makerspaces in a variety of community contexts that serve a diverse group of learners who do not all share the same resources;
- to identify, develop, and share a broad framework of projects and kits, based on a wide range of tools and materials, that connect to student interests in and out of school;
- to design and host online social platforms for collaboration among students, teachers, and the community;
- to develop programs especially for young people that allow them to take a leading role in creating more makers in schools, afterschool programs, summer camps, and other community settings;
- to create a community context for the exhibition and curating of student work in relationship with all makers and making, such that new opportunities are created for more people to participate;
- to allow individuals and groups to build a record of participation in the maker community, which can be useful for academic and career advancement as well as support the student's growing sense of personal development;
- to develop educational contexts that link the practice of making to formal concepts and theory, to support discovery and exploration while introducing new tools for advanced design and new ways of thinking

about making (practically, this means developing guides for teachers, mentors, and other leaders); and

- to develop in all students the full capacity, creativity, and confidence to become agents of change in their personal lives and in their community.

In summary, we can think of organizing this work in terms of places, projects, and practices. The Maker Education Initiative (http://Maker Ed.org), a nonprofit launched in spring 2012, was founded to work on many of the above ideas. Its mission is to create more opportunities for young people to make, and, by making, build confidence, foster creativity, and spark interest in science, technology, engineering, math, the arts, and learning as a whole. One way that the Maker Education Initiative will approach this is by working to help existing organizations, such as libraries, to build the capacity to engage and develop young makers. Empowering makers of all ages to play an active role in introducing students, and educators, to making will be a key component of these efforts.

Finally, I would like to share a quote by John Boyd, which gets at why making is a gateway to understanding why science and technology matter. Boyd wrote that the goal of education is "to make evident how science, engineering, and technology influence our ability to interact and cope with an unfolding reality that we are part of, live in, and feed upon."[1]

The kind of change we seek in education is part of the change that we are seeing all around us, the kind of change we seek in ourselves. If those interactions with the world we live in inform and inspire us to create, then we are makers.

NOTE

1   Frans P. B. Osinga (2007). *Science, strategy and war: The strategic theory of John Boyd.* New York: Routledge, p. 220.

REFERENCES

Brown, S. and Vaughan, C. (2009). *Play: How it shapes the brain, opens the imagination, and invigorates the soul.* New York: Penguin.

Dweck, C. S. (2006). *Mindset: The new psychology of success.* New York: Random House.

Piaget, J. (1973). *To understand is to invent: The future of education.* New York: Grossman.

CHAPTER 2

HAVE FUN—LEARN SOMETHING, DO SOMETHING, MAKE SOMETHING

THOMAS KALIL

At the second-ever White House Science Fair in February 2012, President Obama manned a bicycle pump in the State Dining Room to power an "extreme marshmallow cannon" capable of shooting a marshmallow 175 feet (over half a football field). This device was invented by a 14-year-old from Arizona, Joey Hudy, who, after the demonstration, handed the President his business card, imprinted "Don't Be Bored, Make Something."

Joey's peers at the Science Fair exhibited items such as a UV-light lunchbox that sanitizes the food packed in the morning until a student opens the box to eat lunch; patent-pending dissolvable sugar packets that reduce waste; and a lightweight, portable disaster relief shelter, designed with a water purification system and a renewable energy source to power an LED light for people who have been displaced.

These students are part of a growing community of makers, people who design and make things on their own time because they find it intrinsically rewarding to make, tinker, problem-solve, discover, and share what they have learned. They put things together, they take things apart, they put things together in a new and different way. They do things such as make *Guitar Hero* into a robot microcontroller or build a solar-powered charging device inside an Altoid tin. Why? For the sheer pleasure of figuring out how things work and repurposing those things at will.

Note: Chapter 2, "Have Fun—Learn Something, Do Something, Make Something" by Thomas Kalil, has been adapted from his article "Extreme Marshmallow Cannons!" published on June 13, 2012, by Slate.com. To view the original article, please see www.slate.com/articles/technology/future_tense/2012/06/every_child_a_maker_how_the_government_and_private_sector_can_turn_kids_on_to_science_and_engineering_through_making_.html.

What makers love is the essence of science: learning and doing. It is this spirit that President Obama wants to invigorate and harness by giving more people the ability to be makers. The maker spirit is in the air. We see it in growing numbers of vibrant maker communities, the Makeshops and "hackerspaces" organizing around projects, technologies, and physical places around the country. We see it in the extraordinary numbers of people who attend the yearly Maker Faires around the country.

Every child is born curious, eager to understand the world around us and to take charge of how he or she will live. For whatever reason, that innate curiosity and eagerness to learn has been damped down for too many of us, especially for K-12 students. The 2010 international PISA test scores (U.S. students scored 23rd in science and 31st in math among the countries taking the test) are disheartening and disturbing.

The spirit and practices of the maker community, however, present an enormous opportunity for educators of the young, particularly those who teach science, technology, engineering, and math (STEM) education, whether in formal or informal educational settings.

President Obama considers science, technology, engineering, and math (STEM) education a top priority because of its potentially crucial innovative contributions to the country's economic well-being. And he has made the connection between STEM and making explicit.

He has extolled the value of making to many different audiences. In his inaugural address, he honored and celebrated the "risk-takers, the doers, the makers of things." He told the National Academy of Sciences:

> I want us all to think about new and creative ways to engage young people in science and engineering, whether it's science festivals, robotics competitions, fairs that encourage young people to create and build and invent—to be makers of things, not just consumers of things.
>
> (Obama, April 2009)

When launching his *Educate to Innovate* campaign, he said:

> Students will launch rockets, construct miniature windmills, and get their hands dirty. They'll have the chance to build and create—and maybe destroy just a little bit—to see the promise of being the makers of things, and not just the consumers of things.
>
> (Obama, November 2009)

The President believes in making because he knows that hands-on, project-based approaches are a particularly effective way to teach. After all, who would teach kids how to play football by lecturing to them about football for years and years before giving them a ball and letting them play?

The Maker Movement is a naturally powerful vehicle that can advance a number of goals essential to a strong society. It improves STEM education by getting kids excited about science and technology, the way chemistry sets inspired previous generations of scientists and engineers. It promotes values that are ends in themselves, such as creativity, problem-solving, collaboration, and self-expression. And it promotes a long tradition of hobbyist communities that became hotbeds of innovation. As Steve Wozniak, co-founder of Apple and designer of the Apple II computer, pointed out, "Without computer clubs there would probably be no Apple computers." Many innovations of the personal computer industry were developed by members of Silicon Valley's Homebrew Computer Club. Today, makers are becoming entrepreneurs, leading the development of industrial robots, 3D printers, and smart devices that integrate hardware, software, sensors, and Internet connectivity.

A number of important technology trends are helping to democratize the Maker Movement and facilitate its inclusion in American schools everywhere, whether in inner cities or small rural districts. The tools needed to design and build just about anything are becoming more affordable and easier to use, in the same way that the move from the mainframe to the PC to the smartphone has democratized information technology. Although nothing compares to actual human interaction in local communities, the Internet has made it easier for makers to share blueprints, software, CAD files, and step-by-step instructional videos and cartoons.

One exciting response to President Obama's calls to action is the Maker Education Initiative (MEI). The goal is to make "Every Child a Maker." Launched with leadership from Dale Dougherty, a White House Champion of Change and founder of Maker Faire and *Make* magazine—with support from founding sponsors such as Cognizant, Intel, and O'Reilly Media—this initiative seeks to create more opportunities for young people to make, and, by making, to build confidence, foster creativity, and spark interest in STEM, the arts, and learning as a whole. MEI will focus on expanding the number of makerspaces in both school and afterschool settings, developing hands-on projects for young people of all ages and interests, and recruiting mentors who can share their passion and expertise with the next generation of makers.

Federal agencies are promoting Making in a number of ways. DARPA, the agency that gave us the Internet and GPS, is investing heavily in the tools needed for design and manufacturing. One thing they have done is to launch MENTOR, a program that will empower students from 1,000 high schools to design and build things such as robots and go-carts. DARPA and the Department of Veterans Affairs are partnering with TechShop to open new locations near Washington, DC and Pittsburgh for veterans and researchers to work on DARPA projects in flexible manufacturing. NASA is promoting DIY space projects, such as "smartphones in space," dramatically increasing the number of people involved in space exploration. The White House Office of Science and Technology Policy is encouraging all agencies to provide R&D funding for entrepreneurs with good ideas for low-cost instruments and kits for makers and citizen scientists.

Of course, empowering every child to become a maker will require more than the government alone. A large, powerful coalition of interested parties will be needed as well. For example:

- Companies concerned about the lack of students with strong skills in STEM and manufacturing could support makerspaces in schools and afterschool programs, and give their employees time off to serve as mentors.
- Youth-serving organizations that reach millions of boys and girls could recruit makers to develop programs at the national, state, and local levels.
- Science museums could serve as "hubs" for making in the regions they serve by creating makerspaces and providing professional development for teachers. The New York Hall of Science, the Pittsburgh Children's Museum, and San Francisco's Exploratorium are already demonstrating what is possible when science museums devote their expertise and social capital to making.
- Individual makers could serve as mentors and leaders of local chapters of organizations such as the Young Makers Club.
- Foundations and philanthropists could provide matching grants to communities interested in embracing making, in the spirit of Andrew Carnegie's support for public libraries. Philanthropists should make a special effort to ensure that girls and under-represented minorities are included in Making.

POSSIBLE RESULTS AND QUESTIONS FOR THE FUTURE

If we make the most of these opportunities, I am confident that we will see the following:

- More students will become excited about excelling in STEM subjects and pursuing STEM-related fields.
- More students will be empowered not just to get a job, but to create the industries and jobs of the future. More graduates will pursue mechanical or electrical engineering as opposed to financial engineering.
- More inventors will develop an idea to address the grand challenges of the 21st century, such as solar cells as cheap as paint or tumor-eating bacteria.

- More citizens will be able to engage effectively in policy debates on scientific and technological issues, such as energy, climate, sustainability, and bio-ethics.

The history of innovation teaches us that new ideas are almost always the result of novel combinations of existing ideas. So, just imagine more two-way traffic between the maker and STEM education communities—in terms of people, partnerships, ideas, and tools. Here are some issues to think about:

- What projects and initiatives should the maker and STEM communities be co-designing and co-creating?
- What big ideas, compelling goals, and concrete "next steps" would inspire individuals, companies, foundations, educators, museums, nonprofits, and government agencies to work together?
- To be more specific, what would career and technical education look like after a maker makeover?
- What would teams of students build with access to a 3D printer, a tech shop, powerful but easy-to-use CAD tools, and an experienced mentor? What foundational knowledge and practical skills would they acquire along the way, and what real-world problems could they solve?
- What are the biggest barriers to bringing makers and their tools into the classroom and informal learning environments, and what experiments should we launch to overcome or work around these barriers?
- What are the most effective ways to engage women and under-represented minorities in STEM and making?

Making is one of the more powerful tools we have for accomplishing the goals of K-12 education, as well as for advancing American society as a whole. The essence of making is continuously asking questions about how things work and how to make things better. Working together, we can prove that the future in America is, indeed, what we make of it.

References

Obama, B. (2009, April). *Remarks by the President of the National Academy of Sciences Annual Meeting.* Washington, DC: National Academy of Sciences. www.whitehouse.gov/the-press-office/remarks-president-national-academy-sciences-annual-meeting.

Obama, B. (2009, November). *Remarks by the President on the "Education To Innovate" Campaign.* Washington, DC: Dwight D. Eisenhower Executive Office Building, South Court Auditorium. www.whitehouse.gov/the-press-office/remarks-president-education-innovate-campaign.

CHAPTER 3

How Designing, Making, and Playing Relate to the Learning Goals of K-12 Science Education

HELEN QUINN AND PHILIP BELL

Many varied experiences associated with designing, making, and playing (DMP) involve meaningful forms of STEM learning and can be conceived of as relating to important learning goals outlined for K-12 science education. The competencies associated with the pursuits and products of the specialized forms of designing and making relate conceptually to the knowledge and practices associated with science and engineering pursuits and products. To develop this argument, we summarize dimensions of the consensus research literature on how, why, and where people learn science, as well as outline connections to the relevant learning goals envisioned in a recently released policy document for K-12 science education—*A Framework for K-12 Science Education* (National Research Council, 2011a).

One shared characteristic of participants in "design, make, play" projects described throughout this book is a sense of individual agency in the learning and investigation process. Whether a particular project is conducted by an individual or a group, participants are generally motivated by their ability to engage in the work, influence outcomes, and contribute ideas and solutions—as much as by their interest in or need for the product of that work. The target learning outcomes for participants are, at most, very loosely prescribed by those who organize and lead the project. Rather, the goals of the project give focus to the work. Learning is then instrumentally or incidentally accomplished in pursuit of the specific project goal and as participants work through the typical challenges and snags that arise in project work.

DMP participants assemble needed resources, or repurpose existing materials in innovative ways, to produce, test, and refine their material artifacts. The traditional image of students engaged in science instruction at their desks in a school classroom has little in common with this picture. You might thus conclude that discussion of *A Framework for K-12 Science Education* (hereafter referred to as "the Framework"), and of the development of K-12 education standards based upon the Framework, would be out of place in this book. This chapter intends to convince you otherwise.

We argue three aspects of the overlap between the Framework and DMP:

- The Framework offers a new perspective on science and engineering learning, one that can inform and enrich work in informal education programs and everyday learning environments to which DMP efforts belong.
- Standards built from the perspective laid out in the Framework will demand a change in classroom culture toward one with greater student agency in the context of meaningful problem-solving and investigations, as indeed is also the case for the Common Core Language Arts and Mathematics Standards.
- By including engineering practices alongside scientific practices, and by including a set of core ideas labeled Engineering, Technology, and the Applications of Science, the Framework makes explicit contact with the design and making pursuits wherever students may encounter them.

Twenty-six states are working with the Achieve organization to develop "Next Generation Science Standards," which will outline a set of rigorous learning goals for K-12 science education, based on the conceptual foundation provided by the Framework, and it is expected that these standards will be widely adopted by multiple states. Standards-based educational improvement efforts strongly impact formal schooling, and standards also significantly focus some of the work in the informal education sector in terms of program, media, and teacher development work (National Research Council, 2009). It is thus important for the informal as well as the formal science education community to understand important aspects of the Framework and how it relates to specific aspects of these educational enterprises.

THE FRAMEWORK AND INFORMAL SCIENCE EDUCATION

Why do we assert that a document that so obviously targets formal education is valuable more broadly? We briefly outline three reasons: (1) formal and informal education have overlapping, complementary learning goals in terms of science and engineering; (2) informal learning experiences often provide important entry points for the learning of disciplinary subjects; and (3) development, life-course educational outcomes (e.g., becoming scientifically literate or developing engineering expertise) are best understood as "life-wide" learning processes, accomplished across a variety of formal and informal settings over extended periods of time.

Shared Learning Goals

Recent NRC consensus research reports (National Research Council, 2007, 2009) highlight the overlaps between the goals of formal science education and informal science education, which would include design-make-play related pursuits. Formal and informal learning environments typically afford different kinds of learning experiences and support different aspects of disciplinary learning outcomes. However, the multiple venues associated with science learning should be considered part of the same learning ecosystem for science education in that they share the goals of cultivating the same intertwined strands of science learning outcomes. Although the idea is counterintuitive and controversial to some, similar learning processes can be found in formal and informal environments. For example, sustained investigations of the natural world in a classroom involve similar cognitive, social, and cultural practices associated with learning during the extended elective pursuits of individuals and groups in everyday and family settings (e.g., personal hobbies such as robotics or gardening) or afterschool programs. Extended design projects involve similar challenges, whether developed in classroom or out-of-school settings. Such activities provide an environment in which not only are participants engaged in doing, but most often they are also engaged in debate and discussion about what they are doing, reflection upon how best to reach their desired outcomes, and analytic thinking in order to solve problems that arise in the context of the project. Furthermore, in solving problems, participants are motivated to seek and apply the knowledge and skills needed to reach a solution. Thus, while the explicit goal of a project may be a purposefully designed product, almost all such projects, particularly those directed to school-age children, have goals as to the type of learning expected to occur as the product is developed, sometimes explicitly, sometimes implicitly. It is important to recognize a significant overlap between these informal education goals and the goals for science learning articulated by the Framework.

Based on the research literature and prior consensus reports, the Framework conceptualizes science learning as having three dimensions: (1) Scientific and Engineering Practices; (2) Crosscutting Concepts; and (3) Disciplinary Core Ideas. See Table 3.1 for a specification of the elements of

Table 3.1 The three dimensions of the Framework

---

1. Scientific and Engineering Practices

---

1. Asking questions (for science) and defining problems (for engineering)
2. Developing and using models
3. Planning and carrying out investigations
4. Analyzing and interpreting data
5. Using mathematics and computational thinking
6. Constructing explanations (for science) and designing solutions (for engineering)
7. Engaging in argument from evidence
8. Obtaining, evaluating, and communicating information

---

2. Crosscutting Concepts

---

1. Patterns
2. Cause and effect: mechanism and explanation
3. Scale, proportion, and quantity
4. Systems and system models
5. Energy and matter: flows, cycles, and conservation
6. Structure and function
7. Stability and change

---

3. Disciplinary Core Ideas

Physical Sciences
PS 1: Matter and its interactions
PS 2: Motion and stability: forces and interactions
PS 3: Energy
PS 4: Waves and their applications in technologies for information transfer

Life Sciences
LS 1: From molecules to organisms: structures and processes
LS 2: Ecosystems: interactions, energy, and dynamics
LS 3: Heredity: inheritance and variation of traits
LS 4: Biological evolution: unity and diversity

Earth and Space Sciences
ESS 1: Earth's place in the universe
ESS 2: Earth's systems
ESS 3: Earth and human activity

Engineering, Technology, and the Applications of Science
ETS 1: Engineering design
ETS 2: Links among engineering, technology, science, and society

---

each of these at the top level. The learning goals of any significant design-make-play project will have significant overlap with at least the first of these dimensions (i.e., the specialized practices associated with science and engineering), probably also with the second (e.g., structure and function; systems and systems models), and possibly with elements of the third, disciplinary knowledge dimension, particularly, but not uniquely, those of the Engineering, Technology, and Applications of Science category. Given these overlaps, the value of the Framework is that it gives a common language for the formal and informal sector to talk about these goals. They define the base, or floor, of shared learning goals for all residents and citizens in the United States.

Informal Learning Environments Provide Entry Points for Science Learning

Because of some unique qualities of informal learning environments—tied to promoting voluntary and differentiated learning experiences as well as developing and promoting use of compelling educational materials related to contemporary and classic science topics—informal learning environments often serve as entry points in sustained science learning for individuals (National Research Council, 2009). In our research on where, why, and how youth learn science, we find that informal contexts such as hobbies, summer programs, and science centers can provide stimulating educational experiences that help set initial interest in a topical niche of science (for a review of this work, see Bell, Bricker, Reeve, Zimmerman, & Tzou, 2012). If such moments of situational interest are then further supported—through a blend of formal and informal educational experiences—they can open up into an extended learning pathway associated with meaningful learning and expertise development (see also Barron, 2006). These interest- and identity-driven learning processes for science are described in detail in the *Learning Science in Informal Environments* report (National Research Council, 2009), and they are leveraged in the NRC Framework in an effort to ensure equity in science education by recognizing that individual learning is (and should be) heavily influenced by individual, community, and societal interests. The pursuits associated with designing and making invariably, by their nature, open up extended interest- and identity-driven learning pathways for participants—many of which would be relatable to the learning goals and processes identified in the NRC Framework.

Taking an Ecological Turn on Learning

Life-course educational outcomes that are accomplished only with concerted effort and support over extended periods of time (e.g., graduating from high school, becoming scientifically literate with respect to a broad set of disciplinary knowledge and practices, developing engineering expertise involving extensive design knowledge and practices in relation to scientific knowledge) are best understood as life-long, life-wide, and life-deep learning processes, accomplished across a variety of formal and informal settings over extended periods of time in relation to variable cultural value systems that shape everyday moments of activity (Banks et al., 2007). This conceptual model for learning (shown in Figure 3.1) highlights the broad contours of the educational ecosystem.

Recent trends in science education and learning sciences research are focusing on how learning can intentionally be coordinated and supported across settings over time—to provide a more seamless learning experience (for a detailed description, see U.S. Department of Education, 2010). The design-make-play educational experiences could be approached from a similar ecology of learning perspective focused on the learning goals represented in the Framework. For example, a case study of life-long, life-wide, life-deep expertise development highlights how a university K-12 summer program focused on design play might open up a multiyear hobby pursuit doing designing and making activities that can eventually be coordinated with formal educational courses in engineering (Bricker & Bell,

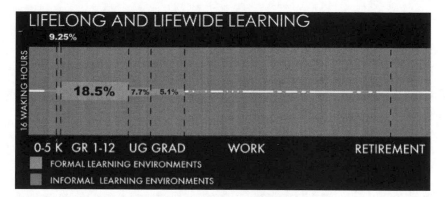

Figure 3.1 This diagram from Banks et al. (2007) shows the amount of time, averaged over a year, that people spend in formal learning environments (i.e., academic-subject-matter school experiences) as compared to the time they spend in other waking activities in informal environments. This diagram was originally conceived by Reed Stevens and John Bransford to represent the range of learning environments being studied at the NSF-funded Learning in Informal and Formal Environments (LIFE) Center (http://life-slc.org). Design, documentation, and calculations were conducted by Reed Stevens, with key assistance from Anne Stevens (graphic design) and Nathan Parham (calculations).

in review). In this detailed case study, a third-grade boy participates in a one-week summer program focused on designing with a commercial toy system, and this launches a series of subsequent design hobby pursuits involving increasingly complex construction and robotics systems, the design of virtual game environments, and ultimately leading the youth to enroll in an elective engineering course in middle school. This young man developed significant expertise in design practices and knowledge through an extended series of pursuits composed of self-organized everyday activities, informal education programs and experiences with his family, and formal education course experiences.

From the perspective of design-make-play communities, the list of practices, crosscutting concepts, and disciplinary core ideas to be embedded in Next Generation Science Standards provides a framework for articulating how the project activity serves the learning goals associated with these topical endeavors. Pursuits in robotics relate to engineering design practices and core ideas of engineering, technology, and applications of science. Pursuits related to do-it-yourself (DIY) construction of scientific instrumentation (e.g., a DIY scanning electron microscope) deeply focus on understanding the atomic model and physical principles in relation to practices that relate to engineering design and data analysis. In summary, we believe that great opportunities arise from having the informal education sector focus on the learning goals outlined in the Framework as well as from designing and offering educational experiences as part of the educational ecosystem for science and engineering education.

Changing the Classroom Culture

Not only the Next Generation Science Standards but also the Common Core English Language Arts and Mathematics Standards demand student capabilities that can be developed only with a change of classroom culture. All three require that classrooms–and group-based learning environments generally—move toward a culture of student participation in discourse and activities that require group problem-solving, investigation, explanation, and argumentation. What differs across the disciplines is the focus of that activity, the detailed nature of the problems to be addressed, and the discipline-specific practices that students must learn to address these problems effectively. By displaying features of the three sets of standards in a single Venn diagram, Figure 3.2 emphasizes both the commonalities across and between disciplines and the discipline-specific elements.[1] All these practices, however, share the feature that implementing them in a classroom context requires a shift in the level and amount of student-to-student discourse that occurs. They all build upon the social foundations of how people learn, and all shift instruction toward dialogic interaction and

These student practices and portraits are grouped in a modified Venn diagram. The letter and number set preceding each phrase denotes the discipline and number designated by the content standards or framework. The Science Framework will be used to guide the production of the Next Generation Science Standards.

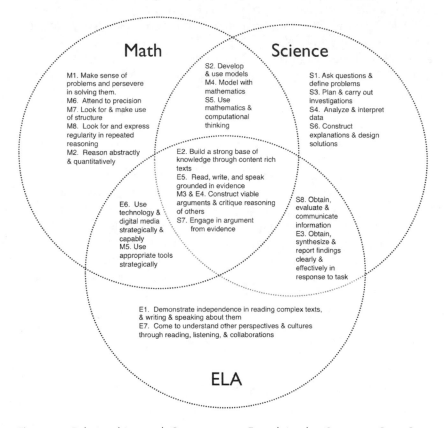

Figure 3.2 Relationships and Convergences Found in the Common Core State Standards in Mathematics (practices), Common Core State Standards in ELA/ Literacy (student portraits), and A Framework for K-12 Science Education (science and engineering practices).

Source: Adapted from figure by Tina Cheuk, Understanding Language, ell.stanford.edu.

sense-making (e.g., National Research Council, 2007). In too many classrooms today, students most often are asked to speak only to give a factual response to a teacher's question.

Of course, particularly at the elementary school level, the image of children sitting at desks in rows doing the same thing at the same time has long been outdated. The pressure of NCLB testing, however, has restored this pedagogical mode to many classrooms for substantial stretches of time, especially those under threat because they have failed to achieve acceptable results for too many students (National Research Council, 2011b). The claim here is that the Framework differs from the drivers of this regression to passive-learner forms of instruction and that the ambitious learning goals outlined in the Framework cannot be achieved by this teaching methodology. What led to this development was that, all too often, classrooms had evolved to a culture of activity and engagement that failed to address important learning goals such as developing, using and critiquing scientific models, or engaging in evidence-based argumentation. To achieve the learning goals of the Framework and the Common Core standards, classrooms must change again, not back to a failed model, but forward to one that learning research demonstrates is more effective: to recognize the central role of active knowledge construction for learners and the social processes of dialogic learning within communities. Such change requires teachers (and school administrators) to clearly recognize that while activity and engagement are important as a precondition for learning that involves conceptual change, activity and engagement are themselves only part of the goal. Each activity must be designed to elicit student thinking and include time for explication of thinking, argumentation, and reflection. Students must engage in a "minds-on" as well as a "hands-on" process to achieve the conceptual growth and development that these standards will demand. Every activity must have a clear connection to specific learning goals and expected student outcomes, as well as requiring and supporting engagement in specific expected practices. For example, students may learn about the conceptual dimensions of habitats by documenting the biodiversity of their schoolyard involving systematic observation, model building, data collection, constructing explanations, and engaging in classroom debates and other forms of communication (National Research Council, 2008).

The Framework introduces defined sets of science and engineering practices that every student is expected to become proficient at using. These practices mirror the intellectual work of scientists and engineers in meaningful ways, support important forms of individual and social learning processes, and provide learners with a more authentic image of disciplinary work. In this sense, the set of practices refines and expands the idea of "scientific inquiry" and "engineering design" as a legitimate and, indeed, essential activity for students. It spells out essential components of that activity, all too many of which have been lacking or underemphasized even in classrooms where students are engaged in activity labeled as inquiry or design. In many science classrooms, students are introduced to established scientific models but not asked to develop, use, or critique their own models of natural phenomena. Or, students are engaged in a design task but not given support in important conceptual dimensions of this engineering work involving defining or delimiting the problem space or optimizing a design solution. If, as is expected based on the Framework, standards (and the assessments that test students' progress toward them) expect students to demonstrate familiarity with and skill in applying these practices in the context of a particular problem, then classrooms where students are actively engaged in the full range of the identified practices as an integral part of their science learning will become more common.

One aspect of this change will be that students experience more design-make-play-related activity in the context of their science classrooms. Well-designed design-make-play learning experiences in informal settings can also support student enthusiasm for, as well as competence and engagement in, these practices. Design-make-play pursuits can be viewed as engaging participants in authentic sequences of these practices within specific compelling contexts. For example, the design and construction of hydroponic gardening systems from everyday materials opens up a complex project space that melds engineering design expertise with an understanding of life science concepts. Another example comes from the emerging hobbyist area of do-it-yourself biology where individuals (e.g., citizen scientists, biologists, computer scientists, artists) are working in unconventional contexts to engineer biological molecules and systems. This synthetic biology work, sometimes referred to as "bio-hacking," involves a sophisticated coordination of scientific and engineering practices (e.g., modeling and engineering design), disciplinary ideas (e.g., growth and development of organisms), and crosscutting concepts (e.g., structure and function).

The need to integrate "content" and "practice" learning goals is nowhere more evident than in the format of the draft science standards released for public review, where, true to the goals of the Framework, each performance expectation will require the student to demonstrate some understanding of a disciplinary core idea by applying this understanding in the context of some disciplinary practice, linking also to crosscutting concepts as appropriate. For example, high school students engaged in an engineering project might be asked to "refine a design by conducting several rounds of tests, modifying the model after each test, to create the best possible design that meets the most important criteria."

Such a change in classroom culture cannot occur without significant teacher professional development, designed to support teachers in effectively implementing such a change. Teachers who have never experienced these practices in their own science education will have difficulty implementing them in their classrooms. The knowledge and experience of the informal sector, and of the DMP movement within it, can provide learning experiences for teachers that will be important in this context.

INCLUSION OF ENGINEERING DESIGN IN THE FRAMEWORK

The Framework makes explicit that the goals of science teaching in schools must be broader than the production of more scientists, or even of more scientifically "literate" adults, if "literacy" is interpreted, as it often is, as knowing more facts. To quote:

> The framework is designed to realize a vision for education in the sciences and engineering in which students, over multiple years of schooling, actively engage in scientific and engineering practices and apply crosscutting concepts to deepen their understanding of core ideas in these fields. The learning experiences provided for students should engage them with fundamental questions about the world and how scientists have investigated and found answers to those questions.

Further, it states:

> studying and engaging in the practices of science and engineering ... should help students see how science and engineering are instrumental to addressing major challenges that confront society today, such as generating sufficient energy, preventing and treating diseases, maintaining supplies of clean water and food, and solving problems of global environmental change.

Given the increasing role of sophisticated technologies in everyday life, there is increasing demand for citizens to be technologically literate about the built world and for students to understand and consider entering engineering- and technology-related fields that use science (National Research Council, 2002). The Framework argues that all students should learn how science is utilized, especially in the context of engineering design, and come to appreciate the distinctions and relationships between engineering, technology, and applications of science. This means that students need to develop problem-solving and thinking skills to understand the science and engineering enterprises and the scientific basis of familiar engineered technologies, as well as to be able to apply that understanding appropriately and effectively in their personal lives and communities. For example, citizens need to understand the trade-offs associated with different forms of energy production; they need to understand how new crops are being engineered and with what benefits and risks; they need to understand the trade-offs associated with a range of biomedical devices that are used to augment human health. The fact that the word *engineering* was centrally included in the NRC Framework is no accident. Inclusion of some aspects of engineering, in particular engineering design, in the Framework is a deliberate decision to broaden the curriculum, both because engagement

Table 3.2 Comparison of practices in science and in engineering

1. Asking Questions and Defining Problems

Science begins with a question about a phenomenon, such as "Why is the sky blue?" or "What causes cancer?" and seeks to develop theories that can provide explanatory answers to such questions. A basic practice of the scientist is formulating empirically answerable questions about phenomena, establishing what is already known, and determining what questions have yet to be satisfactorily answered.

Engineering begins with a problem, need, or desire that suggests an engineering problem that needs to be solved. A societal problem such as reducing the nation's dependence on fossil fuels may engender a variety of engineering problems, such as designing more efficient transportation systems or alternative power generation devices such as improved solar cells. Engineers ask questions to define the engineering problem, determine criteria for a successful solution, and identify constraints.

2. Developing and Using Models

Science often involves the construction and use of a wide variety of models and simulations to help develop explanations about natural phenomena. Models make it possible to go beyond observables and imagine a world not yet seen. Models enable predictions of the form "if . . . then . . . therefore" to be made in order to test hypothetical explanations.

Engineering makes use of models and simulations to analyze existing systems to see where flaws might occur or to test possible solutions to a new problem. Engineers also call on models of various sorts to test proposed systems and to recognize the strengths and limitations of their designs.

3. Planning and Carrying Out Investigations

Scientific investigation may be conducted in the field or the laboratory. A major practice of scientists is planning and carrying out a systematic investigation, which requires the identification of what is to be recorded and, if applicable, what are to be treated as the dependent and independent variables (control of variables). Observations and data collected from such work are used to test existing theories and explanations or to revise and develop new ones.

Engineers use investigation both to gain data essential for specifying design criteria or parameters and to test their designs. Like scientists, engineers must identify relevant variables, decide how they will be measured, and collect data for analysis. Their investigations help them identify how effective, efficient, and durable their designs may be under a range of conditions.

4. Analyzing and Interpreting Data

Scientific investigations produce data that must be analyzed in order to derive meaning. Because data usually do not speak for themselves, scientists use a range of tools—including tabulation, graphical interpretation, visualization, and statistical analysis—to identify the significant features and patterns in the data. Sources of error are identified and the degree of certainty calculated. Modern technology makes the collection of large data sets much easier, thus providing many secondary sources for analysis.

Engineers analyze data collected in the tests of their designs and investigations; this allows them to compare different solutions and determine how well each one meets specific design criteria—that is, which design best solves the problem within the given constraints. Like scientists, engineers require a range of tools to identify the major patterns and interpret the results.

5. Using Mathematics and Computational Thinking

In science, mathematics and computation are fundamental tools for representing physical variables and their relationships. They are used for a range of tasks, such as constructing simulations, statistically analyzing data, and recognizing, expressing, and applying quantitative relationships. Mathematical and computational approaches enable predictions of the behavior of physical systems, along with the testing of such predictions. Moreover, statistical techniques are invaluable for assessing the significance of patterns or correlations.

In engineering, mathematical and computational representations of established relationships and principles are an integral part of design. For example, structural engineers create mathematically based analyzes of designs to calculate whether they can stand up to the expected stresses of use and if they can be completed within acceptable budgets. Moreover, simulations of designs provide an effective test bed for the development of designs and their improvement.

6. Constructing Explanations and Designing Solutions

The goal of science is the construction of theories that can provide explanatory accounts of features of the natural world. A theory becomes accepted when it has been shown to be superior to other explanations, in the breadth of phenomena it accounts for, and its explanatory coherence and Scientific explanations are explicit applications of theory to a specific situation or phenomenon, perhaps with the intermediary of a theory-based model for the system under study. The goal for students is to construct logically coherent explanations of phenomena that incorporate their current understanding of science, or a model that represents it, and are consistent with the available evidence.

Engineering design, a systematic process for solving engineering problems, is based on scientific knowledge and models of the material world. Each proposed solution results from a process of balancing competing criteria of desired functions, technological feasibility, cost, safety, aesthetics, and compliance with legal requirements. There is usually no single best solution but rather a range of solutions. Which one is the optimal choice depends on the criteria used for making evaluations.

7. Engaging in Argument from Evidence

In **science**, reasoning and argument are essential for identifying the strengths and weaknesses of a line of reasoning and for finding the best explanation for a natural phenomenon. Scientists must defend their explanations, formulate evidence based on a solid foundation of data, examine their own understanding in light of the evidence and comments offered by others, and collaborate with peers in searching for the best explanation for the phenomena being investigated.

In **engineering**, reasoning and argument are essential for finding the best possible solution to a problem. Engineers collaborate with their peers throughout the design process, with a critical stage being the selection of the most promising solution among a field of competing ideas. Engineers use systematic methods to compare alternatives, formulate evidence based on test data, argue from evidence to defend their conclusions, evaluate critically the ideas of others, and revise their designs in order to achieve the best solution to the problem at hand.

8. Obtaining, Evaluating, and Communicating Information

Science cannot advance if scientists are unable to communicate their findings clearly and persuasively or to learn about the findings of others. A major practice of science is thus the communication of ideas and the results of inquiry—orally, in writing, with the use of tables, diagrams, graphs, and equations, and by engaging in extended discussions with scientific peers. Science requires the ability to derive meaning from scientific texts (such as papers, the Internet, symposia, and lectures), to evaluate the scientific validity of the information thus acquired, and to integrate that information.

Engineers cannot produce new or improved technologies if they cannot communicate the advantages of their designs clearly and persuasively. Engineers need to be able to express their ideas, orally and in writing, with the use of tables, graphs, drawings, or models, and by engaging in extended discussions with peers. Moreover, like scientists, they need to be able to derive meaning from colleagues' texts, evaluate the information, and apply it usefully. In engineering and science alike, new technologies are now routinely available that extend the possibilities for collaboration and communication.

in design activities can support student learning and interest in science and because knowledge about the engineering design cycle is itself something that all students can benefit from. The Framework takes the position that all students need this knowledge and experience across the K-12 curricular experience, and that, particularly at the K-8 level, it is often a missing element of what is offered to them. In high school, this learning opportunity may occur in a science class, in a career and technical education class, or in some other course. The Framework does not specify the course sequences at this level but simply specifies that all students need opportunities to learn about the engineering design cycle and to engage in design activities. Of course, this opportunity could also be offered or reinforced by experiences outside of school through informal-sector activity; the challenge in that path is to ensure that all students indeed have such opportunities.

The Framework describes eight central practices for science and engineering. Table 3.2 highlights the science and engineering forms of these eight practices. Most are conceptually similar, although two—the starting point (practice 1) and the goal of the process (practice 6)—are substantially distinct. As the table shows, these differences in goals mean that the practices, even when conceptually similar, are used for somewhat different ends in science and in engineering.

In addition to the inclusion of engineering practices, the second engineering-focused element in the Framework consists of two core ideas that highlight conceptual learning goals across the K-12 span. The core idea labeled Engineering Design signifies that there is knowledge about how to most effectively undertake, define, and delimit a design project; knowledge about the design cycle; and knowledge of the need for an iterative approach to explore possibilities and optimize a design solution. The second core idea highlights the linkages between engineering, technology, and science—in terms of how science offers new capabilities for technologies and contributes to engineering designs, how technology and engineering offer tools and extend the reach of science, and how the emergence and broad uptake of new technologies impact society and the natural world. In informal environments, this distinction of knowledge and practice may seem a little artificial—after all, this is knowledge that can be gained through practice. The message here is that if such learning is indeed a goal, it pays to be explicit about what is to be learned, both to guide how activities are structured, and to make sure that participants are encouraged to reflect on what they have done and to help them explicitly recognize the ideas that were implicit as they worked (as outlined in detail in National Research Council, 2009). We believe great opportunities to pursue this engineering education agenda exist across the range of design-make-play pursuits.

Conclusion

A Framework for K-12 Science Education provides both an opportunity and a challenge to those who work in informal learning environments as well as to those in formal science education. It presents a vision as to what is to be learned and how people learn, not where and when it is to be learned. Goals that are central for informal learning environments, such as interest in science and engineering, or identity as a competent maker, are more implicit in formal education. Goals that are more explicit for the formal education sector, such as deeply understanding particular aspects of mechanics, or the relationship between structure and function, are often less of a driving focus for the informal education sector. In fact, however, the goals and complementarities in the ways different environments can support science learning largely overlap. If all students are to meet these goals, then the roles for out-of-school as well as in-school learning are both crucial. We hope and expect that the Framework can serve as a useful tool for guiding participants in meaningful science and engineering learning in the varied pursuits associated with the design-make-play communities across the settings in which they might participate.

Note

1 Analysis by Tina Cheuk is based on Common Core State Standards for English Language Arts and Literacy in History/Social Studies, Science, and Technical Subjects (p. 7); Common Core State Standards for Mathematical Practice, (pp. 6–8); *A Framework for K-12 Science Education: Practices, Crosscutting Concepts, and Core Ideas.*

References

Banks, J. A., Au, K. H., Ball, A. F., Bell, P., Gordon, E. W., Gutiérrez, K., et al. (2007). *Learning in and out of school in diverse environments: Life-long, life-wide, life-deep.* Seattle, WA: University of Washington, The LIFE Center and the Center for Multicultural Education. http://life-slc.org/docs/Banks_etal-LIFE-Diversity-Report.pdf.
Barron, B. (2006). Interest and self-sustained learning as catalysts of development: A learning ecology perspective. *Human Development, 49*(4), 193–224.
Bell, P., Bricker, L. A., Reeve, S., Zimmerman, H. T., & Tzou, C. (2012). Discovering and supporting successful learning pathways of youth in and out of school: Accounting for the development of everyday expertise across settings. In B. Bevan, P. Bell, R. Stevens, & A. Razfar (Eds.), *LOST opportunities: Learning in out of school time* (pp. 119–140). Kluwer, Netherlands: Springer.
Bricker, L. A., & Bell, P. (in review). "I want to be an engineer": Network, framing, and positioning dynamics associated with youth STEM learning and expertise development in and out of school.
National Research Council (2002). *Technically speaking: Why all Americans need to know more about technology.* Washington, DC: National Academy Press.

National Research Council (2007). *Taking science to school: Learning and teaching science in grades K–8.* R. Duschl, H. A. Schweingruber, & A. Shouse (Eds.). Board on Science Education, National Research Council. Washington, DC: The National Academies Press.

National Research Council (2008). *Ready, set, science: Putting research to work in K–8 science classrooms.* Washington, DC: National Academy of Press.

National Research Council (2009). *Learning science in informal environments: People, places, and pursuits.* P. Bell, B. Lewenstein, A. W. Shouse, & M. A. Feder (Eds.). Board on Science Education, National Research Council. Washington, DC: The National Academies Press.

National Research Council (2011a). *A framework for K-12 science education: Practices, crosscutting concepts, and core ideas.* Committee on Conceptual Framework for the New K-12 Science Education Standards, Board on Science Education, National Research Council. Washington, DC: The National Academies Press.

National Research Council (2011b). *Successful K-12 STEM education: Identifying effective approaches in science, technology, engineering, and mathematics.* Committee on Highly Successful Schools or Programs in K-12 STEM Education, National Research Council. Washington, DC: National Academy Press.

U.S. Department of Education (2010). *Transforming American education: Learning powered by technology.* Office of Educational Technology. Washington, DC: Government Printing Office.

CHAPTER 4

NYSCI DESIGN LAB: NO BORED KIDS!

DOROTHY BENNETT AND PEGGY MONAHAN

Design Lab is a place where
You'll tinker with materials,
play around with science,
tackle problems worth solving,
and design things to work.

Design Lab at the New York Hall of Science aims to deeply engage *all* types of science learners in solving personally motivating problems via a creative design process. Developed as a multilayered experience for the general public, teachers, and schools, the project includes a museum exhibition (opening in 2014) involving hands-on, immersive design activities, a series of online instructional resources and tools, and professional development that helps teachers incorporate design thinking into their existing curricula to meet the new science and math standards. From hacking a musical greeting card to creating an audio surprise for a friend to designing working solar ovens from recycled materials, Design Lab is creating new possibilities for young people to identify design problems worth solving, notice design opportunities in the real world, and think creatively about the redesign and reuse of materials to solve everyday problems involving STEM concepts and skills.

Design Lab is a relatively new project for the New York Hall of Science—just about a year and a half old—and is very much a project in process. This chapter discusses some of the things we have learned thus far, our aspirations, and some questions for the future. Early on in the project, we held a retreat to refine the foundational philosophy of what we wanted to achieve. One result of that discussion was a phrase that has become the project's rallying cry: "No Bored Kids!" We do not mean that we want learners to be entertained. We want them to be engaged. We want them to be deeply engaged with problems that they personally find worth solving, and thus with the science content therein.

Unfortunately, most schools have limited access to resources and tools that inspire and motivate students in this way. Science and mathematics are often presented to students as abstract topics devoid of personalized, real-world connections. Students are bored, they are checking out. This is particularly alarming since the most predictive factor in students dropping out of high school and ultimately out of the STEM pipeline is the lack of student engagement with real-world problems in their coursework (Connell, Halpem-Felsher, Clifford, Crichlow, & Usinger, 1995; Jerald, 2006; Rumberger, 2004). When a large-scale survey asked students what would keep them in school, the top responses from underachieving and at-risk students were "opportunities for real-world learning" and "to make classrooms more relevant" (Bridgeland, Dilulio, & Morison, 2006; Rumberger, 2004). There are programs that do connect school studies with real life, but they often target students who are already successful in school and neglect reluctant learners or at-risk students (Bridgeland, Dilulio, & Wulsin, 2008).

Design-based teaching and learning can address these challenges and offer a new and effective approach to STEM education for *all* learners. Design is the iterative selection and arrangement of elements by which people create artifacts, systems, and tools intended to solve a range of problems, large and small. Through design, you learn how to identify a problem or need, how to consider design options and constraints, and how to plan, model, test, and iterate solutions to vexing problems, making higher-order thinking skills tangible and visible. Design-based activities can be intrinsically motivating to children because they engage the desire to make things and learn how things work. Design also responds to the interdisciplinary complexity of life, requiring that multiple areas of expertise be brought to bear on real-world problems, making it a natural approach for integrating STEM into all subject areas. Research shows that actively engaging students in design projects can help learners develop deep conceptual understanding of the knowledge and principles of a domain and support the development of self-guided inquiry skills that are often difficult to teach (Crismond, 2001; Fleer, 2000; Fleer & Williams-Kennedy, 2002; Johnsey, 1993, 1995; Kimmel, Carpinelli, Burr-Alexander, & Rockland, 2006; Kolodner et al., 2003; Lewis, 2005; Linn, 2003; Roth, 1995, 1996a, 1996b; Sadler, Barab, & Scott, 2007; Zubrowski, 2002).

To tap the full potential of design-based teaching and learning, we must invite all learners into content with problems they find personally relevant.

The science geeks, the poets, the makers, the do-gooders, the comedians, and the storytellers are all motivated by different causes. While some children might be excited by an opportunity to design something to help people, others might enjoy designing something for no other purpose than whimsy. Since the definition of "personally relevant" varies from person to person, the nature of the invitation must be broad enough so that each learner finds his or her own skills and interests reflected in the activities. We need to open up the design challenges enough to let learners define their own problems so that, in particular, reluctant learners, who are not already served by current science activities, find something that motivates them.

The true potential of design as a learning approach is that it provides a good foundation for lifelong learning—a process for identifying problems, needs, or goals, as well as gaining strategies for gathering the right resources, information, and materials to tackle problems and generate solutions.

Why Do Design?

Design is not necessarily an efficient way to teach specific STEM content. It is, however, a powerful way to kindle a desire to learn that content. The strength of design-based activities is that, when done well, they are highly motivating and multidisciplinary. Good design problems invite you in with your strengths, and encourage you to use what you already know to define a problem for yourself. They create a strong need to know, giving you momentum toward learning relevant new concepts and skills. At the heart of every good design problem is the opportunity to bump up against rich STEM content in the form of useful information, relevant concepts, and technical skills that help move you further along in enacting or improving your design. For instance, while designing something that would help you survive on a desert island, you might need to investigate the kind of climate you find yourself in, identifying the available flora and fauna, investigating simple water filtration methods, and the strength of materials to create structures that can withstand extreme weather.

Design activities invite divergent solutions, where each solution is as unique as its designer. This makes design activities more aligned with the process of engineering than the process of science. The goal of science is to reach toward the one most elegant and efficient explanation, while the goal of engineering is to negotiate trade-offs to arrive at one of many possible solutions. But that makes it somewhat challenging for educators to incorporate design activities into a standard curriculum where specific content has to be "covered": if learners are going to have such divergent responses to a problem, it is difficult to ensure that they converge on the specific content to be conveyed.

The affordances of design-based activites, however, are highly rewarding for all students. We have observed the following when children are approached through design teaching and learning:

- Children, especially those who think they are not good at STEM, become more motivated and engaged when they experience first-hand how core content and skills are *integral* to solving problems that are personally relevant and engaging, not learning skills taught in isolation. It is more motivating, for example, to learn about scale through the act of designing a piece of furniture to fit yourself than by doing ratio and proportion computation problems.
- When motivated and engaged, students are more willing to persist in the face of difficulties, allowing for deeper learning of content.
- When truly engaged in meaningful problems, students grow to see early failures as necessary iterations leading to successful solutions.

Creating design problems that build on the unique interests, proclivities, and background knowledge and skill sets of diverse learners is difficult, especially when trying to reach reluctant learners who are not readily attracted by typical "go-to" technology activities such as cars, rockets, robots, etc. We have to find new problem contexts that interest these unengaged students. Furthermore, problems that young people are likely to be drawn to in the real world are not neatly packaged to impart some narrow form of content but often encompass multiple content ideas and disciplines.

From the very beginning, Design Lab has worked to build bridges between formal and informal education by drawing on the science museum's power to promote new and engaging ways of seeing the world by coming at a STEM topic sideways and offering opportunities for schools and teachers to make what they teach relevant and empowering through real-world connections. For the general public, Design Lab has been prototyping physical spaces and hands-on activities that can invite visitors to see design possibilities in their everyday lives and to have a sense of agency to change their surroundings in small and big ways. For teachers, Design Lab has been creating formal professional development experiences and an informal tinkering space where educators can find like-minded colleagues, stimulating conversation, and opportunities to be creative, playful, and inventive in coming up with relevant, interdisciplinary teaching approaches for their students. In addition to location-based activities, NYSCI Design Lab is also developing a suite of digital learning resources that will include videos, synchronous and asynchronous webinars, portable apps, and other virtual resources to support design-based learning.

With seed funding from the Verizon Foundation and a research grant from the Office of Naval Research (ONR), over the past 18 months we have also engaged in extensive exhibit prototyping sessions to better understand the kinds of drop-in design activities and invitations into STEM that can be facilitated on the museum floor.

THE TALE OF HAPPY CITY

Through exhibit and teacher prototyping sessions, NYSCI learned about the potential of design-based learning to engage reluctant learners and identified some of the qualities and features that promote engagement and allow for multiple points of entry into STEM. While we have experimented with a broad range of content and activities during this process (e.g., vibrations, motion, electricity and energy, air and pneumatics, and structures) in this chapter, we describe our evolution of a simple activity to introduce children, teachers, and the casual museum visitor to the topic of circuits and conductivity. Affectionately known as Happy City, the activity was tested in multiple venues: on the museum floor as a drop-in experience, at high-traffic venues such as Maker Faire and World Science Day, with teachers in formal and informal professional development sessions, and with school groups in facilitated field-trip classes. The evolution of Happy City has helped us think through some of the guiding principles for developing good participatory design activities that are not too narrowly focused and allow for creative expression.

Circuitry is a topic ripe for design, and the teachers we worked with identified it as a content area worth exploring. Not only is it a common topic in science classrooms, but also we have seen that children get excited when they begin to control electricity. In our early development phase, we challenged ourselves to move beyond creating activities where children investigated what a circuit is. We wanted to develop activities and materials that would enable children to build things that use circuits as a way to interact with and control the world. In addition to understanding that circuits are a loop in which electricity flows, we wanted children to think about the design possibilities in their own lives—the possibility of using circuits to create something they cared about. We needed to create a problem context that gave children enough specificity to get started and to ensure that they explored the content we are hoping they master, and yet was broad enough so that most children could use it to define something personally meaningful. In this case, our task was to prompt learners to create a problem for which they would grapple with completing an electrical circuit that can do something (such as light up an LED).

We began looking at different ways in which circuits can be personalized and fun and that would break out of the mold of conventional batteries and bulbs experiments. Inspired by LilyPad Arduino projects that use conductive fabric, we were looking for an entry-level activity where children could make personalized items such as jewelry, clothing, or accessories that would light up or ring. We experimented with swatches of conductive fabric and felt with conductive thread, excited about the prospect that these unconventional materials would help learners see new possibilities for circuits in their world.

We first piloted this idea with teachers and then in small student groups, and found some intractable problems. We discovered rather quickly that children have difficulty conceptualizing the circuit's "loop" when designing

Figure 4.1 The lights on these "clubbing glasses" blink when she moves.

Source: © Sunny Kam Photography.

with fabric since broad swatches of conductive fabric do not easily translate to the expected "lines" of a loop. While the unexpected materiality did encourage some out-of-the-box thinking (see Figure 4.1), this early frustration hampered everyone's explorations and designs.

We changed the activity to sewing conductive thread onto felt to help make the circuit's loop more obvious, but the process of hand-sewing was so tedious and so physically hard to change that people did not have the time or desire to iterate their designs to find something that worked. We provided more scaffolding to make it possible for children to create things, but then realized we were leaving the realm of design and creating a scripted activity where children were not designing, but merely assembling. We recognized that learning about circuits, as well as how to use unfamiliar materials such as conductive fabric to design anything a person found worthwhile, required significant amounts of time.

FINDING A PROBLEM WORTH SOLVING

The prospect of Maker Faire 2011 made us think more broadly about what we were trying to accomplish with circuits. We still wanted the problem to be personally compelling, but rather than having children create personalized items using novel materials, we considered how to engage them in thinking about circuits in the real world and how they could remix or reuse them to accomplish something worthy or fun. We wanted to communicate that there are many ways to make circuits so long as you have conductive material, a power source, and a load (e.g., a motor or LED), and you do not need hi-tech materials to create them. We knew that at Maker Faire, our booth would have to absorb high traffic from visitors of all ages and skill levels, so we wanted visitors to be able to quickly identify a problem they wanted to solve, drawing from their own experiences, and thus the problem context and materials needed to be fairly easy to engage with.

We arrived at adding "circuits" to a model city known as "Happy City." What if you could add something to a city or city block that would make you smile, laugh, or make it a little happier? A garbage can that said "Thank you" when you threw something in it, a spinning sign that welcomed you to an area, trees with lights that twinkled as you walked by. Rather than work with specialized fabric and thread, we tried using common household or office materials: aluminum foil, pipe cleaners, cardboard boxes, paper clips, binder clips, and tape, along with LEDs and motors.

The idea was easy to communicate and instantly engaging: add something using a circuit to a model city that would make it a happy place. Young and old were completely immersed in this activity and added things ranging from a musical crosswalk, a house that lights up, a breeze hut with motorized fans, a flying house with a helicopter on top, and plenty of pizza places.

HAPPY CITY PROBLEM

Think about something you could build for a model city that would make people happy. How could you use an LED and/or a motor in the city to make your creation do something to spread happiness? Using the materials below, build models with circuits to add to a shared model city.

Materials: cardboard boxes, index cards, aluminum foil strips, binder clips, paper clips, markers, scissors, watch batteries, motors, LEDs, and any other items you can find easily.

As we tried the activity in varied formats and with different audiences, we found that Happy City was successful on different levels, depending on materials, problem framing, time, and facilitation provided.

Happy City promoted a sense of autonomy and ownership while at the same time familiarizing people with circuits and conductivity. Nearly everyone was able to come up with something he or she wanted to add because everyone is familiar with what it is to live in a city, town, or on a block (at least from television, if not in real life). While the activity was still significantly about circuits, the purpose or goal was defined by the learners—they decided how they solved the challenge–promoting a sense of agency.

We knew that a learner's sense of agency is essential to successful design teaching and learning. The following example uses pneumatics rather than circuits as content, but dramatically illustrates the importance of maintaining the learner's sense of agency within the problem statement. The first time we created an activity about pneumatics, we challenged participants to create an assistive device using air that could lift a cup eight inches above the table using balloon pumps, plastic bags, tubing, tape, and cardboard. All the groups arrived at basically the same solution and became more engaged in decorating their devices rather than engaging with pneumatics. We had narrowly defined success, and once it had been achieved, everyone stopped. They were not engaged in the problem context enough to push themselves further. Next, we tried using almost the same materials, but reframed the problem, opening it up for everyone to define the type of the movement he wanted to achieve. We swapped the cup for a flexible plastic silhouette of a person and challenged learners to create an "air-powered people mover" to make this silhouette move in some way.

Both activities challenge the students to make something move. But where the original problem tightly defined both the object's motion (raise it eight inches) and purpose (help someone with limited mobility by creating an assistive device), the new challenge let the students define both for themselves. They were in charge of the narrative behind their creations, which ranged from wake-up devices that raise tired people out of bed, to machines that exercised different body limbs, to launchers for circus acrobats. This range of divergent solutions was in stark contrast to our first incarnation of the problem. By looking at the wide variety of creations and listening to the students' stories, we could tell that they were all deeply engaged in producing something personally meaningful. This reframing kept the learners in control and generated far more experimentation. The challenges that the students posed for themselves were often more difficult than the one we had originally posed, leading them to explore the content of pneumatics more deeply.

GOOD PROBLEM FRAMING: SETTING FIRST

In our professional development offerings, we work to get teachers to think hard about how they frame design problems for their students. Teachers feel an enormous responsibility to cover very specific content, and thus tend to overly specify the parameters for success in their challenge statements. We wanted to experiment with ways of helping them open up the problem framing to invite more students to authentically participate while still engaging with the required content.

To support this process, we adapted Stanford University's d.school problem-framing framework to generate activities (see Figure 4.2) (IDEO, n.d.).

The d.school process starts gently with the content, by encouraging teachers to brainstorm settings in which they might encounter the requisite content. For instance, while brainstorming settings in which students might encounter vibrations, a teacher might think of a shaky subway car, a house during an earthquake, or a construction site with jackhammers and heavy machinery. With those settings in mind, the teachers step away from a content focus, detailing the characters in that setting, and then potential problems that might arise for them. The last step circles back to considering the content in those problems and provides a check that the problems in step three are likely to encourage students to engage with the desired concepts.

Overall, we found this activity extremely useful in getting teachers to think more generatively about problem sets without overly narrowing the focus. Teachers generated a broad range of creative school-based design projects, such as making pothole-resistant asphalt, a technology-based sensor system for finding empty parking spots on NYC streets, and playgrounds that generate energy.

GENERATING AUTHENTIC DESIGN PROBLEMS GIVEN YOUR TOPIC AREA, BRAINSTORM THE CHARACTERS AND PROBLEMS THEY MIGHT ENCOUNTER IN SITUATIONS/SETTINGS	
SETTINGS (PLACES OR SITUATIONS THAT STUDENTS MIGHT ENCOUNTER OR BE INTERESTED IN) EXAMPLE: LOCAL PARK	**CHARACTERS** (AT LEAST 3-6 CHARACTERS WHO MIGHT BE PART OF THIS SETTING) EXAMPLE: ANIMALS, PARENTS, KIDS, PETS
POTENTIAL PROBLEMS (AT LEAST FOUR PROBLEMS TO SOLVE IN THIS SETTING) EXAMPLE: LITTER, HABITAT DISRUPTION, ANIMAL BEHAVIOR, SAFETY OF EQUIPMENT	**STEM CONCEPTS AND BIG IDEAS** (IDEAS NEED TO WRESTLE WITH TO SOLVE THIS PROBLEM) EXAMPLE: INTERDEPENDENCE OF ORGANISMS; LIFE CYCLE, FAILURE IN STRUCTURES

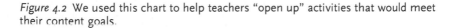

Figure 4.2 We used this chart to help teachers "open up" activities that would meet their content goals.

While encouraging teachers to think of setting first helps them open up their problem contexts, we also found that encouraging children to think about setting first helps them to deeply engage in problem-solving. When facilitating Happy City with school groups, we realized that providing students with additional ways to think about their own experiences increased their participation in the task at hand. We experimented with having students perform a thought experiment on their way to the museum for their field trip:

> *Think of walking down the street, through the park, etc. What do you see? What is your favorite thing to do? What things could you add to your neighborhood that would make people smile?*

Inviting students to think deeply about their neighborhoods before arriving at the museum helped them come up with more ideas of things they wanted to make once they got their hands on the LEDs and motors. This exercise scaffolded the students' problem ideation process and resulted in richer investigations of circuits.

CONTRIBUTING TO SOMETHING BIGGER

One of the most important features of Happy City is the city model itself—the landscape that gets filled with what learners make (see Figure 4.3). The city model serves several purposes:

- It embodies the problem context and helps with problem ideation. A city grid that is half filled with other learners' creations is a powerful introduction to the project and an effective reminder of what kinds of things are in cities, prompting a broad range of responses from participants.
- It anchors the activity as a collective project rather than an individual art project. The act of adding to a vibrant model city is appealing to visitors, since placing their object in a context lets them participate in a whole that is far more impressive than any one person's individual creation.
- It offers a wide variety of examples that are relevant to learners of different skill levels. Once there is a critical mass of projects in the model city, most learners can find an example to inspire them. Participants often gravitate to examples that are just beyond their current skill set, giving them something to strive for. When pruning the city, we do our best to maintain examples that represent a range of skill levels. These inspirational examples serve as effective scaffolds for learners' explorations.

Figure 4.3 Part of a Happy City landscape.

For the original instantiation at the 2011 World Maker Faire, we created a square plywood table with a street grid modeled after a real neighborhood and seeded it with a few buildings, a bridge, a "fountain" made of pipe cleaners that lit up, and a sign that would light up when anyone entered Happy City. People could choose the real estate where their creation would live, in among others' creations. The square table, the centerpiece of the activity space, seemed special—a place where participants wanted to add their contribution. Perhaps even more important, people were able to walk around the tabletop city and see it from different perspectives. The city grid served as a means to provide examples to onlookers of what they might create and how they might improve the city.

Most visitors wanted to find the right place for their creation to live, and the activity was so popular that the city grid filled completely and we commandeered a nearby bench to spawn a suburb. By the end of the day, we had a subway going out to the suburb, things hanging underneath the city (subterranean design), and even a "super baby" that lit up in the middle of the city. This exuberant success led us to think very deliberately about how the products of design could be shared, celebrated, and made relevant.

When we prototyped Happy City on the museum floor as a drop-in activity, we tried using bare tables with no city grid as the city landscape, again seeding it with a few examples we made ourselves and expecting that visitors would fill in the rest. But this time the city did not grow; it just looked like a display of objects on a table and not enough like a city. The facilitators realized they needed to provide more context and they changed the tables into a city landscape. They covered the tables with butcher paper and drew a city grid. Eventually, they experimented with different added features and found that children responded to these features in their designs. A green area of parkland on the map motivated children to create playgrounds. A river inspired bridges and beachfront property. We have now run Happy City at a few festivals and outdoor events, and the facilitators have added local features such as traffic circles, beachfront property, and lakes into the city grids created for those occasions. These features encourage participants to connect these activities to the larger world, and to the broader context all around them.

MATERIALS LITERACY AND SKILLS

Happy City not only encourages children to learn about circuits, but also provides them opportunities to develop physical competencies and skills in building models and using materials in new ways. The materials literacy that develops through design activities can be a potent skill, enabling children to see possibilities in the world around them. In the Happy City activity, we deliberately used familiar materials in order to facilitate this transformation of the everyday. For instance, instead of providing wires, we provided folded strips of aluminum foil. Children were comfortable tinkering with this decidedly non-precious material but were still surprised to see it used in this way.

This idea of materials literacy has become a cornerstone of our work with schools and the exhibit. Through the use of everyday materials, we are communicating the notion that materials can be reused and repurposed depending on needs at hand. When we work with teacher groups, they are especially surprised and appreciative of our use of readily available materials. In our professional development workshops, one particular teacher transformed dramatically from heavy dependence on pre-packaged science kits to being confident that he can assemble his own materials largely by gathering things he already has.

Presenting familiar materials for use in new ways can also focus attention not just on their potential uses, but on their properties as well. It was not uncommon in our sessions to see children testing the other materials (pipe cleaners, paper clips, etc.) to see if they, too, would conduct electricity in the same way as the aluminum foil. The surprise of seeing the aluminum foil strips conduct electricity led to explorations of conductivity: What other materials are good for acting like wires? What are they made of? How can I create my own crude conductivity tester so I know a material can work in my circuit?

BEYOND HAPPY CITY

When we originally created Happy City, one circuit feature we wanted children to experiment with was switches. Opening and closing a circuit not only provides a powerful exploration of a circuit as a loop, but also switches themselves present generative opportunities for design. There are many different types of switches (tilt switches, pull switches, pressure switches, etc.), and the type needed depends on the action that should trigger the circuit to open and close. To zero in on the notion that switches are where circuits meet the real world, we created a DIY video that presents viewers with the task of hacking an audio greeting card for its circuit and reworking the switch so it can be set off to surprise a friend. We initially tried to buy audio circuits for this project, but realized that having people dissect musical greeting cards themselves was important. By ripping open an audio greeting card, people were implicitly given permission to explore other things in their world that might have circuits they could hack (see Figure 4.4).

As a frame for museum visitors and teachers thinking of adapting the hack-a-card activity for their classrooms, we ask people to think about their

Figure 4.4 Hacking a greeting card.

day and the different things they do: How can you use those actions to turn on a switch for your surprise circuit? This was incredibly generative for people unfamiliar with switches. One person created a slip switch that was triggered when someone removed his jacket from a chair. Another person rigged a shoe with a pressure switch so that the song played when someone put on the shoe. Other examples included tilt switches triggered by certain kinds of motion, and contact switches using metal objects in the environment to complete the circuit's loop. By placing the need for the switch in the context of a real-world action, people stretched their skills to meet the demand of the situation.

Looking Forward

To date, we have worked to open up problem contexts to create invitations into STEM for all types of learners, including those who do not gravitate to STEM naturally. To do so, Design Lab developed opportunities for learners to find personally relevant problems to solve while gaining the tools, strategies, and confidence to act as creators, not just consumers, of the designed world. We found that design problems are great vehicles to balance deep engagement with deep content. The challenge is striking the balance between a problem context that is generative enough for learners to define problems for themselves and at the same time integrates compelling STEM content. What makes for a really good marriage of content and context?

We have just begun the process of identifying problem spaces that promote a sense of agency and ownership. The key to making that happen is choosing problem contexts that are not too narrowly defined, providing dynamic ways for sharing and collaborating on design work, and offering engaging materials that call into action interesting applications of STEM concepts and skills. As we extend our reach, we hope to refine the processes for growing a set of strategies and resources for facilitating engagement and deeper learning through learner-centered design problems. Questions for the future include:

- Given that this approach to design necessitates that children follow their divergent interests, what types of resources, examples, and training do museum educators and teachers need to effectively facilitate these activities?
- What tools can be developed to help learners reflect on their process and assess their design work?
- How do we go about sharing and celebrating students' work so that others can learn from it too?

REFERENCES

Bridgeland, J. M., Dilulio, J. J. Jr., & Morison, K. B. (2006). *The silent epidemic: Perspectives of high school dropouts.* A report by Civic Enterprises in association with Peter D. Hart Research Associates for the Bill & Melinda Gates Foundation. Washington, DC: Civic Enterprises.

Bridgeland, J., Dilulio, J., & Wulsin, S. C. (2008, April). *Engaged for success: Service-learning as a tool for high school dropout prevention.* A Report by Civic Enterprises in association with Peter D. Hart Research Associates for the National Conference on Citizenship. Washington, DC: Civic Enterprises.

Connell, J. P., Halpem-Felsher, B. L., Clifford, E., Crichlow, W., & Usinger, P. (1995). Hanging in there: Behavioral, psychological, and contextual factors affecting whether African American adolescents stay in high school. *Journal of Adolescent Research, 10*(1), 41–63.

Crismond, D. (2001). Learning and using science ideas when doing investigate-and-redesign tasks: A study of naïve, novice, and expert designers doing constrained and scaffolded design work. *Journal of Research in Science Teaching, 38*(7), 791–820.

Fleer, M. (2000). Working technologically: Investigations into how young children design and make during technology education. *International Journal of Technology and Design Education, 10*(1), 43–59.

Fleer, M., & Williams-Kennedy, D. (2002). *Building bridges: Literacy development in young indigenous children.* Richmond South, Australia: Australian Early Childhood Association.

IDEO (n.d.). *Educator's guide to design thinking.* Retrieved from: https://dschool.stanford.edu/sandbox/groups/k12/wiki/14340/attachments/e55cd/teacher%20takeaway.pdf?sessionID=1869b6463a7099bc978d839f02b31f2c17a26cf9. Accessed June 30, 2011.

Jerald, C. (2006). *Identifying potential dropouts: Key lessons for building an early warning data system.* Washington, DC: Achieve.

Johnsey, R. (1993). Observing the way primary children design and make in the classroom: An analysis of the behaviors exhibited. *Proceedings of the International Conference on Design and Technology Educational Research and Curriculum Development.* Loughborough, Leicestershire: Loughborough University of Technology.

Johnsey, R. (1995). The place of the process skill making in design and technology: Lessons from research into the way primary children design and make. *Proceedings of the IDATER95: International Conference on Design and Technology Educational Research and Curriculum Development.* Loughborough, Leicestershire: Loughborough University of Technology.

Kimmel, H., Carpinelli, J. Burr-Alexander, L., & Rockland, R. (2006, June). Bringing engineering into K-12 schools: A problem looking for solutions? *Proceedings of the American Society for Engineering Education Annual Conference and Exposition.* Chicago, IL.

Kolodner, J. L., Camp, P. J., Crismond, D., Fasse, B., Gray, J., Holbrook, J., et al. (2003). Problem-based learning meets case-based reasoning in the middle school science classroom: Putting learning by design into practice. *Journal of the Learning Sciences, 12*(4), 495–547.

Lewis, T. (2005). Coming to terms with engineering design as content. *Journal of Technology Education, 16*(2). Retrieved from: http://scholar.lib.vt.edu/ejournals/JTE/v16n2/lewis.html. Accessed May 30, 2011.

Linn, M. (2003). Technology and science education: Starting points, research programs, and trends. *International Journal of Science Education, 25*(6), 727–758.

Roth, W. M. (1995). From "wiggly structures" to "unshaky towers". Problem framing, solution finding, and negotiation of courses of actions during a civil engineering unit for elementary students. *Research in Science Education, 25*(4), 365–381.

Roth, W. M. (1996a). Art and artifact of children's designing: A situated cognition perspective. *Journal of the Learning Sciences, 5*(2), 129–166.

Roth, W. M. (1996b). Knowledge diffusion in a grade 4–5 classroom during a unit of civil engineering: An analysis of a classroom community in terms of its changing resources and practices. *Cognition and Instruction, 14*(2), 179–220.

Rumberger, R. (2004). Why students drop out of school. In G. Orfield (Ed.), *Dropouts in America: Confronting the graduation rate crisis* (pp. 131–155). Cambridge, MA: Harvard Education Press.

Sadler, P. M., Barab, S., & Scott, B. (2007). What do students gain by engaging in socioscientific inquiry? *Research in Science Education, 37*(4), 371–391.

Zubrowski, B. (2002). Integrating science into design technology projects: Using a standard model in the design process. *Journal of Technology Education, 13*(2), 48–67.

CHAPTER 5

IT LOOKS LIKE FUN, BUT ARE THEY LEARNING?

MIKE PETRICH, KAREN WILKINSON, AND BRONWYN BEVAN

When Marcos first arrives in the Tinkering Studio he spends 10 minutes watching as others construct descending sets of ramps on the Marble Machine pegboard. After a while he walks over to a marble run left behind by a previous learner, picks up some ramps and dowels from the floor, and sets to work—spending about an hour changing lengths, angles, and many elements that allow the marble to hit a chime, spin in a funnel, or turn a corner. Each time he makes a change, he drops a marble into the run, and it all goes perfectly until it shoots off the track at one of the two or three tricky spots where alignments aren't quite right. He tries different ways to slow down or redirect the marble so it will make its way past these treacherous turns. He tinkers with the angles of the ramps, creates "guard rails" out of dowels, and adds wooden "backsplashes" to the sharp turns. Finally he has successful test runs that work from top to bottom. He steps back to survey his work. He tells us that it was "a hard activity." He takes out his mobile phone and uses its camera to document what he has accomplished before leaving to find his family.

Marcos, Tinkering Studio, summer 2011

Scenes such as this are common in the Tinkering Studio, a dedicated "making" space in the San Francisco Exploratorium. The studio is thematically organized around sets of materials or phenomena that change regularly. Activities might focus, for example, on work with cardboard, electronic circuits, rotational motion, or squishy things. The space and activities are designed to appeal to people of all ages, and learners in the Tinkering Studio are as equally likely to be adults as they are children. Activity stations and display cabinets are distributed around the studio, so that people can encounter and engage in different ways with the materials or phenomena. Visitors to the Tinkering Studio interact with artists and community tinkerers specializing in these items, and are supported by specially trained Tinkering Studio facilitators to begin to experiment with the materials themselves. In an electricity-themed Tinkering Studio station, people might play with simple circuits, getting bells to ring or strobe fans to whirr, adding a switch and parallel circuits over time. At another station, they might sit in a sewing circle and work with conductive thread to sew belts, scarves, and bags designed to incorporate LEDs, button-cell batteries, and electric circuits. They might interact with a long-standing Exploratorium exhibit called Resistor or with an electrical artwork from a local artist, who might even be in the Studio that day experimenting with circuits made from Play-Doh or other materials. Visitors to the Tinkering Studio are invited to slow down, sink in, and spend time working with phenomena and materials to begin to conceive of, design, and make things themselves. Ideas, models, tools, and facilitators in the studio are carefully curated, but there is no set of instructions, and no prescribed endpoint.

Part exhibition space, part science laboratory, and part atelier, the Tinkering Studio is a new kind of public learning experience. Every day, we see amazing focus, creativity, persistence, and pride developing in people of all ages as they draw on their understanding and imagination to develop

Figure 5.1 Focused work at a marble machine.

Source: © Exploratorium.

and pursue an idea and to make something concrete (even if ephemeral) that represents their ideas and understanding. We are struck by the amount of time people spend working on their ideas—typically an hour, sometimes half a day—and many return regularly as the themes change. This profusion of delight and dedication energizes us and keeps us going—but periodically we are arrested by questions from people who come to observe the studio in action, usually educational policymakers and researchers whose job it is to identify learning in action, who say to us: "*Well, it looks like fun . . . [pause] . . . but are they learning?*"

This question stymied us for many years, mostly because we did not see an inherent contradiction in the notion of people visibly enjoying themselves (engrossed, committed, joyful) and engaging in processes of learning. We were struck by how the visual amalgamation of "fun" and "learning" disrupted so many people's foundational assumptions about what counts as learning, even those who were long-time supporters of learning in out-of-school settings.

In this chapter, we describe what learning looks like in the Tinkering Studio. We begin with how we conceptualize learning in the context of science and engineering, when we see people actively engaged, developing intentionality, generating new ideas, and building solidarity and shared commitment to a practice of design, experimentation, and tinkering. We can point to such characteristics of learning in the Tinkering Studio. The specifics of learning depend on what learners know coming into the experience and how they choose to pursue their interests and ideas through the tinkering activities.

Most of this chapter describes how we design for the conditions that afford such learning. We close with reflections on how our conceptualization of learning and design relates to and supports the vision of science learning advocated by the National Research Council's *Framework for K-12 Science Education* (National Research Council, 2011). We contend that tinkering activities designed to support engagement, intentionality, innovation, and solidarity provide singularly accessible opportunities for learners to engage in scientific and engineering practices that are both epistemologically and ontologically meaningful.

Tinkering manifestly embodies a powerful way to engage learners in science and engineering practices. Through careful design and facilitation, however, we believe that tinkering activities can be made broadly accessible and appealing to even more learners, of widely varying levels of prior interest and experience in science and engineering, including those that do not think of themselves as tinkerers, mechanically minded, or "good" at science.

HOW WE CONCEPTUALIZE LEARNING THROUGH TINKERING

We often describe what happens in the Tinkering Studio as "thinking with your hands" (Sennett, 2009). Learners work for a long time, constructing, testing, and tinkering with their projects until they reach that point of "just so." While cries of delight regularly punctuate the whirring, buzzing, clanging atmosphere of the space, people often work silently and intently with their hands, even when sitting next to friends and family. They ask for tools, for help holding something as they use a hot glue gun; they point to and comment on things that are working or not working. But mostly they are exploring phenomena, testing ideas, and responding to feedback with their hands. We can see, embedded in the things they build, what they are asking and their theories of the properties of the materials or phenomena. We see their thinking especially in how the artifacts change over time, as the learners come to understand, through iterative design and testing, the ways in which light reflects and refracts, the speed and direction of the turning objects based on the ratio of cams and pulleys, the geometric features of shadow makers relative to the light source, or the material properties of cardboard, Plexiglas, and aluminum grids.

Our work draws on constructionist theories of pedagogy (Papert & Harel, 1991) and is based on an expansive view of learning, conceptualized as a process of being, doing, knowing, and becoming. In this way, we move beyond traditional school-like conceptions (knowing), beyond traditional constructivist conceptions (doing), and include conceptions of the socially situated developing self (being and becoming) as central to activities and processes of learning. Our thinking draws on the work of many scholars who have investigated the dynamic relationship of self, setting, activity, and how it supports learning (Herrenkohl & Mertl, 2010; Holland, Lachicotte, Skinner, & Cain, 1998; Stetsenko, 2010). In this view, learning is signaled by ever-expanding participation in social activities that make possible, and that are made possible by, the learner's growing repertoire of knowledge, skills, interests, ideas, and sense of purpose (Vygotsky, 2004).

Critical to learning in the Tinkering Studio are opportunities to engage with the work and ideas of others; to be supported with tools and assistance to develop and pursue one's own ideas; and to develop and evolve these ideas as direct engagement with materials and phenomena provides feedback, creates constraints, and inspires new thinking and solutions.

As designers and students of the space, we see evidence of learning in people's deepening:

- *Engagement*: Active participation, which might include silent or still observation and reflection.

- *Intentionality*: Purposeful and evolving pursuit of an idea or plan.
- *Innovation*: New tinkering strategies that emerge through growing understanding of tools, materials, and phenomena.
- *Solidarity*: Sharing, supporting, and pursuing shared purposes with other learners in the Tinkering Studio, or with the artifacts they have left behind.

When we see these qualities developing in the space or the learners, we know that people are on a trajectory of learning. They are drawing on their resources; they are taking risks with their ideas; they are operating on the edge of their understanding. They are engaging in the different investigative practices of designers, scientists, artists, makers, and engineers. This, to us, is what learning "looks like," and this is what we strive to support in the Tinkering Studio. The specific concepts being learned vary according to the individual's prior experiences and also to the particular activities in the Tinkering Studio. The particular practices learners pursue vary according to their interests and goals—whether more or less evidence-driven, more or less idea-driven, more or less aesthetics-driven. Our goal is to design the experience so that learners can find and pursue a purpose, exercise their creativity and imagination, and confront and solve conceptual challenges, within a STEM-rich tinkering context.

How We Design for Learning

Exploration in the Tinkering Studio is driven by the learner, but it is inspired and informed by the setting: by the materials made available in the studio and by the architecture of how it is made available; by the active work of others in the space; by the archaeological residue of projects left by earlier visitors; and by the modeling and participation of tinkering facilitators, as well as community makers and artists who work in residence for changing periods of time. The environment and activities are surprising, whimsical, and aesthetically compelling—they draw people in, get them going, and keep them engaged through their open-ended and continually complexifying nature.

The Tinkering Studio is located on the Exploratorium's public floor, amid a sea of exhibits, surrounded by a low wall. Museum visitors first see it from a distance; it looks like one more part of the museum's open exhibit space, though visitors might notice that people in the studio seem to be more stationary and focused than elsewhere in the Exploratorium. A low wall and swinging gate serve as a threshold between the open exhibit floor and the Tinkering Studio. Once through the gate, visitors encounter exhibits or art pieces that involve phenomena or materials being explored in the studio that day. While playing with the exhibits or viewing the installations, learners may begin to develop questions or ideas, or they may become curious about the range of activities they see others pursuing at one of the activity stations distributed throughout the space. Drawn to a particular activity, learners begin to interact with the tools, materials, and themes. They might begin to build a contraption that they think will hover in the wind tube. Through working with a collection of materials that includes, among other things, strawberry baskets, pipe cleaners, Mylar, and drinking straws, they might try to build something that is parachute-like, or that has wings. Others might design specifically with thoughts of thrust, lift, weight, and drag already in mind. After testing their contraptions in the wind tube, they might see their object unexpectedly sink or perhaps shoot out of the tube. *Why did it not float as they had intended? What do they need to do to get it to float?* Or perhaps: *Could they make it shoot out of the tube even higher and faster the next time?* As they begin to develop their own questions, construct their own ideas, and "build out" their understanding, they often confront the limits of their knowledge or fluency with the phenomena as they become stuck.

The process of becoming stuck and then "unstuck" is the heart of tinkering. It is in this process that authorship, purpose, and deep understanding of the materials and phenomena are developed.

Figure 5.2 A Wiffle ball with spidery pipe-cleaner legs hovers in a wind tube.

Source: © Exploratorium.

We find that as learners become comfortable with moments when their understanding is challenged by the results of their own designs, they become more engaged, spend more time investigating and/or constructing, and take ownership for and build confidence in their abilities to learn and understand. Indeed, in interviews, when we ask them to describe the history of their artifacts, learners often dwell on these moments of frustration and, most importantly, their solutions to the unexpected challenges to their understanding. These seem to be the most meaningful parts of the process of tinkering. The interviews reveal how important the sense of self is in the interplay of objects and activities in the Tinkering Studio. In an educational context, particularly one that is not mandatory, as in a museum, what helps people persist in their investigations is both the intriguing nature of the materials themselves and the personal investment learners have in their own ideas and understanding. It is the personal accomplishment of becoming unstuck, plus having an artifact to point to—an artifact that may be rickety or lopsided, but yet has resolved the problem that so puzzled the learner— that makes tinkering activities so compelling to the learners. They surprise themselves with their accomplishments. Their ideas, creativity, thinking, and resilience are validated in their own eyes.

In the sections following a brief discussion of the development of the Tinkering Studio, we explain how we design to support this process of inspiration, creativity, frustration, and breakthrough, which we contend is at the heart of generative *making* activities.

Origins of the Tinkering Studio

The roots of the Tinkering Studio come from an MIT Media Lab project called PIE (Playful Invention and Exploration), funded in 2000 by the National Science Foundation. PIE supported a small group of museums to experiment with meaningful ways to engage children with small programmable computational devices called "Crickets," developed by the Media Lab's Lifelong Kindergarten Group led by Mitchell Resnick (author of "Tinkerability," another chapter in this book). Crickets are small computers about the size of a nine-volt battery that can be connected to sensors and motors as well as programmed to collect data, activate a kinetic sculpture as a way to "display" the data, or do other things envisioned by the learner. In testing Cricket-based activities, we noticed that to effectively engage learners' interests and support their creativity and risk-taking, activity designs needed to provide an array of loose parts, support thematic explorations with a variety of possible outcomes, utilize technology and tools as a part (not the focus) of the activities, and provide time to support learners' initiatives. More than a dozen different PIE activities were developed through this project.

In 2003, the Exploratorium received an NSF grant to launch the PIE Institute (led by the first two authors of this chapter, Petrich and Wilkinson) to support a network of museums interested in providing PIE activities for children attending museum-classroom-based workshops. In these museum workshops, it was typically known who was attending, how much time we could give to each activity, how the environment supported the workshop in general, and how to manage loose parts and (sometimes dangerous) tools.

Figure 5.3 Constructing with cardboard in a cardboard Tinkering Studio.

Source: © Exploratorium.

At the Exploratorium, over time we began to move the PIE activities out of the controlled museum workshop and onto the museum's exhibit floor. Tinkering activities in the open floor space needed to accommodate a changing flow of visitors, who came with varying prior experiences and who stayed for self-determined amounts of time. Therefore, we had to think carefully about ways in which to structure the environment and activities so that learners could find their own starting points, tinker at their own pace, be inspired and informed by others, and be free to come and go as their interest and time allowed.

We formalized these experiments in 2008 when we roped off about 400 square feet of space on the Exploratorium's public exhibit floor and called it the Tinkering Studio. The studio was popular from the start. We found that many visitors began making repeat visits to the Exploratorium so they could "do more tinkering." At about this time, we began a research-and-documentation project to understand how our designs and experiments were supporting learning opportunities for museum visitors. We spent the next four years systematically designing, studying, and documenting our work in the Tinkering Studio, incorporating findings into the design and implementation of an expanded, permanent Tinkering Studio at the Exploratorium's new campus at Piers 15/17.

Activity, Environment, Facilitation

Over the last few years, we have produced a set of design principles that articulate key features of the Tinkering Studio that we believe spark and support people's active engagement and learning—in particular, fostering the process of inspiration, creativity, frustration, and breakthrough described above. The design principles were developed through a three-year participatory research project that also involved the study of learning designs in other informal settings. They are currently being further tested to understand how they relate to the learning indicators discussed above and later in the last section of this chapter. Here, we describe these design principles in ways that reference our underlying cultural-historical theory of learning and our constructionist theory of pedagogy.

We describe the principles for activity, environment, and facilitation one by one; however, we stress that we do not encourage a mix-and-match or pick-and-choose approach to the Tinkering Studio. We design for all of these principles at once, though what they may look like will vary at any given time depending on what the Tinkering Studio is doing that month.

Activity Design

Activity design principles encompass how we establish or suggest broad activity goals and pathways, as well as how we select the palette of tools, materials, and phenomena that constitute both the context and the support for learners to make progress toward these goals.

- **Activities and investigations build on learners' prior interests and knowledge.**

We generally design activities that involve familiar, everyday materials and phenomena, but often used in unfamiliar, unexpected ways. For example, when we investigated the theme of time in the Tinkering Studio, we used clocks in different ways. Learners could dissect mechanical clocks. At another table, learners were invited to create metaphorical clocks. At other stations, we engaged people in the familiar concept of time-based animation, in one case through the process of creating strobe-light zoetropes, and in another by inviting learners to contribute to a mural using simple Japanese brushes and ink, and to watch an adjacent time-lapse video that showed the creation of the mural including up to the last minutes when the learner made his or her own contribution. We find that using materials in this way expands the possibilities of resonating with people's prior experiences, whether from a point of familiarity or of surprise and intrigue; this resonant response prompts them to pick up the materials and get started.

- **Materials and phenomena are evocative and invite inquiry.**

We select materials or phenomena largely based on two criteria: their inherent potential to be sensually and aesthetically evocative (to be beautiful, complex, surprising, and observable on their own) and their potential to provide immediate feedback to the tinkerer's actions. The possibility for learners to change an object, produce something new, and quickly see results is essential to the trajectory of experimentation. For example, creating spinning tops is a common science activity, and in designing, building, and decorating tops, learners quickly gather a sense of how symmetry affects their behavior. In the Tinkering Studio, this activity is complexified both by the range of materials, sizes, and scales that one can pursue, but also by the inclusion of aesthetic elements to decorate and personalize the tops, which creates new constraints that can challenge the tinkerer's understanding and mastery of the physical phenomena involved in spinning tops. For example, decorating a top with googly eyes to make a crazy face affects the balance and symmetry and therefore the performance of the top. In general, we tend to select materials that are slightly flawed or that do not fit together perfectly, so that they require more thinking, effort, and ingenuity to get them to work as planned.

- Tools and concepts of science are a means, not an end.

Tinkering Studio activities are designed to provide learners with personally creative and inspiring experiences that are accomplished through working with and developing understanding of relevant science and math concepts, phenomena, and tools. Mastery of the phenomena is the means toward achieving one's goals. For example, in light painting—where tinkerers create tabletop tableaux involving light sources, colored filters, and shadow makers, which are then projected onto a screen—tinkerers are immediately confronted with the relationship of the distance between the light source, the shadow maker (the object), and the screen (on which the shadow is projected) as they experiment with configurations to achieve their desired projected image. These relationships are further explored as the learner continues to tinker, becoming more fluent with, and confident about, the placement of these objects in the investigation/construction. Through such trajectories of learning (Bransford & Schwartz, 1999), tinkerers develop intuitive understanding, facility, and comfort with science and scientific concepts and tools, creating the conditions in which they are more likely to continue to engage with these concepts, including in formalized settings where they may re-encounter concepts they now know well.

- Multiple pathways are readily available.

Activities are designed with multiple pathways for learners to pursue and represent their understanding. First, as discussed above, learners can generally choose from several different (but related) activities at separate activity stations. When exploring circuits, visitors to the Tinkering Studio can sit at one station to connect circuits to make bells ring, move to another station to sew belts or purses with conductive thread, or interact with a small collection of electricity exhibits. Second, activities are designed for multiple possible pathways and outcomes to allow for a greater range of experiments, a more diverse array of starting points, a more varied pattern of tool use, more opportunities for observations, testing, failure, and success. For example, building marble machines could involve creating a precise series of ramps that flawlessly convey marbles from one track to the other, from the top to the bottom of the pegboard wall. Other learners may be interested in more complex ideas such as rolling marbles through a loop-the-loop, or in and out of a series of funnels, or jumping them across gaps in the tracks. The potential for experiments is highly dependent on learners' interests and questions, any of which involves engaging with potential and kinetic energy, trajectory, momentum, conservation of energy, gravity, friction, projectile motion, and more. Thus, there is no one prescribed way through the activity. But it is not *anything goes*: the materials themselves, as well as the ideas and examples in the space that focus people's activities in productive ways, create and constrain possibilities. Designing for multiple pathways expands potential for learners to work with and test their assumptions and understanding, which will vary from learner to learner depending on their prior experiences. Supporting multiple approaches to exploring the phenomena or materials is both helpful and inspirational to learners and also provides tinkering facilitators with evidence and insight into the way learners are understanding the topic at hand.

• **Activities and investigations encourage learners to complexify their thinking over time.**

It is not enough simply to offer multiple pathways or alternatives in an activity; we need to ensure that activities encourage people to challenge and stretch their comfort level and understanding, no matter what level they begin with. Tinkering activities offer simple, attractive starting points to ensure some initial success, but they are designed with ongoing opportunities for complexification as the learner progresses toward understanding a principle, concept, or function. Connecting a light bulb to a battery pack is an early exploration that confronts many learners at the electricity boards activity. The lit-up bulb is initially satisfying, until the learner decides he or she would like to replace the bulb with a motor, or buzzer, or two light bulbs. He or she may decide to add a switch. The complex arts piece on the wall next to the electricity boards station prompts some learners to work toward a similarly cascading set of colorful blinking electrical events. The possibility for the materials to be used in a variety of ways, and in a variety of complex circumstances, is a hallmark of a designed tinkering experience.

Environmental Design

The environmental design of the Tinkering Studio includes the organization of all things (living and human-made) found in the environment. This includes a subdued color palette, natural and warm lighting when available, a collection of approachable materials (as described above), and a human scale to the overall space (something we found essential as we prototyped in the Exploratorium's cavernous exhibit hall at the Palace of Fine Arts). These elements can help learners transition from the free-roaming browsing behaviors of the museum to the more focused activities of a workshop-like setting. The environment should be a comfortable place for learners to experience delight, failure, frustration, and deep engagement over time. The environment should be alive when learners are in the space.

- **Past project examples and current activities are situated to seed ideas and inspiration.**

We design so that the archeology of the environment is apparent when visitors first enter the space. Often this is accomplished by what learners see others working on, and equally often by how the environment honors the work of those who have worked in the space earlier. Cabinets of curiosities, shelves, and niches full of objects and installations from past engagements inform and inspire incoming learners. We also display images and videos highlighting prior or related work. Opportunities for facilitators and learners to refer to someone else's creation, or compare construction techniques or goals, offer a way to seed new ideas and to help solve a problem that a learner might encounter.

- **Activity station design enables cross-talk and invites collaboration.**

We design workspaces in ways that require people to meet and interact with others, even if just to reach tools or take turns projecting images, or to ask for help in holding something steady. For example, rather than segmenting separate spaces for each learner at the pegboard wall for the marble run activity, the entire wall is available for the learners to negotiate together. Learners become natural facilitators when someone is asking for help about something that another has just figured out. We limit the number of tools or particular materials both to avoid over-stimulation and also to encourage sharing and improvisation. These types of adjacencies and designs lead to natural discussions and conversations between learners, an acknowledgment of what each person is working on, and an opportunity for help and feedback at every point along the way.

- **Studio layout supports individual initiative and autonomy.**

While we design for collaboration, we also design for learners to exercise autonomy and not be dependent on the studio facilitator for help, tools, or supplies. We put all necessary materials out on an accessible table, which our visitors can approach at any time as their thinking or needs change. When learners enter the space, a facilitator briefly introduces them to the array of materials available. Activities have no fixed end point or end time, so learners can move from activity to activity as they reach their own transition points or are seeking new ideas or inspiration. They can also return to further complexify their work as new ideas come up in the context of new activities and can be incorporated back into work at another station.

- **Activity adjacencies encourage the cross-pollination of ideas.**

Materials stations are often moved to the edges of the space, away from the design and making area. Walking through the making space to get to the materials table generates encounters with ideas and solutions that learners may not have been actively looking for, but may provide new ideas and breakthroughs. Indeed, although each tinkerer may take a different pathway through an activity, we find that similar outcomes are predictably created as an idea spreads, or is shared in the space. These moments of inspiration roll like a wave through the activity when people are ready for them. For example, at a marble machine, when somebody starts to use tape to create "guard rails," in minutes we will see tape appear across the wall as people pick up on an idea that seems to work. Activity tables are rounded to make it easier for one more learner to join a space at a table. When someone at a shared table invents a new kind of spinning motion on their top, that achievement is immediately experienced by others in close proximity.

Facilitation

Facilitation is key to the operation and impact of the Tinkering Studio. The attitude, support, and outlook of tinkering facilitators create an environment of intellectual safety, creativity, and a genuine interest in supporting the learner's ideas rather than forcing the acquisition of a particular set of procedures or specific facts. Tinkering facilitators understand that their most important job is to support learners to come to care about and persist in developing their ideas. Through the process of that development, learners will be required to grapple with the scientific concepts and phenomena embedded in the materials and activities.

- **The facilitation is welcoming and intended to spark interest.**

A critical role of a Tinkering Studio facilitator is to set the tone and welcome tentative visitors into a creative and exploratory space. Facilitators' enthusiasm creates a starting point for learners who may be cautious about opportunities to publicly create and to demonstrate what they know and do not know in the process. Initial facilitation moves include welcoming people and communicating that there is something in the Tinkering Studio for everyone (whether or not you identify as a "tinkerer" or "maker"), and that the facilitator will be available to help and support the learners as needed. Facilitators typically put materials in front of a new learner and show one or two moves with the materials to get the learner started. They may also point to the work of others in the space to generate ideas or models that learners can work toward.

- **Facilitators try to focus learners' attention, based on individual paths of understanding.**

By observing the moves of the visitor, and by talking to him or her about what he or she is doing, facilitators can identify what ideas or concepts a learner is working with as he or she begins his or her investigation and then make suggestions about tools or ideas accordingly. Many times, facilitators may not need to intervene, once they confirm that the learner is on a fruitful path. Sometimes, the facilitator may find that the learners are on a path that will lead to frustration or getting stuck, but it is important that the learners be allowed to continue until they themselves realize they are stuck. Jumping in to help too early takes authorship away from the learner. Jumping in too late may result in a learner giving up. In the Tinkering Studio, the zone between too early and too late is fairly wide, as the activities and environment tend to maintain people's interest and commitment for a good while. For example, a battery-powered scribbling machine (an activity where an offset motor creates a vibrating-moving-drawing contraption) often completely falls apart when it is first built and set in motion. But rather than providing guidance about how to build and reinforce the design from the start, facilitators let the visitors get feedback first-hand from their own contraption. The scribbling machine's falling apart leads learners to rethink either their designs or the ways in which they have executed them. Facilitators can step in to draw the learner's attention to particular materials (pipe cleaners or wires) or phenomena (symmetry or center of gravity) that are at play in other functioning scribbling machines in the Tinkering Studio. These are facilitation moves that can help learners become unstuck and to recommit to their creative processes.

- **Facilitation should strengthen understanding by helping learners clarify their intentions through reflective conversation.**

An idea that leads to getting stuck is an important learning opportunity, maybe more important than the moments where the learner's idea unfolds flawlessly. A facilitator's role in helping a person come to see and understand why he or she is stuck is as important as their role in helping a person celebrate something that is working. The facilitator's role is not to "quiz" the learner to ascertain whether or what content understanding was achieved, but to continue the investigation by offering subtle challenges, or asking questions that may lead to the complexification of the learner's idea. Learners may feel successful when a construction they create works as anticipated, but it is often important for facilitators to dig a little deeper, to develop a clearer understanding about what the learner knows. Asking the learner to apply the successful idea to another context, or to a new set of materials, or to a new design, often goes a long way in confirming or challenging the learner's grasp of the ideas. For example, in connecting circuits, a young learner who successfully connected a battery and a bulb was surprised when he was unable to successfully connect the wires and terminals to add a switch and a second light bulb. The facilitator stepped in to reposition the materials on the table, clearing away unnecessary wires and more clearly positioning the battery, switch, and bulbs in a circular arrangement to more concretely frame the question about how to approach the circuitry. This simple repositioning helped the boy re-engage with the activity and begin to complexify it further.

How We Recognize Learning in Tinkering

We started this chapter with the question perennially heard in the Tinkering Studio: "*It looks like fun, but are they learning?*" We have tried to describe, in response, what learning looks like to us. Moreover, we have tried to illustrate how learning through tinkering is not serendipitous: it comes about through a process of design decisions and principles that create specific types of opportunities for learning.

The design principles described here have resulted from many years of activity development in which Petrich, Wilkinson, and their collaborators experimented equally with activities, environments, and facilitation. Since 2008, under Bevan's (the third author) direction, the Exploratorium has embarked on a set of research studies to document and understand how our design choices—the interplay of activity, environment, and facilitation—operate to deepen learners' engagement. We have integrated these studies into regular professional development meetings with tinkering facilitators where we review the documentation (video, audio, field notes) and discuss what we see happening, why, and what it felt like in the moment, what we missed, and how to take what we are learning back into our design and staff training programs.

As we undertook these studies, we knew we needed to identify and document learning outcomes and indicators without stopping the tinkering activities or isolating the learners to interview or survey them (i.e., we did not want to "spoil the fun" or disrupt the flow, or decontextualize meaningful personal experiences of accomplishment, both aesthetic and intellectual). We sought naturalistic approaches to documenting learning, which some researchers have argued are critical to supporting creative work in public learning environments (Michalchik & Gallagher, 2010). The primary way we documented our designs for learning was to video people in activity, then review and analyze the video later. We also recorded some

Tinkering Studio conversations among tinkerers as well as between tinkerers and facilitators. From this work, we list four tentative indicators of learning:

1. Engagement
   a. Duration of participation
   b. Frequency of participation
   c. Work inspired by prior examples
   d. Expressions of joy, wonder, frustration, curiosity
2. Intentionality
   a. Variation of efforts, paths, work
   b. Personalization of projects or products
   c. Evidence of self-direction
3. Innovation
   a. Evidence of repurposing ideas/tools
   b. Evidence of redirecting efforts
   c. Efficiences gained through growing fluencies with concepts, tools, and phenomena
   d. Complexification of processes and products
4. Solidarity
   a. Borrowing and adapting ideas, tools, approaches
   b. Sharing tools and strategies; helping others to achieve their goals
   c. Contributing to the work of others

When people are engaged in the flow of tinkering activities designed to support these practices of engagement, intentionality, innovation, and solidarity, they are on a trajectory of learning that is matched to their particular (and evolving) interests, capacities, and commitments. Though most educators respond positively to these constructs, we recognize that this terminology is not yet part of the commonplace language of learning, which is still dominated by a search for evidence of the learner's ability to reproduce (usually in a new context) a fragment of knowledge or skill. For example, many educators are comfortable with a child's being able to verbally define symmetry as evidence of learning but not convinced by (or secure in the knowledge that it can be reproduced) the child's demonstration of his or her mastery of symmetry in creating a spinning top that achieves his or her aesthetic and engineering ambitions. This is an ongoing tension. We believe that tinkering activities have great potential for expanding thinking about what constitutes evidence of learning.

Tinkering and Engineering Practices

The specific STEM concepts and phenomena being learned depend, of course, on the activities engaged in and the age, interests, and prior experiences of the learners doing the engaging. Nonetheless, certain consistent practices in the Tinkering Studio, enabled by the design principles described above, cut across particular conceptual domains, such as electricity or optics. For example, in both domains, learners design, test, respond to feedback (data), and redesign/retest. In our work to identify and articulate learning in the context of tinkering, we turned with interest to the recent *Framework for K-12 Science Education: Practices, Cross-Cutting Concepts, and Core Ideas* (National Research Council, 2011). In particular we examined the document's description of engineering practices, which include:

1. defining problems;
2. developing and using models;
3. planning and carrying out investigations;
4. analyzing and interpreting data;
5. using mathematics, information and computer technology, and computational thinking;
6. designing solutions;
7. engaging in arguments from evidence; and
8. obtaining, evaluating, and communicating information.

The concept of scientific and engineering *practices* is powerful because of its inherent conception of learning as processes of being, doing, knowing, and becoming. The Framework does not define learning solely as the acquisition of facts or mastery of skills, but rather includes engagement with the practices that scientists and engineers use to develop new understandings of materials and phenomena. This more inclusive definition potentially moves the discourse about learning away from memorization of abstract facts to the development of affinity for and fluency in the ways of knowing, doing, and being (the epistemologies and ontologies) of engineers or scientists. Engaging in increasingly complex scientific and engineering practices perforce entails growing mastery of facts, concepts, and skills, but always in the context of pursuing and expanding understanding about questions that matter (for whatever personal reason) to the learner.

What can tinkering offer to the task of implementing the forthcoming Next Generation Science Standards and ideas about engineering practices? We contend that a primary distinction between tinkering activities and other types of engineering activities (such as many robotics programs and design challenges) is that in tinkering the set of constraints that learners are working with and toward are developed in relation to the goals, interests, and capacities of the learner himself or herself. That is, there is no injunction about a building reaching a certain height or a ball rolling down a ramp at a certain speed or a robot traveling a certain distance. Such constraints matter a great deal in the real world, to the people who have already committed to a lifelong profession of engineering, and for whom real consequences (e.g., public safety or job security) pertain if they are ignored. But they may matter less to those who have not yet committed to a STEM profession. However, in tinkering, learners create both goals and constraints for themselves, based on their prior experiences, and also evolve these goals and constraints as their understanding and mastery of the phenomena and materials develop. For example, a teenager initially seeks to make a marble roll down a five-foot pegboard at the slowest possible rate. Once he has control over the speed of the marble, he might become intrigued by the sounds the marble makes when bouncing off chimes placed on the pegboard. This might lead him to switch goals to make the marble produce a descending sequence of tones as it travels down the pegboard. The design and engineering practices remain the same. However, the purpose and pathways that drive engagement and persistence are authored by the learner (or by a group of collaborating learners), and are therefore more likely to matter to the learner and support his persistence. Thus, we contend that tinkering makes an important contribution to STEM education and to the adoption of the forthcoming standards because it embeds engineering practices in purposeful and valued activities, just as these practices are embedded are in the real world.

Authentic purpose is essential to the largely unarticulated distinction between STEM skills and STEM practices. Skills can be taught in ways that are disembodied from purpose or meaning. Though a student can come to understand how to conduct an observation through a series of exercises entailing observing and making notes, whether or not the student learns to observe, and what it means to observe, is not a given. Students can be coached to design experiments, but if they have no stake in the experiment or its results, the exercise becomes at best a schooling practice rather than a scientific practice. The practices of STEM are never disembodied from purpose and the social context that gives those practices meaning. Tinkering activities provide a unique opportunity to engage learners in the processes of developing a purpose, pursuing and mastering the STEM concepts, phenomena, and tools essential to realizing that purpose, as well as engaging in that pursuit in the social context of a creative tinkering community.

Moreover, successful tinkering activities emphasize the processes of pursuing ideas, becoming frustrated, and achieving breakthroughs through one's own ingenuity and persistence, which are essential aspects of science practices that rarely emerge in most designed science activities. In this sense, tinkering activities, whether offered in or out-of-school settings, provide learners with unique opportunities to develop affinities, experiences, and identities with practices of science and engineering that can serve as a strong foundation upon which future and lifelong learning can flourish.

CONCLUSION

It looks like fun, but are they learning? We hope that in this chapter we have shown that if learning is conceptualized as more than the ability to reproduce facts and skills in decontextualized settings, if it is understood as engaging in practices that draw on facts and skills to advance valued and purposeful activity, and if learning activities are designed within a STEM-rich context, such as we have illustrated through examples of the Tinkering Studio, then *yes, they are learning*. But they are not only learning, and learning how to learn, as evidenced by their iterative processes of creation; they are also learning, and learning how to learn, in ways that scientists and engineers learn. That is, they are deeply engaged, in personally meaningful ways, in the evidence-based practices of science and engineering, with the artifacts themselves providing evidence *for* learning as well as evidence *of* learning, in a creative and joyful learning environment that looks like . . . we have to say it . . . a lot of fun.

ACKNOWLEDGMENTS

The Tinkering Studio is the creation of a number of staff and volunteer supporters. Special thanks go to Walter Kitundu, Luigi Anzivino, Ryan Jenkins, Lianna Kali, Nicole Catrett, and Thomas Carlson. The work of the Tinkering Studio has been developed through support from the National Science Foundation (ESI-0452567), the Gordon and Betty Moore Foundation, the Met Life Foundation, and by research conducted through grants from the Institute for Museum and Library Services and the Noyce Foundation.

REFERENCES

Bransford, J. D., & Schwartz, D. L. (1999). Rethinking transfer: A simple proposal with multiple implications. *Review of Research in Education, 24,* 61–100.

Herrenkohl, L. R., & Mertl, V. (2010). *How students come to be, know, and do: A case for a broad view of learning.* New York: Cambridge University Press.

Holland, D., Lachicotte Jr., W., Skinner, D., & Cain, C. (1998). *Identity and agency in cultural worlds.* Cambridge, MA: Harvard University Press.

Michalchik, V., & Gallagher, L. (2010). Naturalizing assessment. *Curator: The Museum Journal, 53*(2), 209–219.

National Research Council (2011). *A framework for K-12 science education: Practices, crosscutting concepts, and core ideas.* Committee on Conceptual Framework for the New K-12 Science Education Standards, Board on Science Education. Washington, DC: The National Academies Press.

Papert, S., & Harel, I. (1991). *Constructionism.* New York: Ablex Publishing Corporation.

Sennett, R. (2009). *The craftsman.* New Haven, CT: Yale University Press.

Stetsenko, A. (2010). Teaching-learning and development as activist projects of historical becoming: Expanding Vygotsky's approach to pedagogy. *Pedagogies: An International Journal, 5*(1), 6–16.

Vygotsky, L. S. (2004). *The essential Vygotsky.* R.W. Rieber & D. K. Robinson (Eds.). New York: Kluwer Academic/Plenum.

CHAPTER 6

DESIGNING MAKERSPACES FOR FAMILY LEARNING IN MUSEUMS AND SCIENCE CENTERS

LISA BRAHMS AND JANE WERNER

How MAKESHOP came to be through a description of the Museum's approach to design, and how this approach has been translated into the design of MAKESHOP.

Makerspaces are places where groups and individuals of diverse ages, genders, and backgrounds come together to "make": to mess around at the crossroads and fringes of disciplines such as science, technology, engineering, art, and math. Motivated by a resurgence of interest in do-it-yourself (DIY) culture, the Maker Movement has grown to embrace the potential for creativity and innovation made possible at the intersection of the physical and digital. The opportunity for learning through making has sparked tremendous national recognition and financial support; acknowledged by the White House to be a potential alternative to traditional science, technology, engineering, and math (STEM) education (Kalil, 2010; *PBS Newshour*, 2011), as a stimulus for political and economic rebirth (*Economist*, 2011), and as a possible key to the retooling of libraries into tool-lending centers (with tools and equipment such as 3D printers, CAD stations, and laser cutters) that promote free access for all (e.g. Torrone, 2011). Now, museums and science centers are expressing growing interest in developing makerspaces within their existing designed environments.

Historically, makerspaces and their predecessors—hackerspaces, tech shops, and fab labs—have attracted adult and youth members and thus provided making resources appropriate for particular age groups. When makerspaces are incorporated into museums and science centers, they must be adapted to the expectations and needs of the populations served by these institutions. The majority of visitors to children's museums and science centers in America are families (Museum Audience Insight, 2010), who use these institutions as resources for shared leisure and learning. As such, families have become a research focus for museum studies and scholars of informal learning (Ellenbogen, Luke, & Dierking, 2004). The field of museum evaluation and research has identified typical learning practices of families in conventional museums (e.g., Crowley et al., 2001) and established principles for effectively designing conventional exhibits for these visiting groups (Borun & Dristas, 1997), as well as developed methods for measuring associated discipline-based and behavioral learning outcomes (e.g., Serrell, 1998).

The growing presence of makerspaces in museums and science centers presents a great opportunity to the fields of informal learning research and practice. Today's makerspaces are unlike most conventional family-centered exhibits. Makerspaces encompass open-ended making opportunities with shop tools and equipment, raw materials such as wood, textiles, and solder, and often require the active presence and participation of skilled and knowledgeable facilitators. The family conversations and behaviors that can be heard and seen as families sew, solder, and build together are distinctly different from those observed through past museum learning research (Brahms, 2012).

As makerspaces are incorporated into the fabric of museums and science centers, we must reimagine the role these institutions will serve in the lives of their visitors as places of cultural consumption, and now, creative production. Researchers and practitioners may work together to advance understandings about family participation and learning in such multifaceted spaces, to design spaces that support and enable productive and complex making practices, and above all, to engage young children and families early in rich and sustained authentic making experiences.

MAKESHOP at Children's Museum of Pittsburgh is a 1,800-square-foot exhibit space that provides a rich, supportive informal learning environment for children and families to engage in authentic making experiences with the *real stuff*—materials, tools, processes, and ideas—of making. *MAKESHOP* is a collaborative project of Children's Museum of Pittsburgh, Carnegie Mellon University's Entertainment Technology Center (ETC), and the University of Pittsburgh Center for Learning in Out of School Environments (UPCLOSE). As leading informal learning, design, and research organizations, each of the three partners brings a unique perspective and area of expertise to the project. Through a collaborative process of iterative design, the museum and its partners have developed and discovered the essential features of *MAKESHOP* at the Children's Museum, a space that supports visitors' making as a dynamic and shared process.

THE REAL STUFF

Children's Museum of Pittsburgh characterizes itself as an arts and cultural organization. With the mission of providing innovative museum experiences that inspire joy, creativity, and curiosity, the museum seeks to offer its visitors, staff, and community opportunities to *think differently*. Inherent in this organizational intent is a willingness to take risks, to look beyond traditional margins of practice for expertise and inspiration, and to trust in the process of collaborative design.

The museum's guiding philosophy is "play with real stuff," which promotes an organizational commitment to the use of authentic materials and processes in its exhibits and programming. This philosophy is manifest through all aspects of the museum's planning and practices, from the composition of its staff to the design choices it makes. Intrinsic to this approach is a deep respect for the museum's visitors, and the belief that a well-designed and beautiful environment, using sustainable and quality materials, affords visitors—children and adults alike—a comfortable and empowering museum experience.

The "real stuff" philosophy came about at a time of great organizational change, both physically and conceptually. Not long after Werner (this chapter's second author) became Executive Director in 1999, the museum launched a large-scale capital campaign to sustainably re-imagine and expand. This entailed transformation on all levels of organizational practice and presence, from the museum's physical structure to its organizational partnerships, to the experiences it offers its visitors.

Today, the 80,000-square-foot LEED silver-certified facility combines design excellence, historic preservation, and environmental sensitivity (Figure 6.1). The museum is now home to five partner organizations that work with or on behalf of children, as it serves its local community by leading large-scale restoration and organizational-bridging projects. The museum's attendance continues to grow, with nearly 250,000 people visiting the museum in 2011.

THE MUSEUM'S DESIGN PROCESS

When designing all visitor experiences—from singular components to large-scale thematic traveling exhibitions—the museum engages the design

Figure 6.1 Children's Museum of Pittsburgh.

Source: Anthony Musmanno.

process of collaborative ideation, prototyping, iteration, and reflection. Ideas are often generated from individual practitioners' areas of creative interest or artistic pursuit, which are then shaped by a site-specific set of design principles of practice refined through years of collaboration (see the box below). Essential to this process is the frequent prototyping of designed experiences on the floor with visitors throughout the exhibit's development. Prototypes range in scope from rough models or mock-ups of an idea to test visitor appeal or methods of approach, to nearly complete components in need of slight adjustments to enhance or extend visitor engagement. Thus, exhibits are never complete: there is always room for improved interaction design.

Partnering with learning researchers from the University of Pittsburgh Center for Learning in Out of School Environments (UPCLOSE), the museum has evolved a process of prototyping that invites the visitor to collaborate actively in the development of exhibits. This process enables the museum to evaluate, research, and expand the experiences it provides by continually addressing the learning needs of its visitor community. Through observation of visitor behavior with exhibit components, designers identify

CHILDREN'S MUSEUM OF PITTSBURGH PRINCIPLES OF DESIGN AND PRACTICE

Play with Real Stuff: The museum's design philosophy promotes an organizational commitment to integrate authentic and exposed materials and processes in its contemporary exhibits and overall design.

Design Process: The museum employs the design process of collaborative ideation, prototype, iteration, and reflection. Frequent prototyping aspects of designed experiences, on the floor with visitors, has become the essential characteristic of the museum's approach to exhibit development.

Sustainability: The principles of reducing cost and environmental impact of exhibits are realized through the choice of products and materials, and the potential for reuse or repurposing of the components.

Flexibility: Elements of the space are constructed to allow for varied use, reconfiguration, and repurposing. Museum experiences encourage flexible thinking, experimentation, and allow for emergent outcomes from visitors.

Accessibility: The museum designs components, environments, and signage that are usable by all people without the need for adaptation or specialized design due to age or ability.

Multilayered: Visitor experiences are designed to allow for repeated and varied use. Exhibits enable frequent visitors to experience familiar exhibits anew and encourage visitors of any age to engage in experimentation and discovery.

Shared Experience: Designed experiences purposefully encourage shared interaction among visitors of diverse ages.

Simple and Intuitive: Through simple, straightforward design, exhibits enable intuitive engagement and use by visitors of all ages. This becomes a functional as well as aesthetic practice, allowing the museum to keep instructional signage to a minimum, and to broaden visitor use and accessibility.

Robust: Designed for the explicit audience of children and families, all exhibit elements are built to withstand extensive and aggressive visitor behavior.

projected and surprising instances of and opportunities for visitor learning. Through successive iterations, as well as deep consideration of the museum's philosophy and design principles, these recognized learning opportunities are cultivated and layered into the evolved design. In so doing, the museum creates singular exhibits that enable authentic visitor experiences with real stuff and processes. These designed experiences marry the museum's commitment to clean contemporary design with its philosophical "real stuff" stance, exposing the materials and processes of use while maintaining a fresh appearance.

MAKESHOP AT CHILDREN'S MUSEUM OF PITTSBURGH

MAKESHOP, in principle and practice, evolved as both a natural extension of the Children's Museum's approach to designing visitor experiences, and as a timely response to institutional challenges and opportunities. As the idea of *MAKESHOP* emerged, two trends were taking shape in the museum's institutional community. As places of informal learning, libraries began designing research-based, media-rich creative environments for youth (e.g., *YouMedia* Chicago), widening the perception and use of digital media as learning tools for creative production in informal environments. Simultaneously, a narrowing trend of identifying and designing primarily for children age 5 and younger began among children's museums across America. At the time, the Children's Museum of Pittsburgh knew that older children, beyond the age of 5, still encompassed a significant percentage of the child-visitor population (28%) (UPCLOSE, 2011). Additionally, recent studies (UPCLOSE, 2005, 2011) found that among the museum's permanent arts and science-based exhibits, children age 8 and above favored those that offered visitors active and prolonged opportunities for creative production, exploration, invention, play, and co-activity among family members. Parents reported that these spaces were markedly enjoyable and empowering for their older children. Moreover, observations of visitors in these spaces noted distinct and different behavior patterns among family units compared to those displayed in other areas of the museum. Rather than sitting back and watching their children play, parents actively engaged in creative and exploratory activities with and alongside their children, pulling their own silkscreen print and modeling their own sculpture.

In light of these trends and history of success, in 2010 the museum began to work with Carnegie Mellon University's Entertainment Technology Center (ETC)—a premier graduate program for the pioneering of educational media projects, games, and interactive software for children—and the University of Pittsburgh Center for Learning in Out of School Environments (UPCLOSE)—a leading learning sciences research lab that studies informal learning spaces—to create a space for the museum's older-child demographic, age 8 to 12, that would marry the strength of the museum's "play with real stuff" culture with technology, visitor-produced content, and informal learning research and evaluation. Also around this time, two other influential factors began to coalesce for the museum. First, we began participating in the national conversation around making through affiliation with *Make* magazine, and second, a network of local organizations committed to the integration of the arts, science, and technology to inspire learning and creative play—Pittsburgh's Kids + Creativity movement— gained significant momentum.

The partners envisioned *MAKESHOP* as a well-equipped workshop space where children age 8 and older could experiment, collaborate, and create, using digital media and physical materials. Working alongside adult makers, or facilitators, skilled in a variety of areas, older children would purposefully engage in the design process of ideation, prototyping, iteration, and reflection to integrate digital and traditional technologies in their making experiences. Visitors to *MAKESHOP* would be welcomed with the question "What do you want to make today?" Teaching artists, guest makers from the community, and fellow children in the space would help visitors realize their project vision by engaging in the design process. In addition to serving and extending the museum's general visiting audience, *MAKESHOP* would be a new home for the museum's youth afterschool program, a resource for pre-service and continuing teacher professional development as well as for complementary community programming. It was with this vision that the partners set out to test, assess, and discover the most generative combination of physical resources and structure for productive visitor and staff making in our context.

Prototyping *MAKESHOP*

In April 2011, the museum dedicated a small open-concept exhibit space, and three staff—a museum educator, the museum's research fellow (this chapter's first author), and the program manager—as thought partners, along with $5,000, to prototyping this idea before creating a permanent installation. Although *MAKESHOP*'s original target demographic was the older child, when we began prototyping the average age of child visitors to the Museum was between 4 and 5 years old. One or more adults—often parents and/or grandparents—always accompany children of this age, as well as their older siblings, to the museum.

From the beginning, we recognized that making experiences would need to accommodate a wide range of age, skill level, and capacity for engagement. How this would take shape was a guiding question for our iterative design process. While the vision for *MAKESHOP* was of an open-access workshop where digital and physical making would intersect, we sought to prototype medium-based themes (electronics, sewing, and wood) independently so as to develop a deep understanding of the affordances of and limitations to the making process each new medium presented to visitors and facilitators.

ElectricShop

We began prototyping the theme of electronics, iteratively designing a range of tabletop experiences to introduce and extend visitor understandings and manipulation of electronics. At the entrance of the space, we placed a table full of circuit block components, assembled in-house (Figure 6.2): LED lights, small motors, buzzers, and repurposed electronic toy parts, such as propellers and wheels fastened to wooden blocks with their wire leads exposed and attached to conductive nails. Children and families connected different components to a battery station with alligator test leads. The variety of components and loose test leads enabled visitors to explore through observation, test through trial and error, and further widen the possibilities for learning created from the simple act of closing a circuit. This accessible manipulation of parts, supported by the expertise of the facilitation staff, scaffolds visitors' understanding, identification, and application of core concepts and the language of electronics, including the concept of a circuit as a pathway of energy transfer through the power supply, wires, and light; of switches as controllers of energy flow; and of polarity. Circuit blocks proved to be a valuable experience accessible to all visitors, as well as accommodating to individual and shared exploration. For some visitors, circuit blocks became an introduction to an extended making experience with electronics, whereas, for others, the combination of blocks, batteries, and leads provided a meaningful making experience in and of itself.

To complement the experience of creating a circuit, families joined facilitators in disassembling electronic devices with screwdrivers and pliers, and discovered how things work from the inside out at our "take-apart"

Figure 6.2 Experimentation with electronic circuit blocks in ElectricShop.

table. Here, visitors explored the inner workings of old printers, compact disc players, and electronic toys (Figure 6.3). The interior components were then repurposed at our "reassembly and fabrication" table, where visitors turned them into newly constructed electronic devices. Together, families and staff work through iterative combinations of complex and parallel circuits, a variety of vibrating "bots" made of found materials and offset motors, and a creative array of conductive switches used to turn their "bots" on and off—everything from paper clips and brass tacks to magnets and hairpins (Figure 6.4).

Throughout the prototyping of ElectricShop, the museum formulated foundational understandings about the facilitation of meaningful making

Figure 6.3 "Take-apart" in ElectricShop.

Figure 6.4 "Reassembly and fabrication" in ElectricShop.

experiences with children and families. Paramount is the utility and inherent value of simple exploratory experiences with tools, materials, and processes that enable visitors of any age to begin making without encountering many barriers to participation. We extended this participatory goal (Jenkins, Purushotma, Clinton, Weigler, & Robison, 2006) through the development and use of scaffolds, or multiple and varied supports for meaningful visitor participation, to enable visitors to incorporate advanced concepts at their own pace, empowering parents and children to become each other's mentors through active exploration and conversation. Finally, through this initial prototyping phase, we began to recognize the affordances of open making, where the goal of the making experience is left up to the visitor—individual or group—and supported by the gentle guidance of a skilled facilitator; empowering the visitor through the production of his or her own ideas, as well as allowing for the innovative blending of materials and processes.

SewShop

We continued prototyping as summer approached, bringing with it crowds of energetic family visitors. We harnessed the creativity and vitality of three talented ETC students willing to serve as facilitators and thought partners for developing *MAKESHOP* during the museum's busiest months. The expanded *MAKESHOP* team, composed of museum staff, the UPCLOSE research fellow, and ETC interns, initially worked together to develop and test complementary scaffolded and open-access "real stuff" experiences around the theme of sewing. The team agreed that a central intention was to prototype the use of the sewing machine with visitors of diverse ages and proficiency levels, but we questioned how best to facilitate such open making experiences with somewhat delicate and potentially dangerous equipment.

We designed a careful sequence of tabletop experiences to support learning about the sewing process, as well as use of materials and tools. The design included the presentation of diverse fabrics so visitors could explore texture, color value, and weaves; a tabletop loom so visitors could contribute to a large woven runner made of wide ribbons that introduced the fundamental over-under-over process of sewing; and handmade wooden frames with stretched latch hook canvas to encourage needle threading and practice with the rhythm of hand-sewing (Figure 6.5).

Within the first few hours of prototyping, we quickly discovered that all these designed experiences paled in popularity to visitors' desire to use the sewing machines. Visitor interaction with the machines usually began by observing the sewing process—as staff members or knowledgeable visitors demonstrated the sequential steps of operating the machine. Many children, from toddlers to teenagers, had never seen a sewing machine

Figure 6.5 Sequencing experience in SewShop.

before or questioned how their clothing and textile accessories had been made. Remarkable was the immediate and inherent value of the most basic aspects of sewing, as young visitors cherished fabric pieces they had joined together, no matter how simply, as consequential products of their making experience. Notable as well was the relative speed with which visitors picked up the process and learned to use the sewing machines smoothly. They began making everything from pillows to purses to pincushions to LED-lit bracelets with fabric, thread, and a whiz through the sewing machine.

The general appeal of the machines triggered a bottleneck in activity, motivating the strategic distribution of facilitation—one staff member per machine and one dedicated to hand-sewing and construction—as well as the measured timing of activity. Material consumption was rapid as project trends swept the museum—if one visitor made a pillow, there would be 100 small pillows floating around the museum by the end of the day. While the vast majority of visitors took their made treasures home, some willingly left their projects behind to serve as inspirational examples for future young makers.

Among the countless patterns of visitor activity and associated techniques for facilitation observed and employed through prototyping SewShop, the staff became acutely aware of and interested in the various types of *adult* participation in the making process. While some adults hesitated to encourage use of the machine, claiming lack of experience, fear of breaking the machine, or assuming the experience was "too advanced," "too dangerous," or "too girly" for themselves or their child, many took its presence in the museum as an invitation for use—both knowledgeable and experimental. Although this freedom did lead to a few broken needles and a great many jammed machines, it also initiated occasions for learning and unique moments of intergenerational conversation among visitors and staff.

Many parents became consequential co-learners, collaborators, and facilitators of their family's making experience—feeding the fabric through the machine together with the small child seated on the adult's lap; supporting their children's choice of material and creative direction; requesting facilitator coaching at specific points in the making process; and encouraging their children to continue the project or process at home. Frequently, staff would overhear parents and grandparents telling children stories of personal and familial history—when they learned to sew or how they or their parents made their childhood garments by hand—as well as expressing an intention to dig an old sewing machine out from storage to use with their children or grandchildren. Conversely, parents often became barriers to their children's innovative design process. As staff would invite children to envision the product they would like to make, parents would often quickly suggest the replication of another visitor's object; or they frequently limited the amount of time and attention of their children's making experience; or took control of the process entirely, compelling the children to observe rather than actively create. This breadth of parent participation was enormously instructive for staff. Through prototyping SewShop, we confirmed our assumptions that *MAKESHOP* would afford families' meaningful opportunities for intergenerational learning, but we also saw how adults could interfere with this process. Our response was ongoing assessment and the accumulation of facilitation techniques and scaffolds—from signage to space design—to directly guide parent participation so as to indirectly enhance children's making experiences.

WoodShop

Through the prototyping of ElectricShop and SewShop, we began to evolve a framework for designing collaborative open-access making experiences with families. This framework included a commitment to scaffold the processes of making within the given theme, so as to provide easy entry for all—adults and children alike—to intuitively begin and develop facility with materials and processes. We recognized the diversity of inherent and emergent roles among family members during the making process, and the need for the designed experience to reflect and respect these roles. Similarly,

JANE WERNER'S REFLECTIONS ON A DAY IN SEWSHOP

On my daily walk through the museum around 3 p.m. I stopped into SewShop. I walked over to the sewing machine area where a grandmother and her granddaughter were working on sewing a butterfly with the help of a facilitator. The grandmother told me that they had so much fun the day before that they had come back. This conversation prompted another mother to chime in, saying that she and her family had come at 10 a.m. that day, expecting to stay an hour or two, and were still there. They hadn't stopped making even for lunch. Her 9-year-old son showed me the stuffed whale he was working on, and then she showed me a sand shark her younger son, about seven, had made. At the other end of the spectrum, the day before, a man between 70 and 80 was sitting all by himself sewing away on a pincushion he was making for his wife. I think SewShop is working!

we developed an appreciation for the strengths and limitations of the facilitation staff, and the need to balance the level of facilitation among the making experiences offered.

Within this evolving framework, we designed a variety of introductory tabletop experiences as scaffolds to the materials and processes of woodworking. This included the sensory experience of exploring different types of wood, a table dedicated to the experience of sanding and shaping wood with assorted tools (sandpaper, files, etc.), and an area where visitors could physically touch many woodworking hand tools, deprived of their sharp parts (e.g., a hand drill without bits), as well as a cardboard construction area, where visitors could experiment with methods and materials of joinery (e.g., doweling, butt joints, dovetail joints, tape, glue, nails).

In addition to these introductory experiences, the team designated a workshop space, wherein facilitators would assist visitors in their application of basic woodworking processes through the making of full-scale projects. While visitors had tentatively approached the sewing machines, often seeking permission or instruction, a surprising majority of visitors entered the WoodShop without hesitation, freely reaching for potentially dangerous tools, materials, and equipment. To balance visitor interest with facilitator resourcefulness and ease visitor approach, as well as encourage and assess visitors' exploratory use of the materials, tools, and processes of woodworking, the team quickly began a daily process of iteratively prototyping and reflecting on different spatial configurations, methods of facilitation, and crowd control.

Separating the tabletop experiences from the workshop with a low wall immediately reduced the speed at which visitors approached the woodworking tools. This separation also encouraged parents of very young children to appreciate the relative fit between the introductory experiences and their children's level of interest and engagement. For many young children, the repetitive experience of sanding a small piece of wood or matching the size and function of simple hardware parts was quite satisfying.

The inherent nature of woodworking enabled us to prototype an important aspect of the *MAKESHOP* vision: the visitor's active and iterative design process. While we had verbally ushered visitors through this process during the prototype of SewShop, we sought to formalize and make explicit the steps of the design process through which visitors were traveling while making. All visitors who approached the workshop area were asked what they wanted to make. The children were given an index card and pencil and encouraged to sketch their intended project at the "ideation table" outside the workshop space. This focused children, helped them take ownership of their making process, and enabled adults and facilitators to more fully understand the child's vision for his or her project (Figure 6.6). Once the sketch was complete, visitors were invited into the workshop and asked to think about which materials they would need to make their design. Facilitators worked with children and adults to gauge the length of time and attention children were willing to commit to their projects (which usually took between 20 and 40 minutes to complete). Facilitators guided the visitors' making, from wood and hardware selection, through instruction on tool use (e.g., where to hold a hammer, how to safely clamp wood for drilling and sawing), to procedural suggestions (e.g., when to drill a pilot

Figure 6.6 "Ideation" sketches in WoodShop.

hole, which type of joint to use, measuring techniques, productive order of construction). Through this rather individualized process, children and their accompanying adults learned mechanical principles and processes, acquired additive skills and techniques, experienced feelings of motivation, frustration, accomplishment, and empowerment, made mistakes and discoveries, and produced an array of unique and personalized projects (Figure 6.7).

Figure 6.7 Making personalized products in WoodShop.

The physical design of the workshop evolved to allow for meaningful, safe, and efficient facilitation and visitor participation. In the middle of the workshop sat a construction table, where visitors assembled and finished their projects with simple hand tools such as hammer and nails, staple gun, files, and sandpaper (Figure 6.8). Around the perimeter was a series of workbench stations, each equipped for a different operation. One was dedicated to the use of the miter saw, one for drilling using clamps and vises, and one for more delicate work with the coping saw. This evolved space design not only helped with flow, but it also helped facilitators recognize the participants' intentions and choices throughout their making process, by way of their physical movement between workbenches and the construction table. Limited supplies were provided in open-access bins, so as to encourage thoughtful material selection and discourage material waste.

The workshop area was equipped to handle independent older children (above age 7), as well as child-adult co-makers of any age. The team worked to find the safest adult-to-child ratio that would allow for meaningful making experiences in our compact space, and accordingly limit the number of safety goggles and workshop aprons to accommodate this comfortable capacity.

Throughout prototyping WoodShop, adult involvement continued to be a focus of facilitator interest and learning. Parents and caregivers exhibited patterns of involvement with their children's making endeavors similar to those in SewShop: the communication of skilled practices and making

Figure 6.8 Prototyping space design in WoodShop.

traditions between generations; the empowered and instructional initiative of experienced adults; and the willingness to learn a new trade alongside their child; as well as adults' encumbered perceptions of gendered practices, fear of novel experiences, and lack of trust in children's vision and intent. Parents both underestimated and overestimated children's levels of interest, motivation, strength, and focus—important properties of the woodworking endeavor. Aware of these participation patterns, staff continued to refine appropriate facilitation techniques to encourage families to explore materials, tools, processes, and equipment outside the workshop space before diving into an involved woodworking project.

ITERATION AS AN INHERENT ASPECT OF THE DESIGN PROCESS IN WOODSHOP

Sam, 8 years old, began his WoodShop experience by making a detailed sketch of the television he wanted to build. After selecting his materials and learning how to use certain tools, Sam began to modify his design. The size and shape of the available wood lent itself better to an open-front design, turning the static wood of the sketched screen into a puppet theater for live performances. Upon completing his project, Sam compared the final product to his initial sketch. Unprompted, he explained his iterative process and the design choices he had made along the way. "I think it's better this way [as a puppet theater]," he said, "this way, I can make up whatever show I want to see!"

DESIGNING IN NEW DIRECTIONS

Through collaborative prototyping and reflective practice, we developed a proof of concept that was true to the Museum's approach to design, visitor experience and learning, and to each partner's interests. With a more comprehensive understanding of the opportunities for learning and contextual change made possible for visitors and staff when messing around with diverse materials of making, we set out to design the permanent *MAKESHOP* exhibit. Central to the design concept was the need for the architecture of the space to communicate the authentic spirit of making to the museum's core audience by way of the museum's "real stuff" philosophy (i.e., to be a space where tinkering, testing, play, collaboration, and possibility are celebrated). The permanent exhibit design, built in response to the extensive prototyping described above, is intended to welcome and engage visitors of all ages, genders, and levels of ability, communicate flexibility and accessibility of thought and use, encourage collaboration across generations, and provide all makers with supportive open access to the materials, tools, and processes that bring innovative ideas to fruition.

Opened in October 2011 in the museum's most prominent gallery, *MAKESHOP* now provides museum visitors open access to physical materials and digital media resources to produce a robust place for curiosity, exploration, creativity, and innovation (Figure 6.9). The 1,800-square-foot space is divided into three large areas. Upon entering *MAKESHOP*, visitors encounter a carpeted area designed to be a comfortable introduction to the

Figure 6.9 MAKESHOP at Children's Museum of Pittsburgh.

materials and processes of making. Here, visitors may construct life-size structures by combining components made of wood, industrial felt, rubber, and plastic, with metal screws and bolts; investigate electricity with an ever-growing assortment of circuit blocks; test out evolving physical and digital prototypes of activities and exhibits, and explore printed and digital resources, books, and images to generate ideas and inspiration for possible projects. Beyond this area lie the open-access workshops where a dedicated facilitation team comprising skilled makers, artists, and educators with specialties in digital media, sewing and flexible materials, electronics, woodworking, and informal learning engage visitors with the diverse materials and processes of making. Here, these "practitioners of making" enable visitors to translate their ideas into tangible products and further prototype playful and innovative blendings and juxtapositions of materials, tools, and ideas every day.

THE ENTRANCE TO MAKESHOP, WITH MISTER ROGERS' SWEATER

Fred Rogers of *Mister Rogers' Neighborhood* lived and worked in Pittsburgh and was a good friend of the Children's Museum. Mister Rogers' sweater, the one his mother knit for him to wear on the show, is displayed prominently at the entrance of *MAKESHOP*. It reminds us that one way to show we care for someone is the simple act of making something for him or her. We see such acts of love and kindness daily in *MAKESHOP*. We think Fred would be pleased.

Figure 6.10 MAKESHOP activity reaching new audiences.

Source: Larry Ripple and Renee Rosensteel.

MAKESHOP continues to develop through ongoing research and reflective practice among partners. Digital making resources are now being carefully prototyped, evaluated, and consistently integrated into the permanent *MAKESHOP* exhibit space and activity. With the intention of advancing field-wide use of digital media as an integrated tool for facilitating conversation, exploration, and productive making among young families, the museum, the ETC, and UPCLOSE continue their work together to develop digital experiences that thoughtfully and intentionally consider the child, the family, the content, and the context of use. Each academic semester, a student design team from the ETC works with the UPCLOSE research fellow, and representative *MAKESHOP* staff to develop a digital component for the space. Projects have included a digital system that captures visitors' reflections of their making process, and a tangible block interface that enables children of any age to engage in a simple form of computer programming. As these digital projects are developed by the ETC, the *MAKESHOP* facilitation team creates complementary making endeavors that integrate scaffolds or extensions to the project. For example, the tangible block interface has become a scaffold to more advanced computer programming activities such as visitors' guided and independent use of the MIT Media Lab's programming language Scratch and a series of e-textile workshops. In addition, *MAKESHOP* has become a site of local and national playtesting, as designers of digital learning products and educational games iteratively test their designs with families in *MAKESHOP*.

The identification of common patterns of family activity has enriched our understanding of our visitors and the affordances for meaningful museum participation that open-ended making experiences provide. While *MAKESHOP* undoubtedly benefits our original target demographic of children above age 8—the numbers, frequency of visit, and length of time spent in the space for children of this age has already increased—our prototyping and ongoing practices indicate that *MAKESHOP* has also become the site of meaningful making experiences for family groups of diverse ages and compositions (Figure 6.10). By broadening our design and research to include the distinct social participation patterns of young children and their significant adults, we have developed a deep appreciation for the unique opportunities for collaborative family learning through making that *MAKESHOP* presents by way of its seamless integration into the Children's Museum, a familiar place of informal family activity (Figure 6.11). Although adults may not expect to encounter the types of experiences *MAKESHOP* provides when they enter the Children's Museum, such as soldering a microcontroller, building an electric guitar, or sewing an LED light into their clothing, by and large they do expect to set aside time to play, imagine, and explore with their children. This expectation, combined with the exhibit design and facilitators' willing invitation to make, enable consequential family engagement to take place.

As we have widened our target visitor age range, we have also evolved our understanding and approach to scaffolding visitor experience, from their point of entry into the space, to the range of making experiences provided, through the outcomes of making and learning such experiences afford. Initially, we envisioned that *MAKESHOP* activity would be guided by children's ideas, with the introductory question "What would you like to make today?" For many visitors, young and old, material and/or tool

Figure 6.11 Collaborative family learning in MAKESHOP.

exploration, as well as the rehearsed execution of related making processes or techniques, are important and equally productive points of entry into meaningful family making experience. We now intentionally design to encourage learning progressions in *MAKESHOP* that are varied, flexible, and open-ended, which include opportunities for engagement with "real stuff" (materials and tools), processes and ideas, and that consider the proximal learning outcomes of visitor experience as well as the cognitive, social-emotional, physical, and digital resources that make learning possible. Such outcomes include knowledge and skill development and transfer, but also include changes in the way parents and children relate to and collaborate with one another, as well as shifts in children's interests and identities as people able to play with materials, tools, processes and ideas, and to build and innovate. These outcomes may emerge through a single visit, or may be a part of an evolving trajectory of participation (Greeno & Gresalfi, 2008) that spans weeks, months, or years, and extends beyond the museum, connecting contexts of family learning (Brahms, 2012).

As museums and science centers design makerspaces, we must consider the unique learning trajectories of young makers and the ways in which thoughtful design can support productive family participation in making. This involves looking beyond the traditional definitions, measures of success, and outcomes of learning currently associated with stem disciplines toward the broad range of opportunities for learning—discipline-based, social, and affective—that making affords when situated in informal learning environments designed for families.

Research has shown that family learning in physical and digital designed environments is highly dependent on parent involvement, both tacit and explicit (Barron, 2006; Barron, Martin, Takeuchi, & Fithian, 2009; Ito et al., 2010). Parent perceptions and awareness of opportunities to learn, parent knowledge and confidence regarding content, and parent perception of their role in their children's or family's learning experience significantly influence the potential for child and family learning (Barron et al., 2009; Schauble et al., 2002). When designing making experiences, museums should consider the critical role parents and grandparents play in their children's potential for learning, as these significant adults share personal stories and perspectives, provide rich explanations, scaffold understanding, and model values and dispositions. Such productive social practices can be enriched through design, as the materials, tools, processes, and ideas of making become vehicles for family learning that transcends conventions of gender, generation, and ability.

Makerspaces are highly localized environments of social learning that embrace a vast and expanding array of expertise, as they necessarily encourage participants' innovative thought and practice: to use and combine materials, tools, and processes in new ways to solve problems and push society in new directions. When designing museum-based makerspaces for family participation, we must embrace emergent forms and outcomes of learning, by creating making environments that enable children and their families to comfortably begin their making experience; to discover, connect, and develop points of personal and shared interest; and to chart paths of participation that integrate family members' individual, shared, and evolving resources and relationship to digital and physical marketing. Through the purposeful design of makerspaces for family learning, museums and science centers can enhance their role as dynamic, reliable, place-based cultural resources for children and families.

As we continue to imagine, develop, and design making experiences for all visitors to the Children's Museum, we look forward to further exploring the patterns of family participation intrinsic to *MAKESHOP* through our ongoing empirical research and prototyping practices. By attending to these patterns and practices, we will advance understandings of the family museum experience and of the potential for learning made possible through making.

Acknowledgments

Funding for *MAKESHOP* was provided by the Grable Foundation, the Claude Worthington Benedum Foundation, the John D. and Catherine T. MacArthur Foundation, and an anonymous foundation.

References

Barron, B. (2006). Interest and self-sustained learning as catalysts of development: A learning ecology perspective. *Human Development, 49*(4), 193–224.

Barron, B., Martin, C. K., Takeuchi, L., & Fithian, R. (2009). Parents as learning partners in the development of technological fluency. *International Journal of Learning and Media, 1*(2), 55–77.

Borun, M., & Dritsas, J. (1997). Developing family-friendly exhibits. *Curator, 40*(3), 178–196.

Brahms, L. (2012, April). Designing for meaningful disciplinary participation in museums. Paper presented at *Digital Media Arts: Learning, Assessment, and Design*, symposium conducted at the annual meeting of the American Educational Research Association, Vancouver, Canada.

Crowley, K., Callanan, M. A., Jipson, J. L., Galco, J., Topping, K., & Shrager, J. (2001). Shared scientific thinking in everyday parent-child activity. *Science Education, 85*(6), 712–732.

Economist: Technology Quarterly (2011, December 3). More than just digital quilting, pp. 3–4. Retrieved from: www.economist.com/node/21540392. Accessed December 10, 2011.

Ellenbogen, K. M., Luke, J. J., & Dierking, L. D. (2004). Family learning research in museums: An emerging disciplinary matrix? *Science Education, 88*(51), 48–58.

Greeno, J. G., & Gresalfi, M. S. (2008). Opportunities to learn in practice and identity. In P. A. Moss, D. C. Pullin, J. P. Gee, E. H. Haertel, & L. J. Young (Eds.), *Assessment, Equity, and Opportunity to Learn* (pp. 170–199). Cambridge, UK: Cambridge University Press.

Ito, M., Baumer, S., Bittanti, M., Boyd, D., Cody, R., Herr-Stephenson, B., et al. (2010). *Hanging out, messing around, and geeking out: Kids living and learning with new media.* Cambridge, MA: MIT Press.

Jenkins, H., Purushotma, R., Clinton, K., Weigler, M., & Robison, A. (2006). *Confronting the challenges of participatory culture: Media education for the 21st century. Building the field of digital media and learning.* Chicago, IL: The John D. and Catherine T. MacArthur Foundation. Retrieved from: http://newmedialiteracies.org/files/working/NMLWhite Paper.pdf. Accessed December 15, 2011.

Kalil, T. (2010, September 29). Remarks on innovation, education, and the maker movement. New York Hall of Science. [Transcript] Retrieved from: http://radar.oreilly.com/2010/10/innovation-education-and-the-m.html. Accessed December 15, 2011.

Museum Audience Insight (2010, April 20). Who's coming to your museum? Demographics by museum type. Retrieved from: http://reachadvisors.typepad.com/museum_audience_insight/2010/04/whos-coming-to-your-museum-demographics-by-museum-type.html. Accessed December 15, 2011.

PBS NewsHour (2011, June 29). Can DIY movement fix a crisis in U.S. science education? [Transcript]. Retrieved from: www.pbs.org/newshour/bb/science/jan-june11/makerfaire_06-29.html. Accessed December 15, 2011.

Schauble, L., Gleason, M. E., Lehrer, R., Bartlett, K., Petrosino, A., Allen, A., et al. (2002). Supporting science learning in museums. In G. Leinhardt, K. Crowley, & K. Knutson (Eds.), *Learning conversations: Explanation and identity in museums* (pp. 425–452). Mahwah, NJ: Lawrence Erlbaum Associates.

Serrell, B. (1998). *Paying attention: Visitors and museum exhibitions.* Washington, DC: American Association of Museums.

Torrone, P. (2011, March 10). Is it time to rebuild and retool public libraries and make "techshops"? *Makezine.* Retrieved from: http://blog.makezine.com/2011/03/10/is-it-time-to-rebuild-retool-public-libraries-and-make-techshops. Accessed December 15, 2011.

UPCLOSE (2005). *Children's Museum of Pittsburgh Evaluations and Reports.* Unpublished evaluation report. Pittsburgh: University of Pittsburgh Center for Learning in Out of School Environments.

UPCLOSE (2011). *Children's Museum of Pittsburgh Visitor Survey.* Unpublished evaluation report. Pittsburgh: University of Pittsburgh Center for Learning in Out of School Environments.

CHAPTER 7

THE ULTIMATE BLOCK PARTY
Bridging the Science of Learning and the Importance of Play

JENNIFER M. ZOSH, KELLY FISHER,
ROBERTA MICHNICK GOLINKOFF, AND KATHY HIRSH-PASEK

THE PLAY CRISIS

We are in the midst of a crisis. A play crisis. Play is a rapidly diminishing staple for today's children. From 1981 to 1997, children's playtime dropped by a staggering 25% (Hofferth & Sandburg, 2001). A more recent analysis shows that this low level of play was maintained between 1997 and 2003, but that during this time, children spent more time studying and less time outdoors, playing sports, or involved in passive leisure activities (Hofferth, 2009). Despite scientific findings that link play and recess to increased levels of attention and increased learning (for a review, see Hirsh-Pasek, Golinkoff, Berk, & Singer, 2009; Pellegrini, 2005; Pellegrini & Davis, 1993; Pellegrini, Huberty, & Jones 1995), recess has been eliminated in thousands of schools in the United States to allow for more time for academic study (Elkind, 2008). Dr. Edward Zigler, father of the Head Start program, has written that "play is under siege" (Zigler, Singer, & Bishop-Josef, 2004).

The issue is not simple. Much of the pressure to increase time spent in school and decrease play is fueled by international test results which found U.S. 14-year-old students, rank 17th among industrialized nations in reading, behind Finland, Poland, and Japan; 23rd in science; and 30th in math, 13 slots behind Slovenia (Fleischman, Hopstock, Pelczar, & Shelley, 2010). While our paltry rankings are not news, what *is* news is that science has made major progress in uncovering how children learn. The last three decades of *science of learning* research has produced a wealth of empirical data that highlight the power of play on development. Ginsburg et al. (2007), in a white paper for the American Academy of Pediatrics, emphasize that free and unstructured play is essential for all domains of development— not just physical health. Free, unstructured play helps children reach physical, cognitive, and social milestones. Further, it aids in managing stress and promotes resiliency. Play is imperative if children are to thrive in a 21st-century world. As the world has changed, so too have the knowledge and competencies needed to succeed—such as creativity, critical thinking, collaboration, communication, confidence, and content—all of which begin in the sandbox during play and take us to the boardroom (Hirsh-Pasek et al., 2009; Hirsh-Pasek & Golinkoff, 2010).

Playful learning, encompassing both free- and guided-play activities, provides children the opportunity to actively engage, explore, and discover the world around them and integrate their learning based on principles defined by developmental psychology and learning sciences research (Bransford, Brown, & Cocking, 2000; Fisher, Hirsh-Pasek, Newcombe, & Golinkoff, in press; Meltzoff, Kuhl, Movellan, & Sejnowski, 2009). *Free-play* activities—those that are fun, voluntary, flexible, have no extrinsic goals, involve active engagement of the child, and often contain an element of make-believe—allow children to practice new skills, test out ideas, and expand their play (Johnson, Christie, & Yawkey, 1999; Pellegrini, 2009; Sutton-Smith, 2001). From dress-up to stacking blocks to creating art, research suggests that free play fosters mathematics, language, and early literacy in children from diverse backgrounds. Additionally, children learn and practice how to share, communicate with others, focus attention on a task, test new ideas, and generate novel solutions—all of which are necessary for later academic success.

In *guided-play* contexts, adults create flexible, interest-driven, child-centered play experiences that encourage children's natural curiosity, engagement, and thinking (Fisher et al., in press). Adults are seen as collaborative partners who actively facilitate the learning process in at least two ways (e.g., Berk, 2001; Vygotsky, 1978). First, adults might enrich the environment with objects or toys or games that provide self-driven experiential learning opportunities and focus children on the dimension of interest. To promote spatial thinking, for example, adults may put blocks in a child's free-play area. Second, adults may facilitate children's learning by gently scaffolding their discoveries using a variety of techniques, including commenting on children's insights, co-playing with them, asking open-ended questions, suggesting ways to explore and play with the materials in ways that children might not have thought to do, or creating games that help them hone their knowledge and skills (e.g., National Research Council,

2009). Building on the previous example, an adult may challenge children to "design and build the tallest skyscraper" in the room and, after the activity, ask children to compare skyscrapers and figure out why some toppled over while others did not. Evidence shows education programs that incorporate free- and guided-play activities, such as Tools of the Mind and Montessori, promote long-term academic achievement (e.g., math, vocabulary) as well as increased inventiveness, curiosity, social skills, and motivation beyond traditional, structured programs (e.g., Alfieri, Brooks, Aldrich, & Tenenbaum, 2011; Bodrova & Leong, 1996, 2001, 2007; Burts, Hart, Charlesworth, & Kirk, 1990; Burts et al., 1992; Diamond, Barnett, Thomas, & Munro, 2007; Golbeck, 2001; Hirsh-Pasek, 1991; Lillard & Else-Quest, 2006; Marcon, 1993, 1999, 2002; Stipek, Feiler, Daniels, & Millburn, 1995). The data paint a clear picture: the "active and engaged child"—one who explores, interacts, and engages in the environment—is the child who is best prepared for the future (Chi, 2009).

Despite this, 65% of children age 4 to 11 experience more than two hours of TV a day, while more than one third (37%) experience fewer than six active-play sessions a week (Anderson, Economos, & Must, 2008). These same children are exposed to more highly regimented education programs in place of play (Miller & Almon, 2009). For example, the "Baby Einstein" phenomenon changed the environment of many homes in America. Experimental studies show that very young children are unable to learn vocabulary from educational videos (Krcmar, Grela, & Lin, 2007; Roseberry, Hirsh-Pasek, Parish-Morris, & Golinkoff, 2009) and, in fact, increased television watching among 8- to 16-month-old infants is associated with decreased vocabulary compared to little to no television watching (Richert, Robb, Fender, & Wartella, 2010). Furthermore, television watching leads to decreased communication between mother and child compared to book reading or playing with toys (Nathanson & Rasmussen, 2011) across early childhood. Despite these findings, 40% of children age 3 months and 90% of 24-month-olds are already regularly watching screen media (i.e., television, video, and DVDs) (Zimmerman, Christakis, & Meltzoff, 2007). Others have found that highly structured educational activities in early childhood result in limited, short-term gains and, in some cases, negative effects on children's motivation (Stipek & Byler, 2004) and long-term academic outcomes (Marcon, 2002). Child psychologists also worry that a lack of playtime compromises the next generation's academic, physical, and social-emotional health (Fisher, Hirsh-Pasek, Golinkoff & Glick Gryfe, 2008).

While science shows that play is vital for children's learning and development, the message is often lost in the mass commercialization of childhood and the misguided belief that only highly structured activities are the best way for young children to learn (Wong, Fisher, Uribe-Zarain,

Ma, Golinkoff, & Hirsh-Pasek, 2008). How might we reverse this trend? Could a group of scientists start a grassroots effort to change the culture of childhood today? Our plan was simple—channel the "block parties" of the past where families came together to share knowledge and play. In this case, we hoped to bring together the scientific community of researchers studying play, the professional community of educators, social workers, and librarians, nonprofit corporations invested in children such as museums, corporations that work with children, and most important, today's families. Enter: the "Ultimate Block Party."

THE ULTIMATE BLOCK PARTY

On October 2, 2010, over 50,000 people attended our first "Ultimate Block Party" event, held in New York City's Central Park. With the help of a wide range of scientists, community partners, corporate leaders, children's museums, nonprofit groups, volunteers, and even celebrities such as Sarah Jessica Parker and Mariska Hargitay, we hosted the first celebration of the impact of play on development and shared this message first-hand—from the mouths of scientists to the ears of today's parents and families. Since then, thousands more families in Baltimore and Toronto have told us the same thing that New Yorkers did: today's families are ready for a culture change.

Translating the Science of Play. The Ultimate Block Party initiative sought to transform attitudes about how children learn by demonstrating that play can foster important learning skills in science, technology, engineering, and math (STEM) as well as in literacy and the arts. Recognizing that the general public is largely unaware of the explicit connections between play and learning, we developed the Ultimate Block Party to create unique opportunities for families to experience and understand the science of learning in action. We created playful learning activities that families could engage in and linked play to learning in a variety of ways, including an emphasis on how the arts impact children's learning.

Playful Learning Activities and the Playbook. The Ultimate Block Party included 28 activities spanning eight play domains: adventure, construction, physical, creative, the arts, make-believe, technology, and language play. All activities were based on the learning sciences literature and were designed to appeal to a wide demographic audience (e.g., ages, interests, learning ability including learning disabilities, and physical ability). For example, studies show that block and puzzle play promote spatial understanding and mathematics achievement (e.g., Ginsburg, 2006; Ginsburg, Lee, & Boyd, 2008; Levine, Ratliff, Huttenlocher, & Cannon, 2012; Newcombe, 2010; Wolfgang, Stannard, & Jones, 2001); hence, the "LEGO Extravaganza" activity was created for the event. Other activities were based on research originating from the NSF Science of Learning Centers (Gentner, Levin, Dhillon and Polterman, 2009).

A pivotal piece of this outreach was designed to inform parents that play is central to children's learning. We produced an Ultimate Block Party *Playbook* that we gave for free to each family at the event, full of useful information about play. For each of the eight play domains, we introduced parents to "The science behind playing around" and also suggested "More ways to play at home!" In addition, the *Playbook* contained descriptions and a map of the locations of the Ultimate Block Party activities. It also had a list of both scientific and popular resources for more information on the science of learning. Below, we highlight a few of the events we featured and the messages we gave parents to help highlight the science behind the play. Much of the text below appeared in the pages of the *Playbook*. To view the complete *Playbook*, visit www.ultimateblockparty.org.

Where in the World? Adventure Play

How do young children learn to navigate or "get around" in this great big world? Psychologists find that even preschool children have the ability to learn to use a map. Kids' ability to think about space has been linked to achievements in science, technology, engineering, and even in math. A great way to improve this skill is through fun practice using maps and thinking in space or "spatially." The adventure play activities allow you and your child to use a map to find your way around the park, go on a huge scavenger hunt for local "treasures," and play a big game of hide-and-go-seek.

- *Hide-and-Go-Seek* (sponsored by Hali): You will need a phone with a GPS (such as an iPhone or an Android) to play this game. Players are divided into two teams, Hiders and Seekers. Hiders must work as a team to keep each other safe, while seekers must coordinate to find and tag Hiders. The app provides a map, showing other players' approximate locations. Seekers are given exact locations of Hiders who are far away, but as they near the Hiders they must rely on their eyes to tag them. Hiders must judge when a Seeker is too close and figure out when their location is no longer secure.

Building the Future: Construction Play

How do cars work? What holds up a house? Kids love to know how things are made. But did you know that giving kids the chance to build things (such as a block tower) also helps them learn about shapes, space, patterns, and even mathematics? And if children build with others, they practice working as a team, problem-solving, turn-taking, and perspective-taking.

Giving children the chance to build (and even destroy!) new structures gives them the opportunity to become child-engineers! Imagine the wonder! How did those small pieces come together to build something so large and wonderful? The activities in this section will allow you and your child to experience this wonder first-hand. You will get the chance to create a CL!CK moment using LEGO CL!CKs, build your own tallest skyscraper, race a one-of-a-kind model car, and even create your own playground!

- *LEGO Extravaganza* (sponsored by LEGO; Figure 7.1): Families will have an opportunity to build an original design by themselves or become part of a team of builders. The foundation of the activity is a blog (www.LEGOclick.com) that serves up daily musings on those daily moments of brilliance—the "light bulb" or CL!CK moments—when ideas just seem to come together. From innovative activities and experiences to new inventions to everyday fixes, CL!CK moments are the intersection of creativity and problem-solving, and often go unnoticed. For a child, a CL!CK moment occurs when he or she snaps the last brick on his or her LEGO creation and declares, "I did it!" These moments nurture patience and persistence. The reward is a sense of accomplishment and a self-esteem boost that is the foundation for a lifetime of creativity.
- *Imagination Playground* (sponsored by KaBOOM!; Figures 7.2 and 7.3): Imagination Playground is a breakthrough play-space concept conceived and designed by architect David Rockwell to encourage child-directed, unstructured free play. Imagination Playground offers a changing array of elements that allows children to constantly reconfigure their environment and to design their own course of play. Giant foam blocks, mats, wagons, fabric, and crates overflow with creative potential for children to play, dream, build, and explore endless possibilities. Kids learn how to use their imaginations and foster their building skills as they create houses, barns, and simply interesting block configurations. Social skills are also enhanced as kids who have never met before team up to make something together.
- *Skyscraper Challenge* (sponsored by NSF's Science of Learning Centers and in collaboration with the Chicago Children's Museum): Design your own skyscraper and enhance your understanding of the science, engineering, art, and technology behind what keeps the world's tallest buildings standing! Using a variety of materials resembling a large plastic erector set, children were encouraged to build the tallest skyscraper while exploring their knowledge of physics. After constructing their tower, children were asked if it "wobbles," and learned that structures built with a cross-brace for support were much stronger than those built without. What a fun way to become scientific engineers!

Figure 7.1 Children design, make, and play in a sea of LEGOs.

Source: Diane Bondareff.

Figure 7.2 Parents and children alike constructed their own personal playground from giant foam shapes at the Imagination Playground.

Source: Rachel Weaver Rivera and Liza Sullivan.

Figure 7.3 Building structures with massive blocks allowed children to create their own "cities."

Source: Rachel Weaver Rivera and Liza Sullivan.

Get Moving! Physical Play

Following rules, learning self-control, even learning to count—these are things that can be learned through play. When we play games, we add pleasure to the task of mastering our minds and bodies: "Put your hands on your head"; "Simon says, touch your ear." In this seemingly simple task, if you know to touch your ear but *not* put your hands on your head, you are practicing "executive functions" like regulating and controlling your impulses. Research suggests that self-control is critical to success in school. And, as you might guess, when you pay attention, you will perform your classwork better and will also be better at forming friendships. The activities in this section will get your body moving and your brain learning!

- *Pop-Up Adventure Playground* (sponsored by the New York Coalition for Play): Children need to be in charge of their play! At the Pop-Up Adventure Playground, kids have permission to create their own play environments and scenarios. Do not be surprised if kids continually transform this space throughout the day. Children will encounter an assortment of materials such as planks of wood, cardboard boxes, lengths of fabric, mixing bowls, sand, water, leaves, and branches. Stand back and enjoy your kids using this stuff to construct whatever they desire—hideouts, forts, flying ships—the sky is the limit! The play may be loud or quiet, silly or serious. One thing will be true: kids and their imaginations will rule!

Just Add Imagination! Creative Play

Kids love to create—new works of art, music, and dance! Being creative and exercising their imagination is important for kids to become better observers and innovative thinkers. Practicing drawing and painting when you are little helps you learn how marks on a page can express your feelings and ideas. Creating art lets children imagine worlds that might be and songs that never existed. In this section, you find that art can come from everyday materials such as cardboard and sidewalk chalk. Create your own brain art using a seven-foot 3D sculpture, and then design your own kite.

- *Brain at Play* (sponsored by Children's Museum of Manhattan; Figure 7.4): Children's Museum of Manhattan (CMOM) asks: "How does play make the brain hum with activity?" Children paint, collage, and draw on a huge 7-foot, interactive, three-dimensional sculptural "brain" that sparks the connection between play, creativity, and healthy brain development. Pulsing lights flash and portals strategically placed throughout the sculpture inspire children to send "play messages" into the large brain, creating documentation of thousands of children's favorite play activities. These play messages were posted on CMOM's website after the event to help families discover how important play is to their children and inspire them to find new ways to play (www.cmom.org).

Got Rhythm? Music and Dance Play

Music is a language all its own. Emotions, feelings, movement, and ideas are all invoked and expressed through music. Plus, getting up to dance to the beat helps children be active and exercise their bodies. The activities in this section enable children to find their rhythm.

- *Sesame Street Sing-a-Long* (sponsored by *Sesame Street*): Come sing along to some of your favorite classic *Sesame Street* songs with "Gordon" from the Emmy Award-winning series on PBS created by Sesame Workshop. Music can be a playful and engaging way to help children learn about and explore their world as they strengthen their language and literacy skills, develop academic skills, enhance their social and emotional development, and foster artistic confidence and creativity.

Figure 7.4 "How does play make the brain hum with activity?" was the question posed at the Brain at Play activity. Children gladly answered on this huge 7-foot, interactive, three-dimensional sculptural "brain."

Source: Diane Bondareff.

For instance, recent work suggests that even short-term music training may improve preschoolers' performance on tests of verbal intelligence and executive function (Moreno et al., 2011).

Pretend Worlds: Make-Believe Play

How do kids learn to control their behavior when they feel sad or mad or just plain rotten? They play! Scientists tell us that letting kids engage in make-believe gives them a chance to work through their feelings and figure out good ways to respond. Playing make-believe helps children control their thinking and behavior. This "self-regulation" ability is important for kids to learn for future success. Self-regulation goes beyond learning to walk away from the cookie jar when dinner is almost ready. Self-regulation helps kids develop persistence, master tasks, cooperate with you and others, and make good moral choices. Through becoming a restaurateur and consulting with *The Muppets'* Swedish Chef, and even through practicing "clowning around," kids learn to do the right thing.

- *Let's Play Café* (sponsored by the Goddard School; Figures 7.5 and 7.6): Make a reservation at this special make-believe restaurant! Children can pretend they are chefs, create their own placemats, cook imaginary meals, wait on tables, dine, make change, and much more at the Let's Play Café. As children play with their friends in this rich learning environment, they are rehearsing real-life experiences! They negotiate who will be the cook and who the customer at the restaurant, they practice communicating their ideas and feelings to another person, they learn how to balance their wants/desires with those of other children, and they practice sharing. But that is not all! They also gain skills in math, hand-eye coordination, creativity, and problem-solving. This play-and-learning destination is sure to delight children and their families.

Tech-Time! Technology Play

Children specialize in "why" and "how" questions: "Why did my ice cream melt?" "How does it snow?" Children are natural-born scientists who conduct little experiments each and every day. When children question the meaning of events and why they happen, they are improving their powers of observation, reasoning, and prediction while generating excitement about science. Thinking scientifically also fosters creative thinking and hypothesis-testing as children ask themselves how and why a particular thing occurred. And just like scientists, children learn from their successes *and* their failures.

Figure 7.5 A budding chef at the Goddard School's *Let's Play Café.*

Source: Diane Bondareff.

Figure 7.6 A young chef sits down to take an order at the Goddard School's *Let's Play Café.*

Source: Rachel Weaver Rivera and Liza Sullivan.

In this area, kids create their own science projects such as a lively robot and a video game.

• *Geocaching and Dinosaur Train* (Thirteen/WNET and the Jim Henson Company's Dinosaur Train): Join Thirteen/WNET and the Jim Henson Company's Dinosaur Train on a family-friendly outdoor adventure called geocaching! Stop by to learn more about this world-wide treasure hunt and find out what you need to get started on this GPS-driven activity. Geocaching and Dinosaur Train encourage kids to use GPS technology to find "treasures" hidden outside throughout the park. Children will get outside, be in nature, apply their map-reading skills, and make their own discoveries. Learn how you can get started geocaching right here in Central Park!
• *Scratch* (sponsored by Columbia University Teachers College and MIT Media Lab): Why not make your own video game and share it with other kids? Columbia University Teachers College introduces technology by dissecting video games made using Scratch, a programming language developed at the MIT lab. Instructors will teach children how to use the programming language to make their very own games on computers.

Say What? Language Play

Language makes humans special. Spoken and written language allows us to communicate, pass on our traditions and stories, and form relationships with those around us. Research has shown that the amount of language children hear addressed to them–from birth on—influences not only their vocabulary size, but also their school achievement. Language lets children interact with others, express their emotions, and learn about the world. Learning more than one language is easy for children if they are immersed in it and is a gift that lets them participate in an even larger world. For all children, being able to read opens up the universe!

- *Bilingual, Bicultural, Brilliant!* (sponsored by the University of Washington's Institute for Learning and Brain Sciences): Why is it cool to know more than one language? And why is it so much fun to play language games? The activities here demonstrate the benefits of being bilingual and bicultural through simple games and activities. For instance, playing bilingual bingo will demonstrate that speaking more than one language can help children and adults be more flexible thinkers. Children and parents who speak English, Spanish, or a combination of both languages will really enjoy these games.

Facilitators at the Ultimate Block Party

Volunteers. Over 100 volunteers from the community, ranging from high school and college students to teachers and parents, this large cadre of volunteers manned each of the 28 activities at the New York Ultimate Block Party. They were excited to be part of something that brought the word of playful learning to families and were eager to share in this unique opportunity. They were offered materials on the web to read about what the activities offered and how to help parents understand the value of play.

Play Doctors. Members from the NSF-funded Science of Learning Centers and others from the scientific community acted as *Play Doctors* who walked around interacting with families and children. Their primary goal was to facilitate the public's understanding of how play relates to children's learning and development based on scientific research. They wore white lab coats decorated with colored handprints and messages about the importance of play. They also wore pins that said "Play Dr." so that families could identify them as targets to ask questions about the activities.

Experts. Professionals from a wide array of backgrounds, including art, music, law, architecture, finance, museum education, media, and toy companies, acted as *Experts* stationed at the various activities. Experts interacted with children and families, sharing stories about how their play activities promoted interest in their chosen careers.

Assessment and Outcomes

Whom Did the Ultimate Block Party Reach?

The goal of the Ultimate Block Party was to convey the message about the power of play and the science of learning to the community at large. The original Ultimate Block Party event in the Naumburg Bandshell in Central Park, New York City, attracted over 50,000 attendees—82% of whom lived in New York City. Importantly, the event attracted a wide range of attendees of different races and ethnicities: 44% were non-white, and many resident New Yorkers commented that this part of Central Park is most frequently visited by an upper-class and largely white population. Many of those interviewed said that the Ultimate Block Party was a destination rather than simply something that they happened upon in their own neighborhood. Notably, the "age of oldest child" of about half the Ultimate Block Party participants was 5 years or under. Research suggests that early childhood experience is a key factor in later emotional, psychological, and academic development (as reviewed in the May 2010 issue of *Archives of Pediatrics & Adolescent Medicine*). In addition, our June 2011 Ultimate Block Party in Toronto, Canada attracted over 5,000 attendees, and over 10,000 people attended our October 2011 Ultimate Block Party in Baltimore.

Further analysis revealed that our reach was far greater than the number of attendees. By involving community partners, engaging in a press campaign, using social media, and working hard to contact as many people as possible both before and after the event, our public relations partner estimated an on-air or online reach of millions, print circulation of over 1.8 million, and an estimated print audience of more than 4.5 million! Since the event, the Ultimate Block Party has been featured as a full-page story in the *New York Times*, as a cover story in the *Christian Science Monitor*, and a story in the *Chronicle of Higher Education*. The media appear to be supportive of this message, and engaging with local and national news organizations can only help spread the word about the power of play.

Did the Ultimate Block Party Work? Assessing Beliefs about Playful Learning

A key goal of the Ultimate Block Party was to change parents' beliefs about the value of play to learning. A team of researchers from Sarah Lawrence College and Yale University conducted an external assessment of the event to examine the messages conveyed to attendees, how its organization was viewed, and, more generally, people's attitudes about play, to be used for future endeavors and outreach. The research team interviewed 258 parents or caregivers who attended the Ultimate Block Party event in New York

City and Ultimate Block Party volunteers. One objective was to learn whether attendees' attitudes about play changed and, if so, whether change depended on the number of activities individuals visited. We asked questions about the perceived relationship between play and learning. We wanted to discriminate between those who believe play leads to learning versus those who do not. Among those who participated in one activity, only 50% reported this direct relationship. Among attendees who visited two to three sites, 62% reported this relationship, while 83% of those visiting four or more sites reported the same. Thus, the more interaction participants had with the Ultimate Block Party activities, the more they believed that play leads to learning. Furthermore, participants made direct connections between certain activities and learning, demonstrating that they understood the value of spatial learning as instantiated through block play and a geo hide-and-seek game.

LESSONS LEARNED FROM THE ULTIMATE BLOCK PARTY

Since the original Ultimate Block Party in New York City, we have hosted two other parties—one at Fort York in Toronto and one at the Inner Harbor in Baltimore. After three Ultimate Block Parties, we have learned a number of lessons that can be applied to any design, make, or play event.

- *Power from the people.* The Ultimate Block Party would not have been possible without the contributions of countless numbers of individuals. Early on, we relied on guidance from our scientific and business advisory boards, who participated in the formation of this event from the ground up. Our scientific consultants helped make sure that all our activities were based in science and that we were fulfilling our mission of bringing science into the hands and homes of today's families. Because of the scope of the event, we had outside help with public relations and marketing; we also had a production company to help make sure that this massive event went off without a hitch. One of our key partners in the NYC Ultimate Block Party was the Children's Museum of Manhattan. This well-established, trusted, and well-connected partner not only shared our vision, but also facilitated cutting through some of the red tape that inevitably stands in the way of any community endeavor. Our Baltimore Ultimate Block Party was partnered with Baltimore City Public Schools, which allowed us to tap directly into a large school district and highlight this event to underserved communities. The Toronto Block Party occurred in partnership with the Ontario school system, which was heralding its new play-based curriculum.

- *Involving community organizations.* One surprising but unintended outcome was what happened when the Ultimate Block Party brought together community organizations and partners to plan the Ultimate Block Party. This was often the first time these community organizations had come together around the same table. We often heard these groups make additional plans to work together—both in preparation for the Ultimate Block Party but also for future events. The planning committees in all our locations reported that they simply were not aware that so many people, so close by, shared a passion for the promotion of learning and play in childhood.

- *Communication is crucial!* To have a well-attended Ultimate Block Party, communication must happen early and often with a wide range of constituents. Each Ultimate Block Party was up to two years in the making. Over these two years, innumerable emails, phone calls, and emergency meetings occurred to make sure every last detail was covered to ensure successful events. A massive community event requires that everyone—from the event planners to the security staff to the clean-up crews to the legions of volunteers—be on the same page. This means that from the beginning, everyone involved must develop a communication style that works and must be willing to change it as the project changes. What started as a few emails and phone calls between five to 10 people very quickly became a 100-plus-person effort that required constant communication.

- *Professionalism.* We learned that a high-end product commands respect. We made the decision to have at every juncture a consistent brand that was accessible, high-profile, and understatedly elegant. This was indeed an event about parents and families, but it was also one that preserved scientific integrity by offering the finest learning activities. Our production company utilized professionally made signage that lined our walkways and surrounded the event, making it clear to all participants that there were individual activities that were part of a consistent and thoughtful event (Figures 7.7 and 7.8). The look went beyond "street fair" to create more of a museum-moves-outdoors kind of feel. The *Playbook*, too, was published on shiny, glossy, heavyweight paper, and the website has a clean, very sophisticated yet playful look. Playing, making, and designing is serious business and needs to look that way to be taken seriously.

- *Training.* Any community event will benefit from the help of volunteers, but only if these volunteers are well informed to help make a difference in their community. One core aspect of the Ultimate Block Party was incorporating the help of many volunteers. We had two different types: professionals (i.e., researchers and scientists) and community members,

Figure 7.7 We utilized consistent branding/signage to identify different activity centers to help families navigate through the park.

Source: Rachel Weaver Rivera and Liza Sullivan.

and we did not expect everyone to know how best to interact with families in the community. So we trained them. We equipped our Ultimate Block Party volunteers with an extensive handbook outlining our event, our goals, and their responsibilities. We used YouTube to share our goals and aspirations for our volunteers' participation. We also outlined ways to help maximize their impact by advising them on how to interact with a variety of families. For example, we instructed

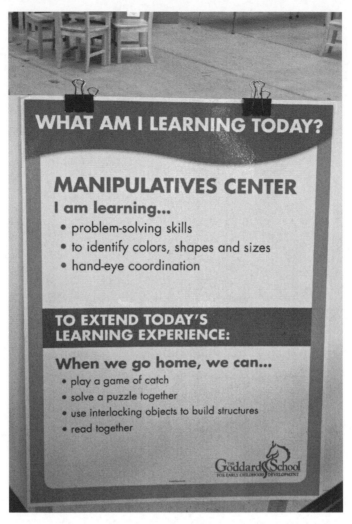

Figure 7.8 Clear signage at the entrance to each activity indicated what parents and children would learn from this activity, but importantly, also how to take the same lessons home.

Source: Rachel Weaver Rivera and Liza Sullivan.

our volunteers to engage in discussion with parents about the motivation of the Ultimate Block Party movement, to point out the learning that existed behind their child's play at the activities, and to highlight ways in which the *Playbook* could help them bring the lessons home. The sheer number of volunteers allowed us to maintain a "presence" throughout all the events to help parents and families learn

Figure 7.9 Will it fall or won't it? A young builder investigates his building's foundation and learns the basics of physics and architecture alongside a helpful caretaker.

Source: Rachel Weaver Rivera and Liza Sullivan.

how important play is in their children's development. Local researchers and professionals and interested community members help expand a dedicated staff. From lending scientific expertise to pointing people in the direction of their choice event, volunteers make an event shine.

• *Social media is your friend.* One of our main Ultimate Block Party objectives was to maximize the number of people who heard about our event. A key strategy is to meet people where they are—and many people are online. We used both Facebook and Twitter to help communicate with families in the area. We blogged about the event on our blog (in addition to blogging about topical issues). We quickly learned that engaging the online community was a maximally effective way to get the word out about our event and our mission. Parent bloggers already active in the community had a long list of followers. They blogged about us too and, in no time, thousands of families from all ethnicities knew about our event. We used social media tracking services (free!) and found that Facebook and Twitter were very effective ways to quickly communicate with our audiences. Before the event, we engaged our community partners, and on the day of the Ultimate Block Party, we posted updates about directions and parking alongside pictures and updates (nothing gets the buzz going more than cyberspace hearing that the U.S. Secretary of Education is at your event with his family!). Social media transformed our ability to communicate directly with today's families. Finally, engaging families online allows the lessons about play and learning to continue, long past the close of an event or exhibit. We still work to keep our followers updated with the newest research on our understanding of the science of learning.

- *Reaching all families.* The Ultimate Block Party was designed to attract all families—rich and poor, black, white, Asian, and Hispanic. To do this, we needed outreach beyond the traditional blogs. We sought out contacts within specialized communities such as Hispanic community centers and schools for deaf children, and in each we offered flyers and commentary in the native language so all felt welcome. This event was completely *free* to make sure that all could attend. Because our event was held outdoors in such an open and easily accessible environment, we did not have a registration process or RSVP system; instead, we encouraged anyone and everyone to walk freely through the event. The event was held rain-or-shine to make sure that all families, even those without access to the Internet, knew that the event was "on" regardless of weather.

- *Nothing was sold!* It was critical to ensure that the families who came felt comfortable at our event. If vendors were selling goods or even handing out advertisements, some families might feel less included than others. To make certain that rich and poor children participated in our activities side by side, we allowed no vendors (not one!) and permitted only subtle signage. Sponsors for each activity were noted on signposts at the entrance to their activity and in the *Playbook*, as well as listed at the entry gate to the main event. The more prominent signs were reserved for connections between the science and the play.

- *Bridge the gap.* One main focus of the Ultimate Block Party was to bridge the gap that exists between today's families and today's scientists and researchers. We wanted to bring the science of play to everyday life. To do this, we charged a scientific advisory board to help us ensure that the science supporting the event was strong and accurate and reached out to local scientists to serve as volunteers and Play Doctors on the day of the event. Local universities can offer scientists (oftentimes in psychology, education, or human development departments) who want to be involved and can contribute to the playing, the making, and the designing. These researchers have often dedicated their careers to finding out how children learn about the world, and many are elated to work closely with their community. They have access to the latest scientific research and can help distinguish between "hype" and the real science that exists.

Moving Forward: Playing for the Future

The Ultimate Block Party is a new approach that puts the science of learning into the hands of families, practitioners, educators, and policymakers. To date, our proof of concept demonstrates that a highly professional approach that allows people to experience learning through play activities is attractive to families of all races, ethnicities, and income levels. It is a concept that travels well across borders and promises global reach and local flavor. And it emphasizes the value in the lost art of play. Society appears ready not only to hear this message, but also to participate actively in this change. The Maker Movement is another stellar example of a grassroots effort that is quickly causing large-scale changes in thinking. In 2006, 20,000 makers—crafters, builders, artists, engineers, researchers, and scientists—gathered in San Mateo, California to celebrate do-it-yourself play of all types. Only five years later, 100,000 makers joined in the play, and two additional sites held their own Maker Faires. From the inaugural success of the Ultimate Block Party in New York City and other cities to the practical explosion of the Maker Movement both nationally and internationally, one message is clear. Society is ready for change—and people are ready and willing to design, make, and play their way into a better future.

Acknowledgments

Workshops around the Ultimate Block Party were generously supported by NSF grant 1058081 to RMG and KHP and 1044384 to Kathy Hirsh-Pasek and Roberta Michnick Golinkoff. Additional funding for the Ultimate Block Party was provided by three NSF Science of Learning Centers: Spatial Learning and Intelligence Center (SILC); Learning in Informal and Formal Environments (LIFE); and the Temporal Dynamics of Learning Center (TDLC). In addition, funding was provided by Temple University and the University of Delaware.

References

Alfieri, L., Brooks, P. J., Aldrich, N. J., & Tenenbaum, H. R. (2011). Does discovery-based instruction enhance learning? *Journal of Educational Psychology, 103*, 1–18.

Anderson, S. E., Economos, C. D., & Must, A. (2008). Active play and screen time in U.S. children aged 4 to 11 years in relation to sociodemographic and weight status characteristics: A nationally representative cross-sectional analysis. *BMC Public Health, 8*, 366.

Berk, L. E. (2001). *Awakening children's minds: How parents and teachers can make a difference.* New York: Oxford University Press.

Bodrova, E., & Leong, D. J. (1996). *Tools of the mind: The Vygotskian approach to early childhood education.* Englewood Cliffs, NJ: Prentice Hall.

Bodrova, E., & Leong, D. J. (2001). *Tools of the mind: A case study of implementing the Vygotskian approach in American early childhood and primary classrooms.* Geneva: The International Bureau of Education.

Bodrova, E., & Leong, D. J. (2007). *Tools of the mind: The Vygotskian approach to early childhood education* (2nd ed.). Columbus, OH: Merrill/Prentice Hall.

Bransford, J. D., Brown, A. L., & Cocking, R. R. (Eds.). (2000). *How people learn: Brain, mind, experience, and school.* Washington, DC: National Academies Press.

Burts, D. C., Hart, C. H., Charlesworth, R., Fleege, P., Mosley, J., & Thomasson, R. H. (1992). Observed activities and stress behaviors of children in developmentally appropriate and inappropriate kindergarten classrooms. *Early Childhood Research Quarterly, 7*, 297–318.

Burts, D. C., Hart, C. H., Charlesworth, R., & Kirk, L. (1990). A comparison of frequencies of stress behaviors observed in kindergarten in classrooms with developmentally appropriate versus inappropriate instructional practices. *Early Childhood Research Quarterly, 5*, 407–423.

Chi, M. T. H. (2009). Active-constructive-interactive: A conceptual framework for differentiating learning activities. *Topics in Cognitive Science, 1*, 73–105.

Diamond, A., Barnett, W. S., Thomas, J., & Munro, S. (2007). Preschool program improves cognitive control. *Science, 318*, 1387–1388.

Elkind, D. (2008). Can we play? *Greater Good Magazine, IV*, 14–17.

Fisher, K., Hirsh-Pasek, K., Golinkoff, R.M., & Glick Gryfe, S. (2008). Conceptual split? Parents' and experts' perceptions of play in the 21st century. *Journal of Applied Developmental Psychology, 29*, 305–316.

Fisher, K., Hirsh-Pasek, K., Newcombe, N., & Golinkoff, R. M. (in press). Taking shape: How teaching practices impact preschoolers' geometric knowledge.

Fleischman, H. L., Hopstock, P. J., Pelczar, M. P., & Shelley, B. E. (2010). *Highlights from PISA 2009: Performance of U.S. 15-year-old students in reading, mathematics, and science literacy in an international context* (NCES 2011-004). U.S. Department of Education, National Center for Education Statistics. Washington, DC: U.S. Government Printing Office.

Gentner, D., Levin, S., Dhillon, S., & Poltermann A. (2009). Using structural alignment to facilitate learning of spatial concepts in an informal setting. In B. Kokinov, K. Holyoak and D. Gentner (Eds.) *New Frontiers in Analogy Research: Proceedings of the Second International Conference on Analogy.* Sofia, Bulgaria: New Bulgarian University Press.

Ginsburg, H. P. (2006). Mathematical play and playful mathematics: A guide for early education. In D. Singer, R. M. Golinkoff, & K. Hirsh-Pasek (Eds.), *Play = learning: How play motivates and enhances children's cognitive and social-emotional growth* (pp. 145–168). New York: Oxford University Press.

Ginsburg, H. P., Lee, J. S., & Boyd, J. S. (2008). Mathematics education for young children: What it is and how to promote it. *SRCD Social Policy Report, XXII.*

Ginsburg, K. R., (2007). *The importance of play in promoting healthy child development and maintaining strong parent-child bonds. Pediatrics, 119*(1), 182–191.

Golbeck, S. L. (2001). Instructional models for early childhood: In search of a child-regulated/teacher-guided pedagogy. In S. L. Golbeck (Ed.), *Psychological perspectives on early childhood education: Reframing dilemmas in research and practice* (pp. 3–29). Mahwah, NJ: Lawrence Erlbaum Associates.

Hirsh-Pasek, K. (1991). Pressure or challenge in preschool? How academic environments affect children. In L. Rescorla, M. C. Hyson, & K. Hirsh-Pasek (Eds.), *New directions in child development. Academic instruction in early childhood: Challenge or pressure?* (No. 53, pp. 39–46). San Francisco, CA: Jossey-Bass.

Hirsh-Pasek, K., & Golinkoff, R. (2010). *The six C's: Developing 21st century skills.* Retrieved from: www.ultimateblockparty.com/about.html. Accessed October 5, 2011.

Hirsh-Pasek, K., Golinkoff, R. M., Berk, L. E., & Singer, D. G. (2009). *A mandate for playful learning in school: Presenting the evidence.* New York: Oxford University Press.

Hofferth, S. (2009). Changes in American children's time, 1997–2003. *International Journal of Time Use Research, 6,* 26–47.

Hofferth S. L., & Sandberg, J. F. (2001). Changes in American children's use of time, 1981–1997. In T. Owens & S. L. Hofferth (Eds.), *Children at the millennium: Where have we come from, where are we going?* (pp. 193–229). Amsterdam, Netherlands: Elsevier Science Publishers.

Johnson, J. E., Christie, J. F., & Yawkey, T. D. (1999). *Play and early childhood development* (2nd ed.). New York: Longman.

Krcmar, M., Grela, B., & Lin, K. (2007). Can toddlers learn vocabulary from television? An experimental approach. *Media Psychology, 10,* 41–63.

Levine, S. C., Ratliff, K. R., Huttenlocher, J., & Cannon, J. (2012). Early puzzle play: A predictor of preschoolers' spatial transformation skill. *Developmental Psychology, 48,* 530–542.

Lillard, A., & Else-Quest, N. (2006). The early years: Evaluating Montessori education. *Science, 311,* 1893–1894.

Marcon, R. (1993). Socioemotional versus academic emphasis: Impact on kindergartners' development and achievement. *Early Child Development and Care, 96,* 81–91.

Marcon, R. (1999). Differential impact of preschool models on development and early learning of inner-city children: A three-cohort study. *Developmental Psychology, 35,* 358–375.

Marcon, R. (2002). Moving up the grades: Relationships between preschool model and later school success. *Early Childhood Research and Practice, 4,* 517–530.

Meltzoff, A. N., Kuhl, P. K., Movellan, J., & Sejnowski, T. J. (2009). Foundations for a new science of learning. *Science, 325,* 284–288.

Miller, E., & Almon, J. (Eds.) (2009). *Crisis in the kindergarten: Why children need to play in school.* College Park, MD: Alliance for Childhood.

Moreno, S., Bialystok, E., Barac, R., Schellenberg, E. G., Cepeda, N. J., & Chau, T. (2011). Short-term music training enhances verbal intelligence and executive function. *Psychological Science, 22,* 1425–1433.

Nathanson, A. I., & Rasmussen, E. E. (2011). TV viewing compared to book reading and toy playing reduces responsive maternal communication with toddlers and preschoolers. *Human Communication Research, 37,* 465–487.

National Research Council. (2009). *Mathematics learning in early childhood: Paths toward excellence and equity.* Committee on Early Childhood Mathematics. Christopher T. Cross, Taniesha A. Woods, & Heidi Schweingruber (Eds.). Center for Education, Division of Behavioral and Social Sciences and Education. Washington, DC: The National Academies Press.

Newcombe, N. (2010). Picture this: Increasing math and science learning by improving spatial thinking. *American Educator, Summer, 29*–43.

Pellegrini, A. D. (2005). *Recess: Its role in education and development.* Mahwah, NJ: L. Erlbaum Associates.

Pellegrini, A. D. (2009). Research and policy on children's play. *Child Development Perspectives, 3,* 131–136.

Pellegrini, A. D., & Davis, P. D. (1993). Relations between children's playground and classroom behaviour. *British Journal of Educational Psychology, 63,* 88–95.

Pellegrini, A. D., Huberty, P. D., & Jones, I. (1995). The effects of recess timing on children's playground and classroom behaviors. *American Educational Research Journal, 32*(4), 845–864.

Richert, R. A, Robb, M. B., Fender, J. G., & Wartella, E. (2010). Word learning from baby videos. *Archives of Pediatrics & Adolescent Medicine, 164,* 432–437.

Roseberry, S., Hirsh-Pasek, K., Parish-Morris, J., & Golinkoff, R. M. (2009). Live action: Can young children learn verbs from video? *Child Development, 80,* 1360–1375.

Stipek, D., & Byler, P. (2004). The early childhood classroom observation measure. *Early Childhood Research Quarterly, 19,* 375–397.

Stipek, D., Feiler, R., Daniels, D., & Millburn, S. (1995). Effects of different instructional approaches on young children's achievement and motivation. *Child Development, 66,* 209–223.

Sutton-Smith, B. (2001). *The ambiguity of play.* Cambridge, MA.: Harvard University Press.

Vygotsky, L. S. (1978). *Mind in society: The development of higher psychological processes.* M. Cole, V. John-Steiner, S. Scribner, & E. Souberman (Eds.). Cambridge, MA: Harvard University Press.

Wolfgang, C. H., Stannard, L. L., & Jones, I. (2001). Block play performance among preschoolers as a predictor of later school achievement in mathematics. *Journal of Research in Childhood Education, 15,* 173–180.

Wong, W., Fisher, K., Uribe-Zarain, X., Ma, W., Golinkoff, R. M., & Hirsh-Pasek, K. (2008, March). "Educational toys": Do parents believe the hype? Poster presented at the International Conference on Infant Studies, Vancouver, CA.

Zigler, E. F., Singer, D. G., & Bishop-Josef, S. J. (Eds.). (2004). *Children's play: The roots of reading.* Washington, DC: Zero to Three Press.

Zimmerman, F. J., Christakis, D. A., & Meltzoff, A. N. (2007). Television and DVD/video viewing in children younger than 2 years. *Archives of Pediatrics & Adolescent Medicine, 16,* 473–479.

CHAPTER 8

SQUISHY CIRCUITS

ANNMARIE THOMAS

This project began when I posed a simple question to an undergraduate research student: *Can we create play dough conductive enough to build circuits with?* This was quickly followed by more questions: If so, what could we do with it? What could others do with it? My research over the last few years has been focused on engineering education at the pre-collegiate level and incorporating play into engineering, so the idea of sculptable circuits was intriguing. While previously existing primarily in rigid board form, circuits can now be sewn and painted (Buechley, Elumeze, & Eisenberg, 2006; Buechley, Hendrix, & Eisenberg, 2009; Qi & Buechley, 2010). Many adults, myself included, have fond memories of playing with play dough, and we thought it would be fun to add electronics to this activity. Could we make circuit building as playful, and intuitive, as manipulating play dough? If so, would this be appealing to individuals, particularly children, who may have no previous exposure to electronics?

Play dough was particularly enticing to our research group because it is something that most children have experience with. Homemade play dough is cheap and relatively easy to make. Additionally, play dough is non-permanent—if you do not like your creation, you can squish it up and start over. Our hope was that by combining something as familiar and easy to use as play dough with electronics, we could create an activity in which circuits could be explored playfully and easily.

Play dough has previously found a place in the physics classroom, typically in resistance-measuring labs (Jones, 1993; Watson, 2000). There, exercises often involve students measuring the resistance of play dough tubes. At the beginning of the Squishy Circuits project, these resistance labs

Figure 8.1 A 3-year-old Squishy Circuit sculptor.

were the only context in which we knew of electricity and play dough being used together. A few months into this project, however, I attended a circuit-bending workshop. Circuit bending is the art of modifying circuits, particularly sound-producing circuits such as those found in toys, typically in order to produce new sounds and music. At this workshop, I was intrigued to see the instructor modify electrical connections on the circuit board by touching it with commercial play dough. Additionally, researchers from the MIT Media Lab's Lifelong Kindergarten group (led by Mitch Resnick, author of the "Designing for Tinkerability" chapter in this book) and the Playful Invention and Exploration (PIE) Network developed technologies for using commonly found objects, including play dough, in circuits to control sound (Resnick, 2006). This work included a project on Musical Play Dough, which allowed users to stretch play dough, connected to a sensor and computer, to create different musical pitches (www.picocricket.com/pdfs/Musical_PlayDough.pdf). We were unable to find any prior work where play dough was used to create circuits with components such as LEDs and motors.

WHAT ARE SQUISHY CIRCUITS?

At the heart of the Squishy Circuit project is a pair of recipes: one for a conductive dough, and one for a highly resistive dough (both can be found on the project's website:www.stthomas.edu/SquishyCircuits). The conductive dough can be treated like a wire (with some resistance incorporated into it), and the high-resistance dough serves as an insulator. By using the dough in combination with components such as light-emitting diodes (LEDs), buzzers, battery packs, and motors, circuits can be created. When setting out to develop the recipes, we agreed that the dough should use only ingredients found in our local grocery store, be non-toxic, and, in the case of the conductive dough, be sufficiently low in resistance that a four-AA battery pack could power a palm-size circuit containing LEDs and a motor.

Given that the play dough resistance-lab activities mentioned above confirm that most commercial play dough is conductive, we were fairly confident that a homemade conductive dough could be created. Our recipe literature search spanned many parenting and school websites, activity books, and craft websites. We measured the resistance of these recipes and developed new ones. Over the course of a summer, first-year engineering student Samuel Johnson developed a recipe that met all three design criteria, using only water, flour, salt, vegetable oil, and cream of tartar. The first pilot test of the project, with middle school students in a summer toy-design class, highlighted that it would be advantageous to also have an insulating dough. Thus, we also developed a highly resistant (hereafter referred to as "insulating") dough made of flour, sugar, vegetable oil, and deionized (or distilled) water (Johnson & Thomas, 2010a).

When we introduce Squishy Circuits to new users, the first circuit we typically have them sculpt is one that lights up an LED circuit. The circuit diagram for a traditional LED circuit is shown in Figure 8.2. Translating the circuit diagram into play dough results in the circuit shown in Figure 8.3. The conductive dough replaces the wire and resistor. Current flows from the battery pack, through the conductive dough, through the LED, and then through the second lump of conductive dough back to the battery pack. Adding insulating dough to the activity allows users to sculpt a circuit where the insulating dough helps prevent the conductive dough lumps from touching each other, which would cause a short circuit (see Figure 8.4).

A **circuit** is a closed path that electricity flows through.

A **conductive** material is one that allows electricity to flow through it. Examples of conductive materials include metals and salt water.

An **insulator** is a material that does not allow electricity to flow through it. Examples of insulators include air, rubber, and wood.

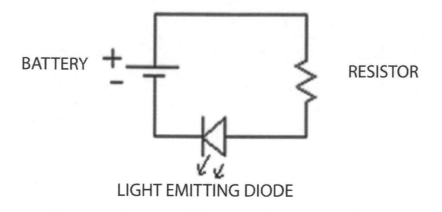

BATTERY $+$ RESISTOR

LIGHT EMITTING DIODE

Figure 8.2 A diagram for a traditional LED circuit.

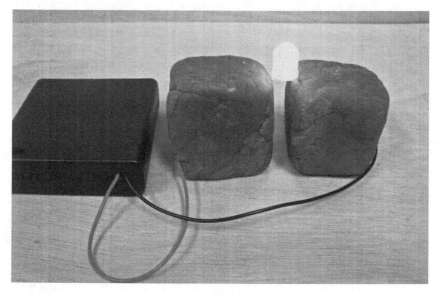

Figure 8.3 The Squishy Circuit interpretation of the LED circuit.

Other Squishy Circuits can be created by replacing, or augmenting, the LED with a motor or buzzer. Typically, when we do Squishy Circuits activities in a facilitated setting, the participants will build these simpler circuits first, then use what they have learned to build more complex circuits, such as those shown in Figure 8.5. In circuits such as those pictured here, the paths of insulating and conductive dough must be planned carefully to allow for more artistic circuits that also perform in the desired manner.

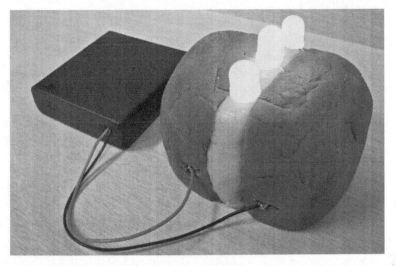

Figure 8.4 LEDs in series (left) and parallel (right).

Figure 8.5 Seasonal Squishy Circuits.

Microcontroller Applications of Squishy Circuits

Once the basic conductive and insulating dough recipes had reached a point where they worked well and other users, such as teachers and families who had found the activity on our website, were reporting good results building basic circuits, we wondered if Squishy Circuits could be used in any further applications. We had begun to receive feedback from people who were using the basic projects and were now looking for other ways to use the Squishy Circuit idea. The resistance of a piece of dough is dependent on its shape, which opens up possibilities in which manipulating the shape of the dough could be used as an input into a microprocessor. We focused our efforts on projects that use the Arduino, an open source microcontroller that has become very popular (Schmidtbauer, Johnson, Jalkio, & Thomas, 2012). Two projects that came out of this exploration are described below. Additional projects are posted on the Squishy Circuits website.

Squishy Sound

In the Squishy Sound circuit, shown in Figure 8.6, the resistance of a lump of conductive dough controls the pitch coming out of the speaker. As the dough is stretched, the resistance increases and the sound played through

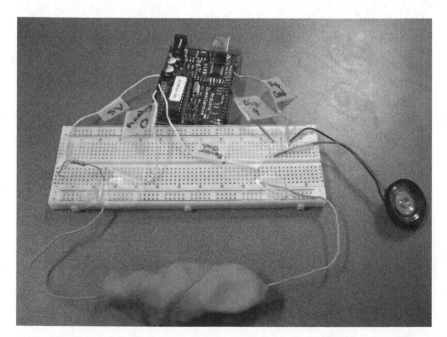

Figure 8.6 The Squishy Sound circuit.

the speaker rises in pitch. As the dough is pushed together, the resistance decreases and the pitch drops. This was the first microcontroller project that the Squishy Circuit team worked on, and is also the one that anecdotally seems to be most popular among visitors to the Squishy Circuits website, as well as at events in which we allow users to interact with the projects. (This circuit works the same way as the above-mentioned Musical Play Dough project.)

Squishy Red/Green/Blue (RGB)

The squishy RGB LED controller uses three of the same resistance-reading circuits as Squishy Sound. Each of the three "input blobs" of dough control a single LED (one red, one blue, one green), as shown in Figure 8.7. The brightness of each LED is mapped to the resistance of the corresponding lump of dough. Thus, as the dough is stretched, the resistance increases and the related LED dims. If the lump is divided into two, breaking the circuit, the light goes out. Manipulating the input lumps creates different color combinations. (This effect is particularly visible when a semi-translucent sheet of plastic is used to diffuse the light.)

Figure 8.7 The Squishy RGB light controller circuit.

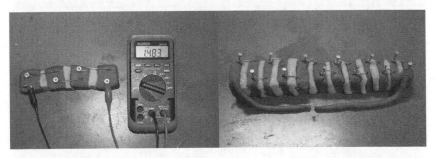

Figure 8.8 Measuring the output from a squishy battery (left), and using a squishy battery to light an LED (right).

Squishy Batteries

An additional activity, developed by undergraduate student Matthew Schmidtbauer and shared on the Squishy Circuits website, is the "squishy battery." Similar to the lemon or potato battery experiments often done in schools, this project uses the electrical potential difference created when two different types of metal are bridged by a lemon, potato, or saltwater. This difference leads to a flow of current, which can be large enough to light an LED. As shown in Figure 8.8, the squishy battery consists of cells made of conductive (purple) dough connected by nails and copper wire. If enough cells are stacked together, increasing the produced voltage, an LED can be lit.

How Squishy Circuits Have Been Used

Based on feedback from educators, parents, and children who tried out Squishy Circuits during the development phase, typically attendees at events and workshops run by the Squishy Circuit team, we decided that other groups and individuals were likely to find this project interesting. We set up a website (see Figure 8.9) for the project, where we shared videos,

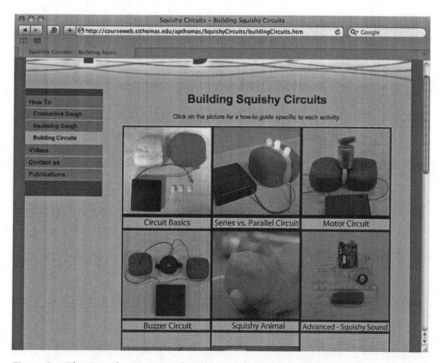

Figure 8.9 The Squishy Circuit website's set of project instructions.

recipes, and instructions, as well as contact information so visitors could ask the team questions. From the beginning, we made it a priority to answer all emails quickly. Parents, students, and teachers from five different continents contacted us. In response to their emails and tweets, we created gluten-free versions of the recipes and posted information on how to substitute lemon juice for cream of tartar (which is hard to find in many countries). Instructions for the project were also published in *Make* magazine (Johnson & Thomas, 2010b), and a short demonstration of Squishy Circuits was posted on TED.com (http://blog.ted.com/2011/04/04/hands-on-science-with-squishy-circuits-annmarie-thomas-on-ted-com).

As time progressed, we found that people using Squishy Circuits wanted a way to share their pictures, stories, and questions about the project. We chose Facebook as a platform where users could assist each other by answering questions and posting about their own explorations with Squishy Circuits.

It was never our goal to provide comprehensive or prescriptive instructions on how to use Squishy Circuits. Our hope was to create content, available on our website, demonstrating possible ways to build circuits as a starting point for others to develop their own projects and ideas. We think the basic simplicity of the project is a large part of its appeal, as it seems to invite users to jump in, play, and develop their own projects and applications. The fundamental principles become evident after a little experimentation with the physical materials, and the materials are inexpensive enough to be used repeatedly for further experimentation with little regard for cost. It is easy to assess whether the project is working (does the LED light up?, does the circuit make sounds?, etc.), and early success can give the user enough confidence to take on more adventurous circuit-building goals.

Squishy Circuits in the Classroom

While we did not initially set out to meet specific academic standards, we have been happy to see teachers find ways to connect Squishy Circuits-based activities to standards they must meet in their classrooms. At the University of St. Thomas, a course for current and future pre-K-12 teachers, "Fundamentals of Engineering for Educators," challenges students to create lessons for their class in which engineering concepts fulfill required academic standards (Thomas, Hansen, Cohn, & Jensen, 2011). Students in the St. Thomas class are exposed to Squishy Circuits, in addition to prototyping boards and more traditional circuit-building methods, as part of the unit on electricity and electronics. A few of the in-service teachers who have taken this class chose to explore Squishy Circuits for their final project.

Bryan Farmer, a high school chemistry teacher at Mahtomedi High School in Minnesota, challenged his class to use their knowledge of chemistry and the engineering design process to create new recipes that improved the current Squishy Circuit dough recipes. The students were responsible for defining "better" and also for analyzing the costs of producing their dough. In addition, they were to imagine that they were an engineering company that would take on chemical engineering challenges.

Adam Beyer, a fourth-grade teacher, used Squishy Circuits to meet the following Minnesota Academic Standards in science (http://education.state. mn.us/MDE/EdExc/StanCurri/K-12AcademicStandards) by having students construct simple Squishy Circuits (such as those in Figures 8.3 and 8.4).

- *4.1.2.2.3 Test and evaluate solutions, considering advantages and disadvantages of the engineering solution, and communicate the results effectively.*
- *4.2.3.1.3 Compare materials that are conductors and insulators of heat and/or electricity. For example: Glass conducts heat well, but is a poor conductor of electricity.*
- *4.2.3.2.2 Construct a simple electrical circuit using wires, batteries and light bulbs.*

One very exciting aspect of watching teachers incorporate Squishy Circuits into their classroom plans has been witnessing their creativity. When we first imagined Squishy Circuits being used in schools, we envisioned their playing a role in classes where teachers had already planned to do circuit-based activities (such as the fourth-grade example above). We have been amazed by how creatively teachers have worked Squishy Circuits into a variety of classes and units. Some examples follow.

Computer Science in the Kitchen

Andrew Davidson, who teaches Introduction to Computer Science at Roosevelt High School in Seattle, used Squishy Circuits to introduce the Arduino microcontroller. The previous semester, he had observed students struggling with wiring prototyping boards. He suspected this was because "it's hard to get a good mental model of a circuit when you're looking at breadboard holes and bunches of wires, and don't see the whole circuit path visually," referring to the standard prototyping boards that are used in many electronics projects. The internal circuit connection paths within such boards are not typically visible. Andrew partnered with a colleague from the school's Family and Consumer Science Department, Wendy Arness. Wendy had her students create big batches of different dough recipes as part of their cooking unit, and emphasized the chemistry interactions with her students. The two classes then combined into mixed groups to build actual circuits. The collaboration was deemed a success by both teachers, and Andrew hopes some of Wendy's students may have been galvanized to take Introduction to Computer Science next year.

Lighting Up Art Class

Art teacher Nadine Charity had never used electronics in her elementary school art class, but our TED talk on Squishy Circuits inspired her to try. Her goal was to "introduce simple circuitry and explore elements of simple sculpture and how light could add another layer of interest to the art" to her second- and third-grade art students. Over two days, her students learned about circuits and created pieces that featured LEDs. Her students spent time building circuits similar to those shown in Figure 8.10, which are based on a circular design and can be made using many LEDs. One highlight for her class was turning out the lights and watching their sculptures glow. Nadine has gone on to present her work to other art teachers, and we look forward to seeing whether this encourages more electronics-focused art projects.

"Squishy Battery Grand Masters"

Through her New York-based education nonprofit organization, Knowledge iTrust, Dr. Karen Kaun developed an inquiry-based program that embeds making into STEM education. When she brought students to present on how to build hydroponic gardens at the 2011 Maker Faire in Queens, New York, she saw Squishy Circuits being demonstrated. Since then, Dr. Kaun has used Squishy Circuits and squishy battery activities with fourteen elementary school teachers and approximately 440 third- to fifth-grade New

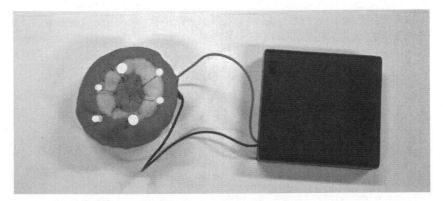

Figure 8.10 A popular Squishy Circuit design, referred to by many as the "wreath" or "sushi circuit."

York City students. She introduces Squishy Circuits in conjunction with other circuit activities that use materials such as snap circuits, alligator clips, and electromagnets. With Squishy Circuits, her students are encouraged to explore variations to circuits and to develop their own creations.

Once her students understand the basics of circuit building, Dr. Kaun asks them to "surprise her." The results have been a number of creative new projects, such as novel squishy switches and even a squishy circuit-based electromagnet. Two girls from PS 107 built what is, to our knowledge, the world's largest squishy battery. After their project did not work during the class period, these girls spent their lunch period making adjustments and finally succeeded in building a large battery (shown in Figure 8.11) capable of lighting an LED. Not content to stop there, these "Squishy Battery Grand Masters" refined their design further and taught other students how to build more efficient batteries. The two girls then shared their battery-building knowledge with more far-flung peers in other schools through a blog and forum. Dr. Kaun says, "I learned how to make better batteries from my students."

ENCOURAGING VERY YOUNG CIRCUIT BUILDERS

We initially thought Squishy Circuits would be most applicable to elementary or middle school classes, but early in the project's development we noticed how appealing they were to even younger audiences. At museum events, the play dough often lured preschool and kindergarten children to our table, and we were excited to see how quickly they picked up on the circuit-building aspects of our activity. At about this time, my nearly 3-year-old daughter began asking me to bring the circuits home for her to play with.

We decided to explore how Squishy Circuits could contribute to a preschool classroom and held two half-hour workshops, one for primarily 3-year-olds and one for primarily 4-year-olds. These very young students were introduced to the concept of electricity flowing through a circuit, then

Figure 8.11 "The world's largest squishy battery," built by students from PS 107 in the Bronx, New York.

Figure 8.12 Preschool students working together on their Squishy Circuits.

guided through the building of a simple LED circuit using conductive dough. (We gave each preschooler a ball of the conductive dough, her own battery pack, LEDs, and motors, but did not introduce the insulating dough.) Once a child could build an LED circuit and turn it on and off by using the dough as a short circuit, he or she was given time to play with the materials (see Figure 8.12). The students seemed quite engaged and excited to build and share. In both classrooms, all students stayed focused on the project for the duration of the activity. Each class developed its own favorite activities; the 3-year-olds spent much of their time playing with the motors, while the 4-year-old class seemed to challenge itself to discover "How many LEDs can I get to light up at once?"

"Green Dough for Go, and Red Dough for Stop"

Paige Beatty, a childcare center program director, used Squishy Circuits with preschool students aged 4 and 5. Here, the activity was part of a larger unit on circuits in which children read books about electricity and then were encouraged to build and troubleshoot circuits. To help her students visualize the concept of conductors and insulators, she dyed the conductive dough green for "Go!" and the insulating dough red for "Stop!" Paige reported that some of her young students took on roles helping their classmates:

Another thing that I noticed was the problem-solving and teamwork between the children when we were working in small groups. Some children understood the concepts and knew what they needed to do to make the circuit work; others had a more limited understanding and weren't able to fix a circuit that wasn't working. The children who got it would happily assist those having more trouble. I was also excited to hear a lot of them formulating their own questions ("I wonder what will happen if I . . .?") and experimenting with the materials.

Observations about Preschool and Squishy Circuits

In both preschools that made Squishy Circuits, parents commented that their children talked about the concepts after the activity had ended. In particular, the children pointed out circuit-related activities such as the power lines they saw on their way to school, or electricians working on a house's wiring.

One challenge we encountered with circuits and young children is the directionality of LEDs. LEDs allow current to flow in only one direction. Thus, if the LED is placed backward into a circuit, it will not light up. This can be frustrating for users, particularly young ones, since it seems like their circuit "doesn't work." With the youngest students, we found that using a different vocabulary helped. LEDs resemble a small gumdrop with two legs, so we tell children that it might help to think of a LED as a person who needs to put on two play dough shoes. If the LED is put into the circuit in the wrong orientation, we can say to them, "Oops! I think the shoes are on the wrong feet," which the children can correct easily by flipping the LED around. Another common occurrence is a child trying to plug both of the battery-pack leads and the LED into a single lump of play dough. This shorts out the LED because the current runs through the dough instead of through the LED, and no light is produced. In this case, we say this is like putting both of the "LED person's" feet into the same shoe. Typically, this is followed by the LED being correctly inserted into two lumps so that the circuit is complete. We have found that this vocabulary allows us to help children build the initial circuit on their own, and once they have successfully lit up their LED they are often more receptive to learning more about how the circuit works.

SQUISHY CIRCUITS IN INFORMAL SETTINGS

Squishy Circuits work well in informal settings where people drop in at activities because they are relatively inexpensive (particularly if only LEDs and battery packs are used), and participants can get started right away with very few formal instructions. We have successfully set up Squishy

Circuit activity tables at family engineering nights at schools, Maker Faires, and activity stations at museums.

Squishy Circuits on a Museum Floor

The Tinkering Studio at the Exploratorium used Squishy Circuits to augment other hands-on circuit activities that they developed. Museum visitors were encouraged to play with the materials at their own pace and to develop their own projects, with staff support available as needed (see Figure 8.13). The Tinkering Studio added a playful assortment of tools, such as cutters and extruders, which led to several creative pieces and techniques. Some young circuit builders discovered that by replacing the battery pack in their squishy LED circuit with a motor, they could use the motor as a generator to light the LED.

A staff member noted that everyone seemed to "be able to jump right in . . . and even very young children had fun building . . ." While children's understanding of circuits afforded by this activity did not seem significantly different from that gained from other circuit activities, it was noted that "The whimsical quality of building with [play dough] also stops most people from dwelling on what they 'should know' about electricity and gives them a tangible substance to test out their ideas" (Jenkins, 2011).

Figure 8.13 A squishy sea urchin in a wooden sculpture.

Source: Exploratorium.

Youth Teachers Make it a Game

It is particularly gratifying when other people take your project and create their own interpretation and execution. That was definitely the case for us when the youth teachers at the Learn 2 Teach, Teach 2 Learn program in Boston used Squishy Circuits to teach creative technologies to others in their community. These youth teachers, assisted by Dr. Susan Klimczak and community technologist Donna Parker, designed and created a "Monopoly-style game" to teach circuits to elementary and middle school students. As the players learn about electricity, power, batteries, solar energy, and other topics, they earn Squishy Circuit building materials, so that they can eventually build the circuit with both batteries and solar cells. At the end of the game, the players receive a sticker that says "I can build with alternative energy! I made a 'squishy circuit' with a solar panel!" to inspire their family and friends to ask them more about what they did.

Super Sylvia's Awesome Maker Show

One of the most viewed videos of Squishy Circuits on the web comes not from our lab, but from Super-Awesome Sylvia, an 11-year-old whose online videos instruct viewers in a wide array of projects (Super-Awesome Sylvia, 2012). Sylvia's episode on Squishy Circuits (see Figure 8.14) covered the chemistry behind the dough recipes as well as how to build the circuits. In its first two months, it received over 75,000 views, and the comments show that many viewers, young and old, were inspired to try the project. Sylvia also developed an interactive video game that allows up to three players to control spaceships by squishing control panels made of conductive dough.

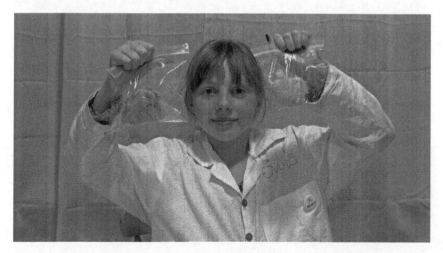

Figure 8.14 Super-Awesome Sylvia teaches her viewers about Squishy Circuits.

Squishy Circuits at Home

Some of the most inspiring emails and blog posts we have seen are from parents who used Squishy Circuits to introduce their children to electronics. Many wrote that they, or their children, had been intimidated by the idea of electricity and circuit building, but that they found the idea of working with play dough rather than prototyping boards more accessible to them. Figure 8.15 shows two sisters sculpting circuits at home.

OUTCOMES

While we have done no formal studies on the learning outcomes of the Squishy Circuit project, anecdotally we have seen some common themes among the emails we have received from parents, educators (both formal and informal), and kids. We repeatedly hear that the Squishy Circuit builders, young and old, had fun. As our goal was to make circuit building playful, we see this as a sign of success. Second, we have heard, and witnessed, persistence among even the youngest circuit builders. Kids seem to want to keep working on their Squishy Circuits to make them more complicated or more aesthetically pleasing. Finally, we have heard from people who mentioned that they found this project appealing because it did not seem intimidating.

One aspect of making project information freely available online is that we will never know many of the project outcomes. That is fine with us! As much as we love hearing from people about how they are using Squishy Circuits, we are also happy to simply know that the information is out there, and that people are using it and seem to be enjoying it. We track the spread

Figure 8.15 Two sisters build Squishy Circuits at home.

of this project by watching for keywords, such as "squishy circuits," on social medium platforms such as Twitter, and through the occasional Google search. In this manner, we have learned of Squishy Circuit workshops around the world, fun stories of families building squishy creations together, and circuit configurations that we would never have thought of.

The most exciting outcome from this project, for us, is that we have seen Squishy Circuits used in such a wide array of designing, making, and playing activities.

ACKNOWLEDGMENTS

The Squishy Circuits project was made possible by grants from the University of St. Thomas Young Scholars program, the University of St. Thomas School of Engineering, and the 3M Foundation, which supported the undergraduate research students (Samuel Johnson and Matthew Schmidtbauer) who worked on this project. Dr. Jeff Jalkio provided valuable insights into the electrical engineering and physics behind Squishy Circuits. Finally, I would like to thank everyone who has given us feedback on Squishy Circuits and generously shared their stories and suggestions.

REFERENCES

Buechley, L., Elumeze, N., & Eisenberg, M. (2006). Electronic/computational textiles and children's crafts. *Proceedings of the 2006 Conference on Interaction Design and Children*, 49–57. New York: ACM.

Buechley, L., Hendrix, S., & Eisenberg, M. (2009). Paints, paper, and programs: First steps toward the computational sketchbook. *Proceedings of the Third International Conference on Tangible and Embedded Interaction*, 9–12. New York: ACM.

Jenkins, R. (2011, July 16). *Squishy circuits 3: In the Tinkering Studio*. Retrieved from: http://blogs.exploratorium.edu/tinkering/2011/07/16/squishy-circuits-3-in-the-tinkering-studio. Accessed December 4, 2012.

Johnson, S., & Thomas, A. M. (2010a). Squishy circuits: A tangible medium for electronics education. *Extended Abstracts of the 28th International Conference on Human Factors in Computing Systems*, 4099–4104. New York: ACM.

Johnson, S., & Thomas, A. M. (2010b, April). 1+2+3: Sculpting circuits. *Make*, *22*, 78.

Jones, B. (1993). Resistance measurements in Play-Doh. *The Physics Teacher*, *31*(1), 48–49.

Musical Play-Dough. (n.d.) Retrieved from: www.picocricket.com/pdfs/Musical_PlayDough.pdf. Accessed December 3, 2012.

Qi, J., & Buechley, L. (2010). Electronic popables: Exploring paper-based computing through an interactive pop-up book. *Proceedings of the Fourth International Conference on Tangible, Embedded, and Embodied Interaction*, 121–128. New York: ACM.

Resnick, M. (2006). Computer as paintbrush: Technology, play, and the creative society. In D. Singer, R. M. Golinkoff, & K. Hirsh-Pasek (Eds.), *Play = learning: How play motivates and enhances children's cognitive and social-emotional growth*. New York: Oxford University Press, pp. 192–208.

Schmidtbauer, M., Johnson, S., Jalkio, J., & Thomas, A. M. (2012). Squishy circuits as a tangible interface. *Extended Abstracts of the 30th International Conference on Human Factors in Computing Systems*, 2111–2116. New York: ACM.

Squishy Circuits (n.d.). Retrieved from: www.stthomas.edu/SquishyCircuits. Accessed December 4, 2012.

Super-Awesome Sylvia (2012). *Squishy Circuits – Sylvia's mini maker show*. Retrieved from: http://sylviashow.com/episodes/s2/e7/mini/squishycircuits-0. Accessed December 4, 2012.

Thomas, A. M., Hansen, J. B., Cohn, S. H., & Jensen, B. P. (2011). Development and assessment of an engineering course for in-service and pre-service K-12 teachers. *Proceedings of the ASEE National Conference*. Retrieved from: http://search.asee.org/search/fetch?url=file%3A%2F%2Flocalhost%2FE%3A%2Fsearch%2Fconference%2FAC2011%2FASEE_AC2011_507.pdf&index=conference_papers&space=129746797203605791716676178&type=application%2Fpdf&charset=. Accessed December 4, 2012.

Watson, G. (2000). Resistivity and Play-Doh. Retrieved from: www.physics.udel.edu/~watson/scen103/colloq2000/problems/playdohexpt.html. Accessed December 4, 2012.

CHAPTER 9

RAFT: A Maker Palace for Educators

Mary Simon and Greg Brown

> RAFT is like a cross between a hands-on science museum, Disneyland, and Costco.
>
> RAFT devotee

Welcome to the Palace!

When you imagine a palace, what do you see? Perhaps you envision a gleaming building filled with precious and unusual objects.

Believe it or not, that is the impression many first-time visitors have when they step into Resource Area For Teaching (RAFT). Our "palace" is not as luxurious as the one in Versailles, but it is just as breathtaking and vast to educators in search of hands-on teaching materials. The endless rows of cardboard tubes, bottle caps, and other surplus materials we collect from local businesses may not cost as much as the crown jewels, but they are equally precious to pre-K-12 teachers in search of inspiration.

To appreciate the educational value of RAFT's materials, consider the following stories:

> "Emma" asked her English Language Learner students to purchase blank notebooks to use as journals. After a few days, she noticed Anthony still had no journal. When she questioned him, she learned he did not want to ask his mother for money because his family was on a tight budget. Emma decided to see if RAFT could help. Our staff pointed her to *Journaling Your Trash*, a low-cost kit that combines an Idea Sheet, outdated corporate letterhead, old file folders, and simple binding materials so the user can create one-of-a-kind recycled journals. (Note: Free copies of Idea

Figure 9.1 Turning light into a rainbow with a RAFT spectroscope.

Sheets can be found at www.raft.net.) Anthony and several other students used the kit to make their own journals. According to Emma, Anthony "wrote and wrote," filling his entire journal. For him, Emma's small investment in the kit was priceless.

"Jana" showed her young students how to build simple spectroscopes using cardboard tubes, stickers, and small pieces of plastic she got at RAFT (see Figure 9.1 and *The Colors of Light* at www.raft.net). The children excitedly compared the rainbow-like patterns created by different lights in their classroom. Later, at a parent-teacher meeting, one mother told Jana what happened when her daughter Sarah came home from school, spectroscope in hand: "Sarah told me all about it. I had no idea she was so interested in science." Thanks to Jana, Sarah is more likely to pursue her interest in science, and Sarah's mother is more likely to encourage her daughter.

In both stories, there is another return on investment worth noting: the impact on the teachers themselves. By visiting RAFT, they elevated their teaching practice and rediscovered the joy of teaching. Stories such as these underscore our belief that RAFT truly is a Maker Palace for educators.

What Is RAFT?

> I go to RAFT for ideas. You get me excited about teaching again. My kids benefit from your creativity.
>
> RAFT member

Figure 9.2 Educators leave RAFT with a armloads of useful materials.

RAFT is a nonprofit, educational, membership organization headquartered in San Jose, California. We run a satellite facility in Redwood City (close to San Francisco) and partner with two independently operated RAFT affiliates in Sacramento and Denver. Our audience includes a growing community of educators who access RAFT via our online resources.

RAFT knows hands-on experiences help students learn best, especially when it comes to learning science, technology, engineering, and math (STEM). We provide innovative, engaging teaching ideas (field-tested Idea Sheets), affordable materials, and the convenience of pre-packaged Activity Kits that support curriculum standards. Other products and services include a full offering of professional development, coaching, and videos that demonstrate how to use hands-on learning resources.

The *mission* of RAFT has remained constant across nearly two decades of operation: "To inspire the joy and discovery of learning through hands-on education."

Our *core purpose* is: "To enable teachers to teach the way kids love to learn."

Our *core values* include heroic customer service, innovation and creativity, and respect for teachers, as well as honesty and integrity in our interactions both inside and outside the organization.

The combined staffing of all RAFT locations is 40 people, with a total annual budget of over $4 million. Roughly half our income derives from educators who become members and pay a portion of the cost of the materials and services they receive. The remainder is contributed by corporate sponsors, individual donors, and foundations.

WHAT DOES RAFT OFFER?

> The free Idea Sheets are incredibly helpful. They suggest projects that can be modified depending on the grade level.
>
> Idea Sheet user

> I love everything, but the kits push me to try new things.
>
> Activity Kit user

> Your classes keep me inspired and nourished. I often take them just for me.
>
> Workshop participant

Figure 9.3 RAFT breadboard circuit.

RAFT Idea Sheets present easy-to-implement, hands-on activities designed around commonly found materials. We offer over 650 free Idea Sheets, each linked to specific curriculum standards, covering virtually all age ranges from pre-K to grade 12 and all Common Core subject areas. Users download them over 500,000 times a year. Many are bundled with pre-packaged Activity Kits that can be purchased at a RAFT location or online. We sell about 50,000 Activity Kits per year, serving nearly one million students. Our main focus is on students from pre-K through middle school.

Here are a few of the design/make/play experiences we have developed:

- *Design experiences*: These projects focus on understanding a need, considering options and constraints, planning, testing, and iterating: *Foil Art, Wrap It Up, Breadboard Circuits*, and *Roller Coaster Math*. After completing these design projects, students have first-hand knowledge of what it is like to be a scientist, engineer, or artist. They develop important 21st-century skills such as critical thinking and collaboration.
- *Make experiences*: Tinkering, creating, reusing, repurposing, and getting connected with materials are all part of these activities: *Hovercraft, Glove-a-phone, Kumihimo*, and *Car on a Roll*. In this era of electronics, the chance to actually build something is a rare and wonderful opportunity. Teachers tell us that many children enter school with great

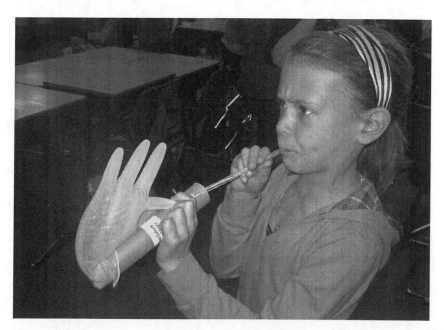

Figure 9.4 Learning about sound firsthand with a RAFT glove-a-phone.

computer skills, but with no idea how to use a screwdriver or even a pair of scissors. Our activities close that gap.

- *Play experiences*: Unbridled curiosity and exploration without preconceived notions of success are central to these RAFT activities: *Freaky Fractals, Foam Dowel People*, and *Building Center*. A crucial ingredient in play is abundance—being surrounded by a seemingly inexhaustible supply of interesting stuff. Having one cardboard box is fun; having 50 opens a world of possibilities for creative play. Students are thrilled at the opportunity to dive into a pile of intriguing materials.

RAFT's physical locations include teacher prep spaces with die cutters, binding equipment, and other useful tools, and they also provide a wide range of professional development services, including one-on-one coaching, teacher workshops, and demonstrations. Our online presence offers a variety of how-to videos, photo galleries, tip sheets, assessment tools, and other resources.

Who Is the Audience for RAFT?

> I have students who are often unable to grasp the concepts unless I can give them a hands-on way of experiencing the lesson.
> Special needs teacher

We design our resources to be useful in all formal and informal educational settings, whether in school or out of school. Many educators are excited to learn that our focus goes well beyond traditional classroom teaching. Roughly two thirds of our 10,000 members work in schools, while one third provide educational services through afterschool programs, summer camps, homeschooling, daycare, scouting, etc.

To foster close ties with our users, our physical sites operate as member-based institutions. Our members see themselves as stakeholders, not customers. They identify with our mission and have a vested interest in the success of our organization. Many veteran educators are very proud to be long-standing members. We work hard to nurture this relationship by getting to know our members and tailoring our offerings to meet their needs.

The RAFT team has consciously considered the many different educator personas arriving at our door. We are especially interested in new users, who are initially overwhelmed by the vastness of our warehouse and the seemingly unlimited choices in front of them. We offer this audience a little hand-holding while they get accustomed to RAFT. For example, a new user may say, "I'm teaching an ocean unit." We have many things that will be useful to this teacher! Experienced members use our copious supplies of paper, foam, and paint to make enormous ocean-themed murals. One enterprising teacher had her students create fantastic jellyfish using RAFT's colorful yarn and huge coffee filters. Several of our Idea Sheets and Activity Kits map directly to ocean-related subjects. We find a way to meet the needs of every audience we serve.

In the final analysis, if you measure an organization's success by the willing participation of its audience, then RAFT is at the top. Our members "vote with their feet" by coming on their own time and spending their own money. Each week, 700 educators visit our San Jose location to fill their minds, fill their cupboards, and recharge their emotional batteries.

RAFT's Place in the Educational Landscape

> I could not do the hands-on activities I do if I didn't have all the equipment and consumables I pick up at RAFT.
>
> Fifth-grade teacher

One of our strengths is our unique position in the educational landscape. Although many organizations provide professional development services for educators, very few focus as tightly on hands-on learning as RAFT does, and almost none combine this training with an enormous warehouse brimming with creative maker materials. And, while many organizations produce pre-packaged kits for STEM education, few of these kits are as carefully designed to make creative use of commonly found objects and surplus materials.

Visitors often tell us they have never seen anything like RAFT. While that is exciting to hear, it also highlights one of our biggest challenges: helping teachers and donors quickly "get" what RAFT is all about. Some have the sense that we are just a big warehouse full of miscellaneous corporate cast-offs. Others think we are a low-cost place to buy commodities such as paper and stickers.

Both impressions are true, but, of course, we are a lot more than that! One way to describe our place in the educational landscape is to imagine an intersection of four roads. RAFT is at the corner where modern teaching practice meets creative thinking, hands-on learning, and playful tinkering. Our products and services are closely tied to the core curriculum and have been shown to improve student achievement (see www.raft.net/student-impact-study). At the same time, we bring a creative, whimsical, and experiential component that gets students engaged.

It is true that some teachers come for basic school supplies. But they leave with intriguing project materials, creative ideas, useful kits, practical training, personal support, and a wonderful sense of community. When we see this happen, we know RAFT is exuberantly fulfilling its mission.

PARTNERS IN RAFT'S SANDBOX

> My goal is to provide learning experiences that focus on process—and RAFT fills the bill.
>
> RAFT member

RAFT would not exist without the 400 local companies who provide 180,000 cubic feet of bulk materials each year. Some material donors have been with RAFT since it opened in 1995. New companies discover us each year.

The RAFT creative team (experienced educators drawn from vibrant classrooms and innovative out-of-school learning environments) gets energy and ideas from like-minded partners who share our passion for playing, designing, and building:

- *The Exploratorium*: Paul Doherty and a long list of other luminaries from this pioneering museum of science, art, and human perception have been deeply engaged in RAFT for years. Many RAFT Idea Sheets were inspired by classic Exploratorium projects.

Figure 9.5 Teachers looking at the world through pinhole cameras.

- *Klutz Press co-founder John Cassidy*: Cass, of the quirky publishing company specializing in kid-activity books cum materials, has added his fingerprints to the format of our published materials and video offerings.
- *Stanford University*: Stanford's long-standing product-design program and its innovative d.school provide exciting opportunities to engage some of the best new design talent in our projects. Stanford students eagerly apply what they are learning to RAFT's real-world challenges.
- *IDEO*: Lively brainstorming sessions sparked by participants from the world-famous global innovation and design firm generate out-of-the-box concepts for new hands-on experiences.

RAFT's Connection to STEM

> My students are now much more interested in science and beg for more.
> Elementary teacher

There are clear links between RAFT content and the NRC *Framework for K-12 Science Education.*

Scientific practices. RAFT Idea Sheets motivate students to make hypotheses, collect data, analyze results, and act like scientists. Clearly, educators who want to teach science successfully must immerse their students in real science experiences. Learning science and math without

Figure 9.6 CDs become wheels on RAFT retractor cars.

interacting with physical materials is like learning to swim without visiting a swimming pool. Everyone needs to dive in! But diving into a science lab can be expensive and risky, especially for an elementary school teacher with a small budget, limited experience, and big concerns that a student might ask a question they cannot answer. To help teachers, RAFT has row after row of huge boxes and barrels displaying low-cost, semi-indestructible items that, with a little imagination, can turn any classroom into a science lab. For example, we offer a myriad of surplus plastic bottles, pieces of tubing, plastic trays, and other items that will work just as well in a school lab as they did in their original industrial application. Two great science projects to look at on our website are *Chromatography*, which uses water and coffee filters to separate the black ink into its component colors, and *The Germinator*, which sprouts seeds in a see-through CD case.

Engineering practices. Humans are designers by nature, eager to seek solutions to problems. We provide engaging engineering experiences that encourage students to develop specifications, build and test prototypes, compare alternative designs, and optimize performance. We offer low-cost electric motors, random pieces of wood, intriguing plastic shapes, and countless varieties of packing materials that can be transformed into engineering prototypes such as those shown in Figures 9.6, 9.12 and 9.15. Here are two fun engineering kits from our collection: *Puff Rockets* (students propel straw rockets through the air) and *On Target with Paper Airplanes* (students collect data to evaluate accuracy of paper airplanes).

Crosscutting concepts. We all know that students are more engaged in learning when they discover connections between different subject areas and between facts and life. RAFT activities help students connect science, math, engineering, technology, art, and language. For example, in an ecology project called *Salmon You Can Count On*, students use scientific sampling techniques to estimate the size of a fish population. The protocol they follow is based on mathematical ratios and proportions. Immersing students in a real-life application of science and math like this one makes both subjects more interesting and memorable. In addition to the salmon project, check out *Anamorphic Art* (which connects science, math, and art skills using a cylindrical mirror) and **Dinosaur Name Game** (which connects science, art, and language when students build models of fictitious animals using classic root words).

Core ideas. We offer hands-on activities focused on all four NRC disciplinary areas. Here are a few examples:

Physical Science:	*Mini Magnet Wands*
Life Sciences:	*Evolution by Natural Selection*
Earth and Space Sciences:	*Shake Table*
Engineering/Technology:	*Staple Remover Catapult*

We have identified over 100 ways to use hands-on activities to both teach and measure student knowledge on Common Core Mathematics content and problem-solving strategies. A great example is *Flip over Fractions*, an Activity Kit that uses scraps of donated cardstock to make "bricks" that help kids understand equivalent fractions or compare parts of a whole.

21st-Century Thinking Skills. Creative problem-solving and teamwork are baked into many of our Idea Sheets and Activity Kits. Two good examples are *Rollback Can* (making a can that rolls back on its own to its starting point, demonstrating energy storage and transfer) and *Leonardo's Arched Bridge* (a self-supporting bridge held together by its own weight).

The Back Story—the Spark that Started RAFT

> The variety of materials inspires me to come up with new ideas I can use in my classroom.
>
> Materials user

> Using common materials or recycled objects to make projects seems to spark the students' imaginations to a fuller extent.
>
> Materials user

The seed of the idea for RAFT was planted back in the late 1970s, when Founder and Executive Director Mary Simon was a young teacher. Visiting the Boston Children's Museum, Mary was intrigued by a special area created for teachers where she discovered barrels full of interesting odds and ends donated by local companies. Captivated, she immediately recognized that this promising idea could be taken much further.

Figure 9.7 RAFT car on a roll.

In retrospect, her insight was a long time in the making. Even as a child, Mary was fascinated by one particular business discard—countertop laminate samples. She says:

> I have memories of sitting on the carpet at home sorting little laminate samples by color, creating patterns, and making up games to pass the time. Later, as a student teacher, I imagined what I could teach using these colorful pieces. When I turned them into math counters, the little samples made math fun. They are still one of my favorite teaching materials.

Math and science were always Mary's favorite subjects to teach:

> I would scrounge for materials to create hands-on projects that helped kids understand . . . helped them see . . . helped them get it . . . and, perhaps just as importantly, helped them have fun. And, I realized it was just as important for me to enjoy teaching as it was for the kids to enjoy learning.

Mary quickly found a kitchen-and-bath store that would give her their old collections of countertop laminate samples. She located a plastic molding company that would save surplus bits and pieces for her. She even convinced the guard at the local paper dump to let her drive her small Toyota pickup in and load up with posters, cardboard tubes, and other treasures.

Mary was thrilled by the generosity small business owners showed once they understood what she was doing with their stuff. She developed a cadre of supporters. She admits, "I was addicted to the thrill of the hunt, and the high of seeing my students crowd around my desk to see what we were going to do today."

Beta-Testing in the Doodad Dump

In 1989, when the Children's Discovery Museum of San Jose was in the planning stages, Mary was hired as an exhibit developer. This created an excuse to take her fascination with surplus materials to a whole new level! With an official business card and keys to the museum's large truck, she built up a willing community of businesses to provide a steady stream of cast-offs. Mary created an exhibit, the Doodad Dump, where kids could use manufacturing and business discards to create wild and wonderful works of art such as the lion mask in Figure 9.8. Tables with glue guns filled the room. Robots, oddball animals, futuristic vehicles, and free-form sculptures were happily constructed and eagerly carried home. One day, renowned educator Howard Gardner visited the museum and noticed how the children using the Doodad Dump stood elbow-to-elbow, focused intently on their creations. The experience was so engaging that many of the children were "in the zone," oblivious to the chaos around them.

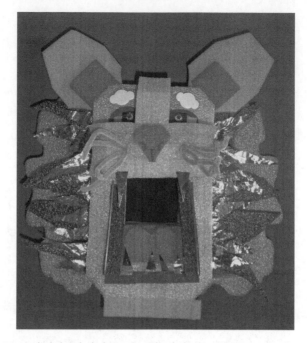

Figure 9.8 Discarded doodads become a lively lion.

Most weekday visitors to the museum were students on field trips. Mary vividly remembers a teacher standing by the Doodad Dump and saying:

> Just look at my fifth graders. I can't get them out of here. At school when I say that it's time for art, they moan and groan. All we have is construction paper and they're sick of it. Where can I get these types of materials?

Soon after that conversation, the museum gift shop started selling empty grocery bags to teachers for five dollars, and they could fill their bags with doodads to take back to school. Mary had to ramp up the quantity of collections, fast!

In the process of reaching out to more companies, Mary found that most businesses had other useful materials, such as office products and desk items, which, while not appropriate for the Doodad Dump, would be valued by teachers.

Mary also noticed that the kids put a lot of engineering into the creations they built in the Doodad Dump:

> With a little help from someone with more background in math and science, I knew the students could produce musical instruments,

measuring devices, and lots of other things that were not simply works of art. I knew that if I could collect more of the treasures out there, and then bring together a group of people who could see the potential of these materials, teachers in every subject would benefit.

RAFT OPENS ITS DOORS

In 1994, Mary decided to start a nonprofit organization dedicated to creative hands-on teaching: "I wanted to create the place I would have loved to have had when I was a teacher ... a place of imagination and fun, a place of abundance." She called this place Resource Area For Teaching (RAFT) and it addressed the three common barriers preventing many teachers from using hands-on activities in their classrooms:

Access to Ideas. If educators want to help kids learn about air pressure, where can they find grade-appropriate, hands-on activities focused on this topic?

Time. If teachers want to build electrical circuits, they need wire, lights, switches, and batteries. How will they find the time to collect these things?

Money. How can teachers afford to buy materials for an entire class when they are expected to pay for supplies out of their own pockets?

Mary knew that if she could overcome these barriers and get more teachers to use hands-on activities, donors would step forward to help.

It all came together in 1995, when RAFT opened a 20,000-square-foot warehouse filled with fabric, plastic, wood, rubber, widgets, doodads, and more, all gathered from local businesses.

As before, it was a challenge to help potential new material donors understand what we needed from them. They would assume we wanted a financial contribution, or perhaps a donation of their finished products. To help them get the idea, Mary built a large, flat, wooden box with a hinged lid; inside she glued about 40 different items such as small springs, plastic shapes, fabric scraps, CDs, and the items shown in Figures 9.9 and 9.16:

> Before they shooed me out the door I would open the box and say, "Do you have anything like this?" They would take a quick look and say, "We do have things like that! We throw them away. We'll start saving them for you."

As materials arrived, Mary checked their potential for use in math or science activities. Other staff and volunteers looked for art and language applications. The team wrote up directions for each new activity in a format we now call the "RAFT Idea Sheet," which also shows clearly how the experience aligns with related curriculum topics. We are still producing new

Figure 9.9 Just about any surplus material can be creatively repurposed.

Idea Sheets today. For some Idea Sheets, we create an accompanying Activity Kit. The kits are available as "onesies" (single units) or larger sets that enable every student, or team, to have a complete set of materials.

By the end of the first year, RAFT was serving 1,000 teachers, as well as scouting groups, summer camps, and a variety of afterschool programs.

As we grew, we began to offer professional development workshops. Teachers could earn college credit in the form of Continuing Education Units (CEUs) as they learned how to apply hands-on teaching techniques.

GROWING EXCITEMENT

In 1999, our fourth year of operation, we purchased a 36,000-square-foot warehouse with classrooms, offices, and workspaces. This was no small feat in Silicon Valley, where commercial real estate prices are sky high. We continued to grow quickly, and we were very happy when a local philanthropist donated a second similarly sized warehouse in 2007. Our hard-working volunteers use the new facility to sort incoming materials and build kits for teachers.

Between 2007 and 2009, two key funders created windows of opportunity for RAFT to open affiliate operations in Sacramento and Denver. During this time, we also added a satellite branch in Redwood City to better serve the entire San Francisco Bay Area.

Today, our four locations welcome visitors from all over the country. Often, these first-timers are brought to RAFT by local friends who are already members and enthusiastic advocates of hands-on teaching. When the new people see what we have created, they invariably become very excited and want to know if our kits are available online. In response, we are expanding our website to include a growing list of our most popular kits and to create a vibrant online community of users.

It is very satisfying to find that RAFT now hosts teachers who were children themselves when the Doodad Dump opened. The teachers innocently tell Mary, "This reminds me of that exhibit at the Children's Museum." Little do they know how it all started!

THE SECRETS BEHIND RAFT'S SUCCESS

> The materials are soooo cheap—every one of my students can make a vehicle and take it home. They have a vested interest in the vehicle because they built it, which improves the quality of their work.
>
> Activity Kit user

We recently brainstormed a list of the not-so-secret ingredients that make RAFT such a successful maker environment, and here is what we came up with:

Focus. We are singularly focused on hands-on activities, which teach essential thinking skills and design practices. The results are tangible, and the feedback is obvious: Did the light bulb light up? Did the rocket take off?

Figure 9.10 Cardboard tubes are a favorite maker material at RAFT.

Content. Our creative educational content makes important concepts easy to understand. We build on existing knowledge using familiar materials. Kids find DNA suddenly more accessible when it is modeled with beads and pipe cleaners. All our content is mapped to curriculum topics and is searchable by grade level.

Abundance. "Abundance" means both a wide variety of items, and a large quantity of each item. Makers get excited when they see 10 different types of bottle caps. That kind of variety stimulates all sorts of ideas. The same maker is also excited to discover a whole barrel full of identical caps (for example see Figures 9.10 and 9.11). The sheer volume will stimulate a whole different set of ideas and applications. It is worth noting that abundance is rare in today's teaching world. The color, variety, and low cost of our materials are a major attraction. When members see the 180,000 cubic feet of materials we bring in each year, they are drawn like bees to honey. They scoop up treasures by the bagful and say, "I don't know what I'm going to do with this . . . but I'll think of something!" One teacher jokingly suggested that we make a deal with a storage company so members can rent lockers to store all the materials they collect.

Affordability. Access to a lot of materials is great, but they have to be reasonably priced. Many of us find it hard to relax and play with materials that are expensive. Low-cost materials allow all students to experiment with many ideas and to take their creations home, thereby extending the learning experience. Thanks to our material donors, we have a plentiful supply of useful creative materials available at low cost.

Convenience. Pre-packaged Activity Kits come with complete instructions and require a minimum of teacher preparation time. We provide easy

Figure 9.11 Bottle caps become game pieces, googly eyes and more.

access to teacher-friendly tools such as die cutters, laminators, etc., in our teacher centers. Our bulk materials are well organized and neatly displayed.

Coaching. We challenge teachers to be their best and offer useful coaching to help educators at all stages of their careers. We offer practical workshops, inspiring institutes, and fun drop-in events. Our website includes videos and other resources to help teachers implement hands-on teaching methods. Peer-to-peer coaching is commonplace here.

Caring. A magical element of RAFT is its welcoming environment. We are both serious and playful. When educators enter RAFT, we respect and celebrate them. They leave feeling smart, capable, and inspired.

Fun. Kindergarten teacher Mrs. B kept a big chest of materials labeled "RAFT" in her classroom. The kids got to use the materials for play, building, art, etc., and they looked forward to Monday mornings when they could see what was added to the chest over the weekend. (They decided the letters on the box stood for "Really Awesome Fun Things.") One child told Mrs. B he did not want to go on to first grade unless his new teacher had a RAFT box too.

THE IMPACT OF RAFT

> I am an avid design challenge user, having my students solve problems with odds and ends with an end-project purpose. Upon seeing that I would be his teacher, one student remarked, "Oh, you're the teacher? I guess I'll have to start thinking!"
>
> RAFT member

> Our test scores are improving and I am convinced that the tangible application of knowledge has helped my students.
>
> RAFT member

Now more than ever, the world needs scalable, low-cost educational solutions that inspire lifelong learning. RAFT offers exactly that! As noted earlier, we now work with over 10,000 teachers in four regions and impact nearly one million students. Our members tell us that roughly half the children they work with are low-income or underserved.

Here are the fundamentals of RAFT's theory of action:

1. Academic studies have demonstrated that hands-on teaching increases student learning and knowledge retention. A meta-analysis of 15 years of research on the advantages of hands-on learning, including 57 studies of 13,000 students in 1,000 classrooms, demonstrated that students in

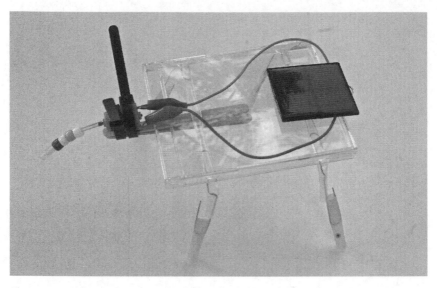

Figure 9.12 Solar energy comes to life in the RAFT solar jitterbug.

activity-based programs performed up to 20% higher than groups using traditional or textbook approaches. The greatest gains occurred in creativity, attitude, perception, and logic (Bredderman, 1982).

2. Research shows that access to a well-trained teacher is the single most important factor in students' educational success. The National Assessment of Educational Progress (NAEP), also known as "The Nation's Report Card," found that teachers who conduct hands-on learning activities on a weekly basis outperform their peers by more than 70% of a grade level in math and 40% of a grade level in science (U.S. Department of Education, 1999).

3. RAFT trains and motivates teachers to deliver effective hands-on learning experiences. Teachers tell us their involvement with RAFT has increased their motivation and confidence: 90% report they are doing more hands-on activities and offering a wider variety of hands-on activities as a result of their interactions with us (RAFT, n.d.).

4. Teachers who use our materials and training have confirmed that their students learn more and retain information longer than with conventional curriculum. Virtually all (99%) report that their students are more engaged in learning and retain knowledge longer as a result of their hands-on experiences (RAFT, n.d.).

For an objective assessment of the impact of hands-on learning in RAFT teachers' classrooms, we hired Rockman et al., a well-respected research and evaluation firm based in San Francisco. Together, we developed and implemented a simple rubric to quantitatively assess student knowledge gains. The observer was asked to keep a running record of what happened during each hands-on activity using the coding categories shown in Table 9.1:

Table 9.1 Impact assessment

Coding Category	Definition	Example
Student Engagement	Students stay on task throughout the hands-on activity, and engage in behaviors that indicate curiosity or interest.	Students ask questions related to the activity.
Content Thinking	Evidence that students are thinking about the content, absorbing it, and applying it.	Students apply a formula the teacher has given them.
Group Dynamics	Pro-social behaviors such as helping, resolving conflicts, and working together.	Two students disagree on an answer. They ask another student for her opinion.
Educator Facilitation	Anything the teacher does to facilitate the hands-on activity.	The teacher brings a show-and-tell sample and explains how activity relates to real life.

We also assessed student engagement in learning. Just prior to the post-test, students were asked to circle all the words describing the activity they had just finished.

Table 9.2 Engagement indicators

Fun	Community	Asking questions
Working alone	Intelligent	Finding answers
Creative	Boring	Solving problems
Rewarding	Learning	Dislike
Like	Working hard	Working with others
Challenging	Play	Easy
Thinking	I'm good at it	Hard

Virtually all (98%) students circled positive statements such as "I'm good at it" and "fun" and almost never chose "boring" or "dislike."

The study was conducted in 17 Bay Area fifth- and sixth-grade classrooms comprising students from diverse socioeconomic, ethnic, and language backgrounds. RAFT materials used in the study focused on important math concepts and were representative of our hands-on Activity Kits in general. The gains shown below demonstrate how effectively RAFT's hands-on teaching materials improve student academic performance (see Figure 9.13).

The rubric and protocol can be downloaded at www.raft.net/student-impact-study.

Here is one example of RAFT's impact at Citizen Schools, a well-known provider of career-focused afterschool enrichment:

During a 10-week "Crime Scene Investigation" unit, a group of Redwood City middle school students completed 16 hands-on RAFT activities, including *Fingerprint Detective, Chromatography, Who's the Daddy?*, and more. Young scientists at another Citizen Schools middle school spent 10 weeks learning about a local marshland, using a wide variety of RAFT activities to discover how marshes filter water, prevent floods, and host wildlife. In one experiment, they used trays and beakers to determine how much water an actual sample of marshland soil could absorb. The instructors for both programs felt that the hands-on activities brought their programs to life for their students and made the 10-week sessions much easier for the teachers to plan, prepare, and present. RAFT and Citizen Schools are planning to repeat the pilot—doubling the scale to include four schools.

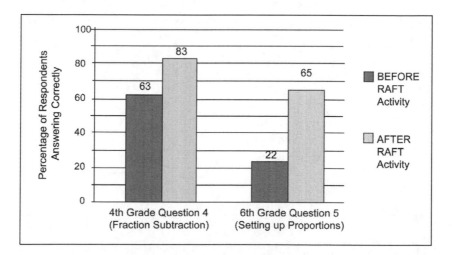

Figure 9.13 Hands-on experience build content knowledge.

VUJA-DE

> Vuja-de—The ability to see something you have seen many times, and see it as if for the first time; the opposite of déjà vu
>
> RAFT dictionary

Our education team is trained to use the attributes of materials to assess their future potential. We do not ask, "What is this?" We ask, "What could it be?"

If RAFT had a mascot, it would be a circle of black rubber about the size of a quarter. We get these circles from a local gasket company: every time it punches a hole in the middle of a gasket, a circle of rubber is created, and this company produces a lot of gaskets. You might be thinking this jettisoned bit of rubber is not much of a mascot. But we use a little vuja-de to look beyond what the circle is to see what it could be. We envision math counters, game pieces, rubber stamps, and more. If a lowly gasket hole can find new life, then every scrap has potential for greatness!

Some experienced makers need little or no help seeing the attributes of a material and coming up with innovative new uses for it (see Figure 9.14). For others, here are three RAFT Idea Sheets/Activity Kits that promote vuja-de thinking:

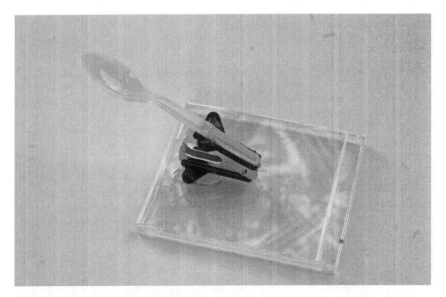

Figure 9.14 A repurposed staple remover powers this RAFT catapult.

Coming Full Circle. The educator challenges groups of students to find connections between seemingly unrelated objects. To begin, each student selects a random item from a pile of stuff, and every group member examines his or her own object as well as those held by others. The leader then explains the challenge: "Form a circle by standing next to people whose objects share an attribute with yours." Identifying a common attribute might be easy—if you have a piece of cloth and the person on your right has a piece of paper, you can say both are flat, both are foldable, both can be cut with scissors, etc. But what if your neighbor to the left has something very different, such as a pencil? What attributes do cloth and pencils share? Maybe both are yellow, maybe the cloth is the same length as the pencil, maybe the two items weigh the same, etc. Fortunately, there are no wrong answers, and a little creativity can always come up with shared attributes, even if far-fetched. *Coming Full Circle* is a bonanza for teachers who want to build their students' skills in critical thinking and creativity.

Thinking like a Real Survivor. Teams of students are challenged to examine an object and brainstorm new applications for it—in other words, they must ignore its conventional function and look at its physical attributes. For example, if given an old CD, the team must forget for the moment that it holds data and focus instead on its other characteristics. It is round, shiny, flat, thin, plastic, springy, etc. Then, using their list of attributes, the students imagine new uses for the object. Their CD could become a wheel for a toy, a signaling mirror, etc.

This Reminds Me of the Fair. Students are encouraged to make quick connections between random objects and their previous life experiences. As in the other activities, the students pick objects from a table. Then, a spinner or large die is used to select one of four themes—anything such as food, game, animal, song, etc. The challenge is to connect the object and the theme, and each student starts by reciting, "This reminds me of [theme]" and ends by giving a little more detail or background. If you pick a button from the pile of objects and the theme is "animal," you might say, "This reminds me of a bear" and explain that your childhood teddy bear had eyes made of buttons.

All these activities stimulate creative repurposing by encouraging observation, inviting people to look beyond the obvious and imagine new potential. Notice how simple and intuitive the activities are. In fact, nothing about the RAFT model is complicated.

Make it Happen!

> I never know what I will find . . . but my creative gears turn when I am at RAFT.
>
> RAFT member

Figure 9.15 Creative ideas take shape at RAFT.

Creating a Maker Palace like RAFT is a "win-win-win" for the community, for teachers, and for students—and it is "green."

When the going gets tough, it helps to reflect on why this is such a worthwhile investment of time and money. Recall Anthony and Sarah, the two students mentioned at the beginning of this chapter. Their lives were changed for the better in one day, with a little pocket change. RAFT provided their teachers with the simple stepping stones these children needed to get on the path to innovation.

It is also motivating to know that RAFT's approach to hands-on teaching has been proven effective. The findings of our teacher surveys and the Rockman evaluation show that we are on the right track. There is nothing iffy about this model. Extending it into the unlimited realm of the maker universe is a logical progression. We are confident that the same methods and materials will work with all maker audiences.

SHARE YOUR IDEAS WITH RAFT

> I am beginning to think like an innovator.
>
> Workshop participant

Share your ideas with us at info@raft.net. Visit a location near you to see RAFT in action. If you are interested in starting a Maker Palace in your community, please contact RAFT!

Figure 9.16 Make it happen!

REFERENCES

Bredderman, T. (1982). What research says: Activity science—the evidence shows it matters. *Science and Children, 20*(1), 39–41. Retrieved from ERIC Document Reproduction Service (ED 216 870).

RAFT (n.d.). *Case for hands-on learning.* Retrieved from:www.raft.net/case-for-hands-on-learning. Accessed December 7, 2012.

U.S. Department of Education (1999). *The NAEP 1996 Technical Report* (NCES 1999-452), by N. L. Allen, J. E. Carlson, & C. A. Zelenak. Washington, DC: U.S. Department of Education, Office of Educational Research and Improvement, National Center for Education Statistics. Retrieved from: http://nces.ed.gov/pubsearch/pubsinfo.asp?pubid=1999452. Accessed December 7, 2012.

CHAPTER 10

DESIGNING FOR TINKERABILITY

MITCHEL RESNICK AND ERIC ROSENBAUM

INTRODUCTION

Make magazine. Maker Faires. Makerspaces. Maker clubs. In the past few years, there has been a surge of interest in *making*. A growing number of people are becoming engaged in building, creating, personalizing, and customizing things in the world around them—making their own jewelry, their own furniture, their own robots. The emerging Maker Movement is catalyzed by both technological and cultural trends. New technologies are making it easier and cheaper for people to create and share things, in both the physical world and the digital world. At the same time, the Maker Movement builds upon a broader cultural shift toward a do-it-yourself approach to life, where people take pride and pleasure in creating things personally rather than only consuming mass-produced goods.

Although most people involved in the Maker Movement are not focused explicitly on education or learning, the ideas and practices of the Maker Movement resonate with a long tradition in the field of education—from John Dewey's progressivism (Dewey, 1938) to Seymour Papert's constructionism (Papert, 1980, 1993)—that encourages a project-based, experiential approach to learning. This approach is somewhat out of favor in many of today's education systems, with their strong emphasis on content delivery and quantitative assessment. But the enthusiasm surrounding the Maker Movement provides a new opportunity for reinvigorating and revalidating the progressive-constructionist tradition in education.

To do so, however, requires more than just "making." Too often, we have seen schools introduce making into the curriculum in a way that saps all the spirit from the activity: "Here are the instructions for making your robotic car. Follow the instructions carefully. You will be evaluated on how well your car performs." Or: "Design a bridge that can support 100 pounds. Based on your design, calculate the strains on the bridge. Once you are sure that your design can support 100 pounds, build the bridge and confirm that it can support the weight."

In these activities, students are making something, but the learning experience is limited. Just making things is not enough. There are many different approaches to making things, and some lead to richer learning experiences than others. In this chapter, we focus on a particular approach to making that we describe as *tinkering*. The tinkering approach is characterized by a playful, experimental, iterative style of engagement, in which makers are continually reassessing their goals, exploring new paths, and imagining new possibilities. Tinkering is undervalued (and even discouraged) in many educational settings today, but it is well aligned with the goals and spirit of the progressive-constructionist tradition—and, in our view, it is exactly what is needed to help young people prepare for life in today's society.

Our primary goal in this chapter is to examine strategies for encouraging and supporting a tinkering approach to making and learning. We view this as a design challenge: How can we design technologies and activities for *tinkerability*? We start, in the next two sections, by giving a fuller description of what we mean by tinkering and why we think it is so valuable as part of the learning process. Then we examine specific technologies and activities we have designed in our research group at the MIT Media Lab, discussing our strategies for encouraging and supporting tinkering.

WHAT IS TINKERING?

The term *tinkering* means different things to different people. It is not uncommon to hear the term used dismissively—*just tinkering*—in reference to someone working without a clear goal or purpose, or without making noticeable progress. But in our view, *just* and *tinkering* do not belong together. We see tinkering as a valid and valuable style of working, characterized by a playful, exploratory, iterative style of engaging with a problem or project. When people are tinkering, they are constantly trying out ideas, making adjustments and refinements, then experimenting with new possibilities, over and over and over.

Many people think of *tinkering* in opposition to *planning*—and they often view planning as an inherently superior approach. Planning seems more organized, more direct, more efficient. Planners survey a situation, identify problems and needs, develop a clear plan, then execute it. Do it once and do it right. What could be better than that?

The tinkering process is messier. Tinkerers are always exploring, experimenting, trying new things. Whereas planners typically rely on formal rules and abstract calculations (e.g., calculating the optimal position for a supporting beam in a structure), tinkerers tend to react to the specific details of the particular situation (experimentally trying different locations for the supporting beam—or exploring other ways to support the structure). In the words of design theorist Don Schoen, tinkerers have "a conversation with the material" (Schoen, 1983).

Sometimes, tinkerers start without a goal. Instead of the *top-down* approach of traditional planning, tinkerers use a *bottom-up* approach. They begin by messing around with materials (e.g., snapping LEGO bricks together in different patterns), and a goal emerges from their playful explorations (e.g., deciding to build a fantasy castle). Other times, tinkerers have a general goal, but they are not quite sure how to get there. They might start with a tentative plan, but they continually adapt and renegotiate their plans based on their interactions with the materials and people they are working with. For example, a child might start with the goal of building a security system for her bedroom, and then experiment with many different materials, strategies, and designs before coming up with a final version.

There is a long tradition of tinkering in many cultures around the world. In almost all countries, local craft traditions have evolved over centuries, characterized by experimenting and tinkering with indigenous materials. In many places, people develop a do-it-yourself mindset, sometimes out of economic necessity, making use of whatever tools and materials happen to be available to them at a given time. This style of interaction is sometimes described as *bricolage*. Anthropologist Claude Lévi-Strauss (1966) describes how people in many parts of the world, acting as bricoleurs, continually improvise with currently available materials to build or repair objects in their everyday lives. Lévi-Strauss contrasts the bricoleur with the engineer, who systematically develops a plan, then gathers the materials needed to execute it.

Tinkering and bricolage are closely aligned with play. Many people see play as a form of entertainment or fun, but we see it somewhat differently. To us, play is a style of engaging with the world, a process of testing the boundaries and experimenting with new possibilities. We see tinkering as a playful style of designing and making, where you constantly experiment, explore, and try out new ideas in the process of creating something. Tinkering can be hard work, and sometimes it might not seem like play. But there is always a playful spirit underlying the tinkering process.

People often associate tinkering with physical construction—building a castle with LEGO bricks, making a tree house with wood and nails, creating a circuit with electronic components. The Maker Movement has reinforced this image, since it focuses on making things in the physical world. But we take a broader view of tinkering. We see tinkering as a style of making things, regardless of whether the things are physical or virtual. You can tinker when you are programming an animation or writing a story, not just when you are making something physical. The key issue is the style of interaction, not the media or materials being used.

WHY IS TINKERING IMPORTANT?

Tinkering is not a new idea. From the time the earliest humans began making and using tools, tinkering has been a valuable strategy for making things. But tinkering is more important today than ever before. We live in a world that is characterized by uncertainty and rapid change. Many of the things you learn today will soon be obsolete. Success in the future will depend not on what you know, or how much you know, but on your ability to think and act creatively—on your ability to come up with innovative solutions to unexpected situations and unanticipated problems.

In such a fast-changing environment, tinkering is a particularly valuable strategy. Tinkerers understand how to improvise, adapt, and iterate, so they are never stuck on old plans as new situations arise. Tinkering prioritizes creativity and agility over efficiency and optimization, a worthwhile tradeoff for a constantly changing world.

Despite its benefits, tinkering is often undervalued in today's society, particularly in formal education systems. Schools tend to emphasize the value of planning, teaching students to analyze all options, develop a strategy, then carry out the plans. That's why students who are natural planners tend to do well in school. But what about students who are natural tinkerers? They often feel left out or alienated, especially in science, technology, engineering, and math (STEM) classes, which particularly emphasize top-down planning. Thus, many students are turned off to math and science, leading to a less scientifically literate populace and a restricted pipeline to STEM professions.

It does not have to be this way. STEM disciplines are not inherently planning-oriented. In fact, expert practitioners in STEM disciplines typically employ much more tinkering in their work than is common in STEM classroom activities (Brown, Collins, & Duguid, 1989). Many of the greatest scientists and engineers throughout history—from Leonardo da Vinci to Alexander Graham Bell to Barbara McClintock to Richard Feynman—saw themselves as tinkerers. In order to broaden participation and foster innovation in STEM disciplines, we must rethink and revise STEM curricula to become welcoming and appealing to tinkerers, not just planners.

Turkle and Papert (1990) argue for "epistemological pluralism"—that is, respecting and valuing multiple styles of learning and multiple ways of knowing. They suggest that logic and planning should be "on tap" (available as needed for particular situations), not "on top" (assumed to be superior). Because the status of logic and planning is privileged, Turkle and Papert worry that many people will be excluded from STEM disciplines not by explicit rules, "but by ways of thinking that make them reluctant to join in." They argue that tinkering and bricolage should be given equal status with logic and planning: "Bricolage is a way to organize work. It is not a stage in a progression to a superior form" (p. 141).

Many educators are skeptical about tinkering. There are several common critiques. Some educators worry that tinkerers might succeed at creating things without fully understanding what they are doing. That might be true in some cases, but even in those cases, tinkering provides an opportunity for learners to develop fragments of knowledge that they can later integrate into a more complete understanding (Hancock, 2003). Others worry that tinkering is too unstructured to lead to success. That critique confuses tinkering with random exploration. The bottom-up process of tinkering starts with explorations that might seem rather random, but it does not end there. True tinkerers know how to turn their initial explorations (*bottom*) into a focused activity (*up*). It is the combination of *bottom* and *up* that makes tinkering a valuable process.

Of course, top-down planning can be valuable too. But in many settings, planning is viewed as the correct approach for solving problems, not just one of several alternatives. Our goal is to end the privileged status of planning, and give equal emphasis to tinkering.

COMPUTATION + TINKERABILITY

Many materials—such as wooden blocks and modeling clay—support and encourage tinkering, enabling people to create houses, castles, bridges, sculptures, and other structures. But what if you want to create things that move, sense, react, interact, and communicate? That typically requires computational tools and materials. Computational materials might not seem very amenable to tinkering, since computation is often associated with logic and precision. And, indeed, computational activities (particularly programming) have often been introduced in ways that appeal more to planners than tinkerers (e.g., learning how to efficiently sort a list of numbers).

In our Lifelong Kindergarten research group at the MIT Media Lab, we are trying to change the ways that young people use and think about computation. We have developed a collection of computational construction kits and activities that explicitly encourage designing and tinkering with computation. In collaboration with the LEGO Group, for example, we developed the LEGO Mindstorms and WeDo robotics kits, which enable young people to build robotics devices that move, sense, interact, and communicate. In the process, young people learn important mathematical, engineering, and computational ideas. Even more important, they learn to think creatively and work collaboratively, essential skills for active participation in today's society.

In this section, we describe two of our group's computational construction kits, Scratch and MaKey MaKey, that are designed explicitly to engage young people in tinkering. In the next section, we use these two kits as the basis for our analysis of how to design for tinkerability.

Scratch

With Scratch (http://scratch.mit.edu), you can program your own interactive stories, games, animations, and simulations—then share your creations online. To create a program in Scratch, you snap graphical programming blocks together into a *script*, much like snapping LEGO bricks together (Figure 10.1). For each character (or *sprite*) in your Scratch project, you need to assemble a set of scripts to control its behavior (Figure 10.2). For a fish sprite, for example, one script might control the motion of the fish across the screen, while another script tells the fish to change directions if it bumps into coral. From a collection of simple programming blocks, combined with images and sounds, you can create a wide variety of different types of projects. Since the launch of Scratch in 2007, young people around the world have shared more than 3 million projects on the Scratch website (Figure 10.3), including interactive newsletters, science simulations, virtual tours, public service announcements, video games, and animated dance contests (Brennan & Resnick, 2012; Maloney, Resnick, Rusk, Silverman, & Eastmond, 2010; Resnick et al., 2009).

As young people create Scratch projects, they typically engage in an extended tinkering process—creating programming scripts and costumes for each sprite, testing them out to see if they behave as expected, then

Figure 10.1 Scratch programming blocks.

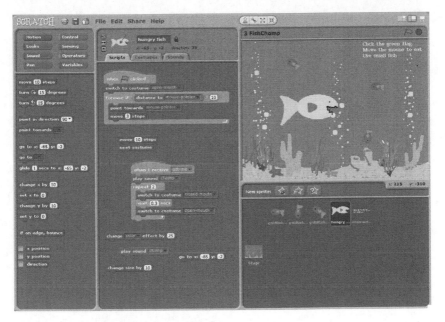

Figure 10.2 Scratch programming interface.

revising and adapting them, over and over again. To get a sense of this process, consider the work of a Scratch community member who goes by the username EmeraldDragon. During her first seven months in the community, EmeraldDragon shared 25 projects on the Scratch website. In one of her first projects, EmeraldDragon created a game in which a user can control the movements of an animated dragon. She created 12 images of a dragon, each with the dragon's legs in slightly different positions, then created a programming script that cycled through the images to create the appearance of motion, much like a flipbook.

EmeraldDragon experimented with different versions of the script to make the dragon move in different directions when the user pressed different keys. When EmeraldDragon shared the project on the Scratch website, she included the comment: "I was just tinkering with the scripts in the game and I finally figured out how to make it so you can run back and forth! I'll fix up the game and put out the new and improved still not yet a game version!"

EmeraldDragon named her project *My Dragon Game (NOT finished)*, to make clear that the project was still a work-in-progress (Figure 10.4). In her Project Notes, she wrote: "I am working on being able to run back and forth without the rock disappearing. Any tips or help?" In the project's Comments section, other members of the Scratch community offered

Figure 10.3 Scratch website and online community.

suggestions. EmeraldDragon soon shared a new version of her project, this time with the name *My Dragon Game (Still NOT finished)*.

EmeraldDragon clearly understood that tinkering is an ongoing process of revision and adaptation. As she wrote in her Project Notes: "This is just a stage in a long process."

MaKey MaKey

With MaKey MaKey (http://makeymakey.com), you can create interfaces to the computer out of any object that conducts electricity (e.g., make a piano keyboard out of pieces of fruit, or use Play-Doh to create a controller for a PacMan game) (Silver & Rosenbaum, 2012). To make a new interface, you connect objects with alligator clips to the MaKey MaKey circuit board (Figure 10.5), which plugs into a computer's USB port. MaKey MaKey pretends it is a computer keyboard, so you can make your own keys. You

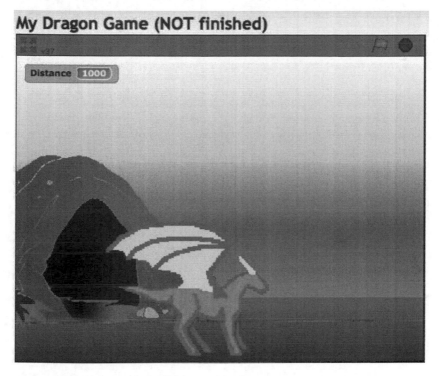

Figure 10.4 EmeraldDragon's game.

Figure 10.5 MaKey MaKey circuit board, with a USB cable and alligator clips.

can replace your space bar, or any other key, with a banana, or with any other object that conducts even a little bit of electricity. MaKey MaKey detects when you touch an object to complete a circuit and sends a signal to the computer that a key has been pressed (Figure 10.6).

Here is a scenario, based on several projects we observed at workshops, that illustrates the workings of MaKey MaKey in more detail. Anna, a 12-year-old girl, is fascinated by a banana piano she saw in a MaKey MaKey video (Figure 10.7), and she decides she wants to make one herself. First, she finds a web page that lets her play a scale on the piano by typing the letters on the home row of her computer keyboard: a, s, d, f, etc. Next, she plugs her MaKey MaKey circuit board into her computer so she can make

Figure 10.6 A MaKey MaKey circuit.

Figure 10.7 Banana piano.

her own keys that trigger piano notes. She lays out a row of bananas and uses alligator clips to connect each one to a different letter on the MaKey MaKey. Then she connects herself to the MaKey MaKey by connecting a lime to "earth" (also known as "ground") on the MaKey MaKey, and holds the lime in her hand. Now, when she touches one of the bananas, a circuit is completed: a tiny amount of current flows from the "a" key input on the MaKey MaKey, through a banana, through her, through the lime, and back to "earth" on the MaKey MaKey. The MaKey MaKey detects the connection, and tells the computer that the "a" key has been pressed, causing the piano web page to play a musical note.

As she plugs in more bananas, Anna makes some accidental discoveries. At first, the bananas are in the wrong order, so instead of forming a scale they play a fragment of a familiar melody. This leads to some playful rearranging of bananas as a musical experiment. During this process, Anna notices that two of the bananas are touching, so that when she touches either of them they both trigger notes, playing a chord. Later, Anna's friend Leo drops by, and together they try making a circuit through both of their bodies. If Anna holds the lime and Leo touches a banana, they can trigger a note by giving each other a high-five—or when Anna taps Leo on the nose. This leads to the idea of making a human drum kit: they find a web page that plays different drum sounds when you press keys, then gather some other friends to connect into the circuit, so each can trigger a different sound.

Later Anna and Leo experiment with different materials. They search around the house and find several items that work well, including Jell-O, pennies, Play-Doh, and the graphite in a pencil drawing on paper. Forming

Figure 10.8 Play-Doh game controller.

Play-Doh into different shapes leads to the idea of making a game controller, with Play-Doh buttons. By connecting the buttons to the arrow keys on the MaKey MaKey, they can play a Mario Bros. game (Figure 10.8).

Through these tinkering processes with MaKey MaKey, Anna and Leo are able to quickly try out new ideas, pursue serendipitous discoveries, experiment with a range of different physical materials, and create their own inventions in different genres.

Designing Kits for Tinkerability

How do you design for tinkerability? Reflecting on the construction kits our research group has developed over the years, we identified three core principles guiding our designs: immediate feedback, fluid experimentation, and open exploration.

Immediate Feedback

The tinkering process typically involves a series of quick experiments—and to do quick experiments, you need quick results. In highly tinkerable construction kits, there is a very short interval of time between making a change and seeing its effect. Many physical processes have this property, of course: when you fold a sheet of paper, you do not have to wait to see the crease. But some physical processes—such as baking, metal casting, or gluing—do require a wait, so tinkering with them is more challenging. Some computational construction kits are stuck in a paradigm from the past, when computation was slow and you had to wait to see the results of your program. We design our kits for immediate feedback, so you can quickly see the results of your actions—and also see a representation of the process as it plays out.

See the Result

In Scratch, you can simply click on a programming block and watch what happens. There are no separate steps for compiling, no separate modes for editing. For most blocks, results are immediate, such as a movement, color change, or sound effect. You learn what the blocks do simply by trying them out. You can even click on a block while it is still in the palette, without even dragging it to the scripting area (where you connect blocks together into scripts).

Ideally, tinkering should be a continuous, ongoing process. In Scratch, you can continue to tinker with Scratch scripts even as they are running. For example, you might start by clicking on a Scratch script to make a sprite move across the screen, then click on other scripts to make them run in parallel (e.g., adding a soundtrack or animating the sprite) while the first script is still running. You can also modify a script while it is running (e.g., changing the number in a *move* block to increase the speed of a sprite) or even insert a new block into the script. This "liveness" allows you to try out many possibilities and see the results immediately, in the context of a running program. The goal is to make people feel they can interact with programming blocks the same way they interact with physical objects.

MaKey MaKey is also designed for immediate feedback. Let's say you make a keypad out of Play-Doh to control a video game character. As soon as you touch the Play-Doh (to complete the circuit), the character on the screen moves. You can also test out the MaKey MaKey circuit board before creating any interface. The board itself has conductive pads that allow you to complete a circuit with your fingers. Touch the "earth" pad (also known as "ground") with one finger and the "space" pad with another finger, and MaKey MaKey will make the computer think that the keyboard spacebar has been pressed.

See the Process

In most programming environments, it is not possible to directly observe the internal properties of the program while it is running. These properties include what the program is doing right now (the current location in its execution) and what the program "knows" (the values of its variables and other data structures). Just as it is sometimes easier to understand what is wrong with a car by looking under the hood (or, at least, by watching the indicator lights on the dashboard), it is easier to fix bugs in a computer program when you can see its internal properties while it is running.

MaKey Makey has some simple indicators of its internal process: LED lights on the board indicate when a circuit has been completed, so you can debug the board and circuit independent of what is happening on the computer screen.

Scratch has a range of features that allow you to monitor programs as they run. Scratch scripts always highlight while they are running, so you can see which code is being triggered when. If you select *single-stepping* mode, each individual block within a script highlights as it runs, allowing for more fine-grained analysis and debugging.

The Scratch interface also has optional monitors that allow you to see the current values of data stored in variables and lists. In most other programming languages, data structures are hidden from view, but Scratch data structures are visible and manipulable, enhancing tinkerability. As a Scratch program runs, you can watch the variables and lists update in real time. You can also type directly into list monitors, modifying the values of items in a list, even while a program is running. The goal is to allow Scratchers to tinker with data—and to gain a better understanding of how the data relate to the rest of the program.

Fluid Experimentation

The tinkering process is inherently iterative. Tinkerers start by exploring and experimenting, then revising and refining their goals, plans, and creations. Then they are ready to start a new cycle of exploring and experimenting, then revising and refining, over and over. The quicker the iteration, the faster the generation and refinement of ideas. To support this style of interaction, we design our constructions kits so that it is easy for people to get started with experimenting—and then easy to continue experimenting by connecting (and disconnecting and reconnecting) objects within the project.

Easy to Get Started

One of the biggest challenges in tinkering with technological tools is the time it takes to get started. When you have an idea you want to express, or some materials you want to experiment with, you want to dive in right away without spending a lot of time setting up. Electronics projects often require basic infrastructure to be set up, such as wiring on a breadboard, before you can start interacting with new parts. Similarly, in programming, some setup code is often required before you can begin expressing new ideas. In order to support fluid experimentation, we design our kits to minimize these setup processes as much as possible.

When you launch Scratch, you can start trying things right away. There is a default character (the Scratch cat), which already has some media to play with: two images that form a walking animation, and a "meow" sound. You can start programming behaviors for the cat immediately: click the *move* block and the cat moves; click the *next costume* block and the cat animates; click the *play sound* block and the cat meows. The blocks start with reasonable default values for their inputs, so you can start playing with the blocks right away, without filling in any inputs.

MaKey MaKey requires no configuration on the computer because it is a plug-and-play USB device that appears to the computer to be a standard mouse and keyboard. The system works with any software or website that responds to keyboard and mouse commands; no special software is needed. The MaKey MaKey circuit board has a fixed arrangement of inputs mapped to keyboard and mouse events, so it also needs no configuration before you begin. You can plug the board into the computer and start making circuits (and keystrokes) right away. Without any setup, you can start experimenting with different physical materials and make your own physical interface.

Easy to Connect

The tinkerability of a construction kit is determined, to a large degree, by how parts of the construction kit connect with one another. In designing connectors for our construction kits, we take inspiration from LEGO bricks: they are easy to snap together and also easy to take apart, and they have just the right amount of "clutch power" to make structures sturdy. This carefully chosen compromise is what makes LEGO kits so tinkerable. Plain wooden blocks are easier to stack up but also easier to knock down. At the other extreme, Erector sets are good for making stronger structures, but the structures are more difficult to put together and take apart. LEGO bricks are in between, enabling quick, iterative experimentation.

In the MaKey MaKey kit, alligator clips are used to attach homemade switches to holes in the circuit board. The clips are quick and easy to use, so you can rapidly test different connections and swap them around, but they provide enough mechanical strength to hold together under the strain of gameplay or musical performance. This makes them more tinkerable than other typical electronics connectors such as female headers (small holes that wires can be fed into but easily slip out of) or screw terminals (which hold wires firmly but require a screwdriver to open and close).

In Scratch, the shapes of the programming blocks constrain how the blocks are put together. When you pull blocks from the palette, it is immediately obvious, from the shapes of the blocks, which blocks can be connected with one another. Unlike traditional text-based programming languages, there is no obscure syntax (semicolons, square brackets, etc.) to learn. Instead, the grammar is visual, indicated by the shapes of the blocks and connectors. Blocks snap together only if the combination makes sense. Of course, the blocks might not behave as you intended, but there can be no syntax errors. If blocks snap together, they are sure to run.

Blocks that take inputs have "sockets" of different shapes, indicating what type of block should go inside. For example, the *move* block has an oval socket, indicating that it expects a number as its input. You can insert any oval shaped block—such as the block that reports the y-position of the mouse cursor. The conditional *if* and *if-else* and *wait-until* blocks have a hexagon-shaped input, indicating that they expect a Boolean (true-false) value as input. For example, you can insert a hexagonal *touching?* block that reports (true or false) whether the sprite is touching another sprite (see Figure 10.1). Some blocks are more tolerant. The *say* block, for example, has a square socket indicating that it can take any type of input (a number, a string, or a Boolean).

The shapes and connectors make it easy to tinker and experiment with the Scratch programming blocks, just as with LEGO bricks. You can snap blocks together, try them out, then disconnect them and try other combinations. The cost of experimentation is low. Also, you can leave some blocks (or stacks of blocks) lying around your workspace (see Figure 10.2), in case you might want to use them later, just as you would with LEGO bricks—unlike most programming environments, where you need to keep your workspace tidy and organized.

Open Exploration

Supporting immediate feedback and fluid experimentation is not enough. It is also important to enable and inspire people to explore a diverse array of possibilities. To do that, construction kits must support a wide variety of materials and a wide variety of genres.

Variety of Materials

Scratch comes bundled with a large library of media intended to spark new project ideas; these media include images and backgrounds, sound effects and music loops, and sprites with programming scripts and media already embedded in them. Scratch also provides several ways to create and import your own media. You can create images with the built-in paint editor, take photos with your computer's camera, or record sounds with the built-in recorder. You can also import images and sounds from your hard disk or the web, simply by dragging and dropping them into Scratch.

Even more important, Scratch provides access to an ever-growing and evolving library of projects created by other members of the Scratch community. You can grab images, sounds, and scripts from other projects and integrate them into your own. Everything shared on the Scratch website is covered by the Creative Commons share-alike license, so community members are free to borrow from one another, as long as they give credit. Roughly one third of the 3 million projects on the Scratch websites are remixes, in which one community member built upon the work of another. The website serves as a continuing source of inspiration, with thousands of new projects shared every day.

Unlike Scratch, MaKey MaKey comes with no materials at all (aside from the circuit board and connectors). Instead, the kit is designed to encourage you to see the world as your construction kit. You can make MaKey MaKey circuits and switches out of anything that conducts electricity—food, plants, pencil drawings, aluminum foil, water, Play-Doh, even your own body. For making structures to support the circuit, you can use any object or material (insulating or conducting), anything from cardboard to beach balls to buckets to hats.

Variety of Genres

When starting out, tinkerers often have no clear idea of what they want to make. So construction kits that support many different genres of projects are useful, providing they offer the flexibility to shift genres as users iteratively adapt and revise their creations over time.

Unlike many software construction kits (such as Gamemaker and Gamestar Mechanic—which, as their names suggest, focus explicitly on games), Scratch enables you to create a wide range of different types of projects, including interactive stories, games, animations, simulations, art, and music. Different parts of the Scratch construction kit are well tuned for different genres. The paint editor and image-effect blocks support animation; *say* and *think* blocks (for making speech balloons) support stories; collision-detection and keyboard-interaction blocks support games; pen blocks (to make sprites draw as they move) support interactive art; mathematical-operation blocks support simulations; and note, instrument, and tempo blocks support music. Because these tools are all in the same kit, a single Scratch project can blend together multiple genres. A tinkerer can start working on one type of project and later decide to morph it into a different genre (or combination of genres) as it develops (e.g., transforming an animation into a game or a simulation into interactive art).

MaKey MaKey also supports creations in a variety of genres, because it can be used to create a controller for any piece of software that can be controlled with a keyboard. For example, you can create a MaKey Makey interface device to control a video game, a sound synthesizer, a video player, a text editor, a web browser, a paint program, or even a Scratch project.

TINKERING WITH TINKERABILITY

In this chapter, we have outlined some of our current thinking on how to design construction kits for tinkerability. But designing construction kits is only part of what's needed. Even the most tinkerable construction kit will not be successful unless it is accompanied by the right types of activities, support materials, facilitation, space, and community. In short, designing *contexts for tinkerability* is as important as designing kits for tinkerability.

It is beyond the scope of this paper to examine these issues in depth. But, in closing, we share a short summary of some key lessons we have learned in designing contexts for tinkerability. These ideas can be useful for educators who want to support young people in the process of designing and tinkering.

- *Emphasize process over product.* While making something is an important part of the tinkering process, too much emphasis on the final product can undermine the experimentation that is at the heart of tinkering. To engage people in thinking about the tinkering process, encourage them to document and discuss intermediate stages, failed experiments, and sources of inspiration.

- *Set themes, not challenges.* Rather than posing challenges to solve (as is typical in many design workshops), propose themes to explore. Select workshop themes that are broad enough to give everyone freedom to work on projects that they care about, but specific enough to foster a sense of shared experience among participants (Rusk, Resnick, Berg, & Pezalla-Granlund, 2008). For example, we might ask workshop participants to design an interactive card for a holiday celebration.
- *Highlight diverse examples.* Show sample projects that illustrate the wide diversity of what is possible, provoking people to think divergently. Keep examples and documentation on display for continuing inspiration.
- *Tinker with space.* Consider how you might rearrange or relocate, to open new possibilities for exploration and collaboration. For example, how can the arrangement of tables and screens help people see each other's work? How can the arrangement of materials encourage clever and unexpected combinations?
- *Encourage engagement with people, not just materials.* In addition to having a "conversation with the material," tinkerers also benefit from having conversations (and collaborations) with other people.
- *Pose questions instead of giving answers.* Resist the urge to explain too much or fix problems. Instead, support tinkerers in their explorations by asking questions, pointing out interesting phenomena, and wondering aloud about alternative possibilities.
- *Combine diving in with stepping back.* While it is valuable for tinkerers to immerse themselves in the process of making, it is also important for them to step back and reflect upon the process.

Our goal is to provide everyone—of all ages, backgrounds, and interests—with new opportunities to learn through tinkering. To do this well, we ourselves need to remain engaged as tinkerers (and meta-tinkerers), playfully experimenting with new ways to design for tinkerability. We see this chapter as just a start. We plan to continue to tinker with and iterate ideas and technologies, continuing to refine our thinking about the nature of tinkering and strategies for enhancing it.

ACKNOWLEDGMENTS

Many members of the Lifelong Kindergarten research group at the MIT Media Lab contributed to the ideas and projects discussed in this paper. We are grateful to Seymour Papert and Sherry Turkle, who have deeply influenced the ways we think about tinkering and learning.

REFERENCES

Brennan, K., & Resnick, M. (2012). Imagining, creating, playing, sharing, reflecting: How online community supports young people as designers of interactive media. In N. Lavigne, & C. Mouza (Eds.), *Emerging technologies for the classroom: A learning sciences perspective.* New York: Springer, pp. 253–268.

Brown, J. S., Collins, A., & Duguid, P. (1989). Situated cognition and the culture of learning. *Educational Researcher, 18*(1), 32–42.

Dewey, J. (1938). *Experience and education.* New York: Simon & Schuster.

Hancock, C. (2003). *Real-time programming and the big ideas of computational literacy.* Doctoral dissertation. MIT Media Lab, Cambridge, MA.

Lévi-Strauss, C. (1966). *The savage mind.* Chicago, IL: University of Chicago Press.

Maloney, J., Resnick, M., Rusk, N., Silverman, B., & Eastmond, E. (2010). The Scratch programming language and environment. *ACM Transactions on Computing Education (TOCE), 10*(4), 1–15.

Papert, S. (1980). *Mindstorms: Children, computers, and powerful ideas.* New York: Basic Books.

Papert, S. (1993). *The children's machine: Rethinking school in the age of the computer.* New York: Basic Books.

Resnick, M., Maloney, J., Monroy-Hernandez, A., Rusk, N., Eastmond, E., Brennan, K., et al. (2009). Scratch: Programming for all. *Communications of the ACM, 52*(11), 60–67.

Rusk, N., Resnick, M., Berg, R., & Pezalla-Granlund, M. (2008). New pathways into robotics: Strategies for broadening participation. *Journal of Science Education and Technology, 17*(1), 59–69.

Silver, J., & Rosenbaum, E. (2012, February 19–22). Makey Makey: Improvising tangible and nature-based user interfaces. Paper presented at the Sixth International Conference on Tangible, Embedded and Embodied Interaction, Queen's Human Media Lab, Kingston, Ontario. *Proceedings of the International Conference on Tangible, Embedded and Embodied Interaction.* New York: ACM.

Schoen, D. (1983). *The reflective practitioner: How professionals think in action.* London, UK: Maurice Temple Smith.

Turkle, S., & Papert, S. (1990). Epistemological pluralism. *Signs, 16*(1), 128–157.

CHAPTER 11

SciGames
Guided Play Games That Enhance Both Student Engagement and Science Learning in Tandem

DAVID E. KANTER, SAMEER HONWAD, RUTH DIONES, AND ADIEL FERNANDEZ

Introduction to Guided Play Games

Several characteristics of children's play are sought-after ideals in learning environments. Players are self-motivated to attend, persist, and discover. They evidence curiosity and creativity and express joy. While play has the potential to support many qualities that one would hope to find in any learning environment, researchers have found that differences in how play is structured influence the extent to which curricular content learning can be supported during such play.

Broadly speaking, play can be classified into two categories: free play and guided play (Fisher, Hirsh-Pasek, Golinkoff, Singer, & Berk, 2011), both child-centered, meaning that the children decide autonomously how to conduct their play. A free play environment, while somewhat difficult to define, is "fun, voluntary, flexible, involve[s] active engagement, has no extrinsic goals, involves active engagement of the child, and often contain[s] an element of make-believe" (Pellegrini, 2009). In guided play, adults set up the environment, enriching it with play objects specifically intended to provide experiences related to curricular content learning opportunities. Adults might further guide play by collaboratively exploring the materials with children, using the materials in ways that might not occur to children, remarking on what children discover, and asking the children open-ended questions (Fein & Rivkin, 1986; Fisher et al., 2011; Resnick, 1998). Studies have begun to show that children are more likely to learn curricular content in a guided play environment than in a free play environment and also that play appropriately guided can be a powerful learning tool (Fisher et al., 2011; Miller & Almon, 2009; Resnick, 2007; Youell, 2008).

A third possible guide to play beyond the nature of the play materials themselves and the role of an adult co-player might further support learning, namely, the rules of a game. Piaget (1962) suggests that rules-based games naturally become part of children's play around the age of 7 to 11 years. This idea that a game and its rules can support content learning during play finds further support in the literature on games. Gee (2003) points out that good games have the potential of helping learners understand the embedded content within the game. Habgood and Ainsworth (2011) describe this as intrinsic integration. With careful design, the target content could be worked into the rules of a game such that the game player can progress in the game only by learning the content. In the case of this study, we were particularly interested in students learning science content. Games have been previously shown to support students learning science content (Barnett, Squire, Higginbotham, & Grant, 2004; Jenkins, Squire, & Tan, 2004).

To the extent to which repeated cycles of gameplay could mirror the scientific inquiry process as students play and replay in an effort to win, a game with rules could even further support science content learning. The rules of the game could be designed to support students asking questions, developing and carrying out investigations, gathering evidence, and proposing explanations based on evidence, i.e., engaging in inquiry (Sandoval & Reiser, 2004; Singer, Marx, Krajcik, & Chambers, 2000) as they strive to win the game. Such inquiry-based practices have been shown to help students improve their understanding of scientific concepts (Kanter, 2010; Krajcik, McNeill, & Reiser, 2008; Marx et al., 2004; Rivet & Krajcik, 2004; Schneider, 2002). Thus, designing the rules of the game to support engaging in science inquiry-based practices should further support the science content learning toward which the play is guided.

We are also particularly interested in guided play games (GPGs) due to the potential they would seem to have to positively impact the affective dimensions of students' learning, namely engagement, a set of interrelated factors having to do with an individual's behavior, emotion, and cognition in a learning setting. Behavioral engagement can include effort, persistence, attention, and asking questions. Emotional engagement has to do with affective reactions to learning, including interest, boredom, happiness, sadness, and anxiety. Cognitive engagement has been defined as the "student's psychological investment in and effort directed toward learning, understanding, mastering the knowledge, skills or crafts that the academic work is intended to promote" (Fredricks, Blumenfeld, & Paris, 2004). Studies have shown that improving each of these three dimensions of engagement can reduce students' tendency to drop out of school (Fredricks et al., 2004; National Research Council, 2003). Newmann, Wehlage, and Lamborn (1992) suggest that engagement can be enhanced by making tasks more authentic, providing more opportunities for students to "own" the tasks and collaborate, and providing more opportunities for fun. This sounds like exactly the kind of playful experience a GPG is designed to provide, and perhaps to a greater degree than traditional classroom instruction can offer.

We were interested to see if playing a GPG could boost student engagement while at the same time improving student learning, reasonably expecting that these two outcomes would strongly mutually reinforce one another. This was our first hypothesis. We also aimed to test a second hypothesis: that GPGs would have an improved impact on engagement and content learning over that found when students engaged in comparable free play.

Designing Guided Play Games

To test our hypotheses, we designed two different GPGs for students to play on the playground. Both GPGs were aimed at helping students understand middle-grades standards-based physical science content. (We chose to work with middle-grades students since that is the age group where the bulk of attrition away from school science occurs; the ability to positively impact engagement and science content learning for this age student might help work against this trend.) The first GPG was a scooter cart game focused on science content learning related to force and motion: the difference between velocity and acceleration, and the relationships among force, mass, and acceleration. The second was a playground slide game focused on science content learning related to energy: how energy can be interconverted from one form to another, specifically potential energy to kinetic and thermal energy, and what factors determine these energy amounts.

The design team was multidisciplinary and included two learning scientists, five teachers, three learning technologists, and one evaluator. After 12 weeks of initial content selection and setting of learning goals, the GPGs underwent three iterative design cycles over a period of 8 months. As we continued to work on designing the games, we found we were able to formalize our above-presented ideas about GPGs as a set of specific design principles to which we subsequently adhered in completing both GPGs. These design principles are as follows:

- *Fun Factor.* Making the game fun to play was one of the most important design principles for the game design. Research on play suggests that while having fun, learners experience prolonged engagement (Piaget, 1962).

- *Control.* We wanted to ensure that the GPG design allowed students to be responsible for the decision-making regarding their own explorations. We wanted the design to enable students to take ownership, meaning that after students understood the rules of the game, they would require an absolute minimum amount of external facilitation or guidance.
- *Knowledge in Action.* This design principle was rooted in the concept of intrinsic integration. To succeed at the game, students would have to employ an acquired understanding of scientific content.
- *Inquiry-based Gameplay.* The rules of the games were designed to encourage repeated cycles of gameplay that promoted prediction, exploration, and reflection, mirroring the scientific inquiry cycle.
- *Playful Data.* To support inquiry-based gameplay, we needed the students to collect data of some sort on which to reflect. Since data would need to be part of the game, we needed a way to present these data in a way that was intuitively easy to understand. We also wanted the data to reflect the playful nature of the game and be less school-like, that is, to not look like tables, graphs, or charts.
- *Personalization.* We needed the experience to be personalized. This would reinforce the fun factor and also reinforce the control design principle by making students feel at the center of their own experience.
- *Reflection.* Besides the reflection that is already part of the inquiry-based gameplay, we focused on additional scaffolds that were necessary to help students see patterns in the data that they and others generated during gameplay in order to use those patterns to improve their performance.
- *Collaboration.* Not only did we want students to enjoy playing the games with others, but we also wanted them to interact and collaborate as they tried to figure out what was required to succeed. Our GPG designs aimed to support students playing in teams and sharing hints or cheats.

Scooter Cart Guided Play Game

In the scooter cart GPG, a pair of students, one driver and one rider, had to match their motion to a target motion and the better their match, the higher their score. The driver pushed the rider on a low-to-the-ground scooter cart down a straight track approximately 50 feet in length (Figure 11.1). The students first interacted with a facilitator who explained how to play the game, helped them navigate the rules of the game, and helped them with the reflection process during the first few cycles of gameplay. The facilitator began by showing the students a video of three different types of motion—constant velocity, low acceleration, and high acceleration—and asked them to replicate any one of these. Winning required creating a motion that matched the ideal for that type. We chose these three kinds of

Figure 11.1 Students having fun playing the scooter cart guided play game.

motion to guide students toward understanding the difference between velocity and acceleration. Also, by pushing the rider on the cart, students would learn about the relationship among the amount of force required to push the cart, the amount of mass sitting on the cart (the rider), and acceleration (the increase in the cart's rate of speed along the straight track).

As the students pushed the cart, we tracked the cart's motion in real time using custom software. A webcam connected to a computer mounted approximately 50 feet away from the track used a computer-vision algorithm to track the motion of the cart against any stationary background.

To start playing, a student waved a flag to select the type of motion they wanted to recreate, and then selected a friend as the rider. The students would make their run and return to the start of the track, where they saw an instant video replay of themselves, with automated overlays using a vertical line to indicate the cart's location at regular time intervals and a green bar showing the force with which the driver was pushing the cart (Figure 11.2). The facilitator helped the students interpret the data during the first few runs by looking carefully at how their vertical lines matched up against those for the ideal motion. As the students became proficient at the game, the role of the facilitator was purposely tapered off, helping students only when they asked for advice.

The design of the scooter cart GPG was grounded in the design principles as follows. The design supported the *fun factor* by letting students push a

Figure 11.2 Playful data representation used in the scooter cart guided play game.

cart fast with a friend on it. The students also had fun watching the instant replay of themselves. The GPG gave students *control* over their gameplay and encouraged them to fail and learn from their failure. Students had control over the kind of motion they wanted to re-create, the selection of the rider and driver, and when to start the run. The GPG focused on *knowledge in action* by making the target physics learning an integral part of the game: the more students learned about the difference between velocity and acceleration and the relationships among force, mass, and acceleration, the better they could match their motion to the ideal and win the game. For example, if the rider was very lightweight, the driver would know that less force was required to push the cart to achieve a high acceleration.

To help students acquire the knowledge needed to perform better at the GPG, the rules supported *inquiry-based gameplay*, even though students probably were not aware of this. The game's design, and the facilitator, encouraged students to make a prediction, do a run, analyze the resultant data for why that run scored a particular way, and draw inferences about what to change to improve the next run. Inquiry was supported by the *playful data* generated during the runs (Figure 11.2). The data were also *personalized* for every student, with the screen split horizontally to show video on the bottom half of the students themselves pushing/riding the cart down the track with an overlay of the vertical motion lines and showing the ideal motion on the top half. Showing these two motions side by side supported *reflection*. Students were easily able to compare their own motion lines and force bar with those of the ideal motion. Reflection was further supported by including a human facilitator as part of the GPG. The facilitator initially encouraged students to observe their data and make comparisons, and to talk about their perceptions of their success matching the target motion and what to change to score better on the next run. Finally, the GPG supported *collaboration* with the students engaging in gameplay and reflection as pairs; the design also supported the reflection being conducted classwide where all students would dialogue to determine what types of strategies would lead to better outcomes.

Slide Guided Play Game

In the slide GPG, students chose different mats to transform energy as they slid down a playground slide. The goal was to slide in such a way so as to end up with the right types and amounts of energy at the bottom of the slide to pass to a computer-based avatar riding in a hot air balloon and get the hot air balloon to hit a target. In this GPG, the students first weighed themselves, and based on the mass, a personalized and achievable target was set for the hot air balloon. Students then choose a mat and descended the slide (Figure 11.3). The amount of kinetic energy the student had at the bottom of the slide would spin the hot air balloon's propeller and push it horizontally toward the target, while the amount of thermal energy due to friction the student had at the bottom of the slide, would raise the hot air balloon vertically toward the target (Figure 11.4). When students were not initially successful in hitting the target, they would try again, working to change their final energy amounts by choosing a different mat, giving themselves an initial push, etc.

The technology supporting this GPG included custom-made light sensors on one side of the slide and high-powered flashlights pointing directly at the light sensors from the other side of the slide. Two light sensor/flashlight pairs placed at the top of the slide could calculate a student's velocity by how quickly she passed the first and then the second sensor. Another pair placed at the bottom of the slide similarly calculated a student's final velocity. These data, together with the previously recorded mass and the height of the slide, were combined to calculate potential energy of the student at the top of the slide, kinetic energy of the student at the top and bottom of the slide, and thermal energy due to friction at the bottom of the slide. It was with these energy values that the students played the GPG.

The design was grounded in the GPG design principles as follows. The design supported playfulness and a certain *fun factor* inherent in letting students slide down a playground slide, including sliding down on mats made of different materials. The design encouraged the students to take *control* of the game by having them choose the type of mat they used to go down the slide and anything else they wanted to change about how to slide. The students also had control over the GPG insofar as the computer would

Figure 11.3 A student having fun playing the slide guided play game (facilitator at left).

Figure 11.4 Playful data representation used in the slide guided play game.

start recording automatically whenever they decided to slide. The GPG focused on *knowledge in action* in that the game required students to use their knowledge of total energy being conserved, how energy is inter-converted among forms, and the factors that determine the various energy types, to end up with the right amounts of the right kinds of energy to get their hot air balloon to hit the target. The better they understood energy, the more reliably they could hit the target no matter where it was positioned.

To help students acquire this knowledge, we again designed for *inquiry-based gameplay*. The game's design, as well as the facilitator, encouraged students to think about what they needed to do to hit the target, do a run, analyze the resultant data for why they missed the target, and draw inferences about what to change to get closer to hitting the target. Once again, students might not even realize they were engaged in inquiry, but they were. The students were working with a *playful data* representation of their energy amounts that was fairly non-traditional, i.e, the movement of a hot air balloon (Figure 11.4). These data were *personalized* in that the game target was set based on the unique potential energy of each student. This GPG also supported *reflection* by showing a looped replay of a student's run, which, along with the facilitator's questions, encouraged her to consider how to improve her performance by thinking about why she missed the target and what to change to perform better on the next run. Finally, the GPG was designed to help students *collaborate* to improve their performance. Students would wait at the bottom of the slide and view the large monitor with the next slider to discuss what happened and what to do differently. Similarly, while students were lined up they were all able to see where the next student's target was set, and this supported them talking with one another about what to do to succeed, making suggestions about, for example, what mat to choose to better their performance.

METHODS

Participants

To gain some preliminary insight into this study's two hypotheses, we recruited 43 8th-grade students from a New York City middle school with a student population that was 62% Hispanic or Latino, 34% black or African American, 3% white, 1% Asian, and 1% American Indian or Alaska Native; 90% of students were eligible for free or reduced-price lunch. We split the students randomly into scooter cart or slide groups, then split each group to play the GPG or engage in free play using that same piece of playground equipment. The numbers of the students participating in the study are presented in Tables 11.1 and 11.2.

Table 11.1 Scooter cart study participants

Group	N	Male	Female
Guided play game	15	8	7
Free play	7	3	4

Table 11.2 Slide study participants

Group	N	Male	Female
Guided play game	12	6	6
Free play	9	3	6

Experimental Conditions

Both GPG groups played the games as described above. Both GPG groups reviewed their runs on the video monitor and then, initially with the help of the facilitator but later without, interpreted the data and decided what do next. In both GPGs, the students were allotted a maximum time of 30 minutes to play.

For both free play groups, gameplay was necessarily different than that for students playing the GPGs. None of the guides to play were employed. The scooter cart and slide and mats were available but all sensors and monitors were turned off. The facilitator was present but his role was strictly that of crowd control. The students could play with the playground equipment however they wished. The scooter free play students notably had multiple students driving and multiple students riding on the cart, and they often did not push the cart along the straight line. Like the GPG students, the free play students were given a maximum of 30 minutes to play.

Constructs: Engagement and Science Content Learning

We deployed multiple constructs and data collection and analysis techniques to explore our two hypotheses and determine (1) the extent to which the scooter cart and slide GPGs impacted the students' engagement and science content learning, and (2) how these student outcomes compared to those observed during free play with the same scooter cart and slide playground equipment.

The first set of constructs is related to engagement, both behavioral, emotional, and cognitive. Engagement is often measured with self-report surveys (Fredricks et al., 2004). To enhance the validity of measurement and to minimize disruption of gameplay, we sought to measure engagement directly through the observation of student behaviors and expressions, physical and verbal.

Attentiveness. Attentiveness is one way we measured behavioral engagement. Video coding was based on observational scales used for measuring playful behavior (Barnett, 1991; Marks, 2000). We developed and used a rubric to code video for the amount of time students were "completely attentive," "partially attentive," or "not attentive at all" while playing. The instances that a student was "completely attentive," "partially attentive," or "not attentive at all" were timed and divided by the average total time the students in that group played to arrive at percentages. Group average attentiveness was calculated by averaging all the individual percentages for the students in a particular group.

Persistence. Persistence is another way we measured behavioral engagement that we considered separately from attentiveness. We wanted to observe how many times students played and for how long. Watching the video, we coded persistence as the number of times a student completed full rounds of gameplay, whether this was the gameplay that was supported by the GPGs or the games students made up for themselves in the free play conditions. In both GPG and free play groups, group average persistence was determined by averaging students' individual persistence tallies for the students.

Fun. In order to get a complete picture of student engagement while playing, we needed to examine some aspects of emotional engagement and thus we looked at whether the students were having fun. Fun was measured in three ways. First, we observed whether or not the students were having fun during play by reviewing the videos for relevant observable behaviors or utterances (e.g. instances where students smiled or laughed, made joyful noises, or vocalized enjoying themselves, or in contrast, appeared to be or stated being bored). Group average fun was determined by averaging individual student's fun tallies. We supplemented this with a post-interview by asking students directly whether or not they had fun during the GPG or free play experiences, as well as how much fun they had as compared to their favorite game.

We supplemented the direct observations of students' fun by asking two self-report items during the post-interview. Students were asked to rate "How much fun was the game/experience?" on a 1 to 5 scale (1 = boring, 2 = average, 3 = good, 4 = very good, and 5 = excellent). We also asked them to rate how the game/experience compared to their favorite game on a 1 to 5 scale (1 = completely boring, 2 = just okay, 3 = almost as much fun, 4 = as much fun, and 5 = more fun than their favorite game). We recorded the individual scores for students and determined group average scores.

Scientific Talk. Scientific talk was considered to be an expression of cognitive engagement. Scientific talk was coded from video and was observed when students supported their arguments with evidence drawn from their GPG or free play experiences (Mortimer & Scott, 2003). Instances of scientific talk were tallied per individual student and group averages for scientific talk were determined. Scientific talk also gives us some insight into the extent to which scientific inquiry-type processes were engendered as had been designed into the GPG to help promote science content learning.

Science Content Learning. Besides the impact on students' behavioral, emotional, and cognitive engagement, we also needed to measure whether students progressed in their physics content learning by virtue of their GPG or free play experience. It is easy to imagine guided play that would be fun enough to boost engagement but at the expense of any science learning, or that the game experience might lead students to improve their science learning but with such a heavy hand that their engagement would slump. To measure impact on content learning we used pre- and post-tests. To maintain the playful nature of the GPG or free play experiences, pre-tests were given at least a week in advance of the students doing the playground activity. The post-test was given the next day. Students who engaged in the scooter cart GPG or free play experiences took a force-and-motion test, and students who engaged in the slide GPG or free play experiences took an energy test. Where possible, questions for both tests were adapted from the Physics Force Concept Inventory (Hestenes, Wells, & Swackhamer, 1992) to be appropriate for these younger students or were identified from standardized test item banks.

RESULTS AND CONCLUSIONS

This study investigated whether GPGs could positively influence behavioral, emotional, and cognitive engagement, and at the same time support science content learning. We compared the outcomes for students who played the GPGs with those of students who engaged in free play with the same playground equipment but without any guides to their play.

For both the scooter cart and the slide GPGs, our results indicated a positive impact on behavioral engagement (attentiveness, persistence), emotional engagement (fun), cognitive engagement (scientific talk), and physics science content learning. The GPGs created impressively high levels of student attention and kept them high throughout the game ("completely attentive" 99% of the time for the scooter cart GPG and 97% for the slide GPG).

The free play students were also attentive ("completely attentive" 80% of the time for scooter cart free play and 100% for slide free play), but they played for a shorter time (on average, 15 minutes for scooter cart free play compared to 30 minutes for the scooter cart GPG; on average, 17 minutes for slide free play compared to 30 minutes for the slide GPG). Students were also significantly less persistent in repeating runs during free play as compared to the GPGs (on average, three complete runs for the scooter cart free play compared to seven for the scooter cart GPG; on average, two complete runs for slide free play compared to four for the slide GPG). This finding was influenced by the fact that the GPG rules supported *all* students having a chance to play the game, whereas in free play, some students did not play at all, perhaps because they felt excluded. So, in the end, guiding the play did not seem to decrease students' playful participation at all and in some ways increased it.

We might attribute the higher levels of attentiveness and persistence for the GPGs compared to free play to the GPGs being more fun (i.e., emotionally engaging). Certainly, the GPGs were created around the design principles of fun factor, control, personalization, and collaboration in an attempt to promote both behavioral and emotional engagement. However, the findings related to fun are not entirely consistent. While both GPG and free play groups self-reported having statistically the same amounts of fun (on average, the students self-reported the experience being between "very good" and "excellent" and between "as much fun" as and "more fun" to play than their favorite game for both the scooter cart and slide GPGs, and also for both the scooter cart and slide free play groups), we actually documented more observed instances of fun with free play than with the GPG students (on average, 13 instances of fun for scooter cart free play compared to seven instances for the scooter cart GPG; on average, 15 instances of fun for slide free play compared to seven for the slide GPG). The finding that free play promoted more emotional engagement seems reasonable, but as you will see, it also resulted in less behavioral and cognitive engagement and less learning. That said, it is hard to know if we should rely on either the self-report or direct observation of emotional engagement as more valid. It is interesting that both the GPG and free play students self-reported an equivalent amount of fun.

To document cognitive engagement, we looked at scientific talk. We observed that the GPG students used scientific talk significantly more often (on average, 21 instances of scientific talk for the scooter cart GPG; on average, 16 instances of scientific talk for the slide GPG) than the free play students (who never used scientific talk during their play at all). This finding indicates the extent to which the inquiry-based gameplay and playful data design principles worked. This finding is particularly interesting because it highlights the extent to which the cognitive engagement engendered by playing GPGs did not come at the expense of behavioral and emotional engagement, which were found at levels similar to or even greater than those found during free play. In this regard, GPGs can be seen to strike an exciting balance, and should the cognitive engagement ultimately support the learning of science content, which we will discuss next, this guided play model might have the potential to keep students both engaged and achieving in science in a virtuous cycle.

Students playing both GPGs improved a significant amount on their content learning tests from pre to post (students improved on the force-and-motion test a statistically significant 1.4 standard deviations after playing the scooter cart GPG; students improved on the energy test a statistically significant 1.2 standard deviations after playing the slide GPG), whereas the free play students did not (there was no statistically significant change pre to post on either test with either type of free play). These findings are consistent with the literature discussed above suggesting that free play does not support content learning as well as guided play. These findings are also consistent with the literature on how games can support science content learning. In sum, we did find evidence of the potential of guided play games to improve students' achievement at the same time as their engagement.

SciGames. It is important to note that after playing the GPGs, students achieved only 60% and 53% of the total points possible on the force-and-motion and energy post tests, respectively. There is room for further improvement in science content learning beyond what the GPGs were able to support. However, if we add more guides for learning to the game, we might risk reducing the positive impact on engagement by effectively tipping the experience from one of student-directed guided play to one that would feel to the student more like guided inquiry, directed by some external authority.

Is there another way we might further improve science content learning while keeping the experience feeling playful to students and thus keeping engagement just as high? It is in this direction that we are extending our work on GPGs with our new SciGames project, work that is being generously supported by the U.S. Department of Education (Investing in Innovation program) and the National Science Foundation (Transforming STEM Learning program), with additional funding from the John D. and Catherine T. MacArthur Foundation, the Motorola Solutions Foundation, and the Bank of New York Mellon Foundation.

SciGames begins using the same GPGs described above, played in the informal playground setting, but with all participating students wearing radio-frequency ID bracelets. We use these bracelets to log students' quantitative data generated playing the GPGs automatically and invisibly while they play. The SciGames system uploads these student-specific data onto a virtual playground application that digitally extends the physical playground into the students' science classroom. In this new virtual space, students will be able to replay their own runs from the GPGs and those of their friends, as well as conduct new rounds of gameplay, including runs that are not possible in the real world, such as runs without friction. Most importantly, the digital application provides specialized tools that support students (with teacher guidance) inquiring deeply into this class-generated quantitative data to look for the patterns that help win the GPGs; due to the knowledge in action design principle that guided the design of the GPGs from the start, winning depends on mastering the underlying scientific principles we wanted students to learn.

We have now determined that GPGs can positively affect student behavioral, emotional, and cognitive engagement in learning. We are excited to see if the SciGames approach can extend the GPG idea and further improved students' science content learning while retaining, if not enhance, the positive impact on engagement we have seen in this study.

Acknowledgments

The material in Chapter 11 is based upon work supported by the National Science Foundation under grant no. DRL-1135202, and the U.S. Department of Education under grant no. U411C110310. Any opinions, findings, and conclusions or recommendations expressed in this material are those of the authors and do not necessarily reflect the views of the National Science Foundation or the U.S. Department of Education.

References

Barnett, L. A. (1991). The playful child: Measurement of a disposition to play. *Play and Culture, 4*, 51–74.

Barnett, M., Squire, K., Higginbotham, T., & Grant, J. (2004). Electromagnetism supercharged! *Proceedings of the 2004 International Conference of the Learning Sciences.* Los Angeles, CA: UCAL Press.

Fein, G., & Rivkin, M. (1986). *The young child at play: Reviews of research.* Washington, DC: National Association for the Education of Young Children (NAEYC).

Fisher, K., Hirsh-Pasek, K., Golinkoff, R. M., Singer, D., & Berk, L. E. (2011). Playing around in school: Implications for learning and educational policy. In A. Pellegrini (Ed.), *The Oxford handbook of the development of play* (pp. 341–363). New York: Oxford University Press.

Fredricks, J. A., Blumenfeld, P. C., & Paris, A. H. (2004). School engagement: Potential of the concept, state of the evidence. *Review of Educational Research, 74*(1), 59–109.

Gee, J. P. (2003). *What video games have to teach us about learning and literacy.* New York: Palgrave/Macmillan.

Habgood, J. M., & Ainsworth, S. E. (2011). Motivating children to learn effectively: Exploring the value of intrinsic integration in educational games. *Journal of the Learning Sciences, 20*(2), 169–206.

Hestenes, D., Wells, M., & Swackhammer, G. (1992). Force concept inventory. *The Physics Teacher, 30*(3), 141–151.

Jenkins, H., Squire, K., & Tan, P. (2004). You can't bring that game to school! Designing supercharged! games and simulations: Genres, examples, and evidence. In B. Laurel (Ed.), *Design research.* Cambridge, MA: MIT Press.

Kanter, D. E. (2010). Doing the project and learning the content: Designing project-based science curricula for meaningful understanding. *Science Education, 94*(3), 525–551.

Krajcik, J. S., McNeill, K. L., & Reiser, B. J. (2008). Learning-goals-driven design model: Developing curriculum materials that align with national standards and incorporate project-based pedagogy. *Science Education, 92*(1), 1–32.

Marks, H. (2000). Student engagement in instructional activity: Patterns in the elementary, middle and high school years. *American Educational Research Journal, 37*(1), 153–184.

Marx, R. W., Blumenfeld, P. C., Krajcik, J. S., Fishman, B., Soloway, E., Geier, R., et al. (2004). Inquiry-based science in the middle grades: Assessment of learning in urban systemic reform. *Journal of Research in Science Teaching, 41*(10), 1063–1080.

Miller, E., & Almon, J. (2009). *Crisis in the kindergarten: Why children need to play in school.* College Park, MD: Alliance for Childhood.

Mortimer, E. F., & Scott, P. (2003). *Meaning making in secondary science classrooms.* Philadelphia, PA: McGraw Hill Education.

National Research Council (2003). *Engaging schools: Fostering high school students' motivation to learn.* Washington, DC: National Academies Press.

Newmann, F., Wehlage, G. G., & Lamborn, S. D. (1992). The significance and sources of student engagement. In F. Newmann (Ed.), *Student engagement and achievement in American secondary schools* (pp. 11–39). New York: Teachers College Press.

Pellegrini, A. D. (2009). Research and policy on children's play. *Child Development Perspectives, 3,* 131–136.

Piaget, J. (1962). *Play, dreams, and imitation in childhood.* New York: Norton.

Resnick, M. (1998). Technologies for lifelong kindergarten. *Educational Technology Research and Development, 46*(4), 43–55.

Resnick, M. (2007). All I really need to know (about creative thinking) I learned (by studying how children learn) in kindergarten. *Proceeds of the 6th ACM SIGCHI Conference on Creativity and Cognition* (pp. 1–6). Washington, DC: ACM.

Rivet, A., & Krajcik, J. S. (2004). Achieving standards in urban systemic reform: An example of a sixth-grade project-based science curriculum. *Journal of Research in Science Teaching, 41*(7), 669–692.

Sandoval, W. A., & Reiser, B. J. (2004). Explanation-driven inquiry: Integrating conceptual and epistemic scaffolds for scientific inquiry. *Science Education, 12*(1), 5–51.

Schneider, R. M. (2002). Performance of students in project-based science classrooms on a national measure of science achievement. *Journal of Research in Science Teaching, 39*(5), 410–422.

Singer, J., Marx, R. W., Krajcik, J. S., & Chambers, J. C. (2000). Constructing extended inquiry projects: Curriculum materials for science education reform. *Educational Psychologist, 35*(3), 165–178.

Youell, B. (2008). The importance of play and playfulness. *European Journal of Psychotherapy and Counseling, 10*(2), 121–129.

CHAPTER 12

MAKING THEIR WAY IN THE WORLD
Creating a Generation of Tinkerer-Scientists

ELLIOT WASHOR AND CHARLES MOJKOWSKI

LET US START WITH A FISH STORY

Back in 2008, you might have noticed this *New York Times* headline: "Fish Tale Has DNA Hook: Students Find Bad Labels" (Schwartz, 2008). Two high school students, the article reported, observing the rising popularity of sushi and sushi restaurants, and perhaps further observing how a lot of raw fish looked the same, decided to find out if the fish served was actually the fish restaurants said it was. With help from one of their fathers (who worked with birds), Kate Stoeckle and Louisa Strauss were able to work with a bit of DNA genetic barcoding. Much to the dismay of many restaurant owners and their customers, Kate and Louisa found that what sushi customers ordered was often not the sushi they were served.

This neat piece of scientific research was not part of any school science project. Indeed, Kate Stoeckle and Louisa Strauss never sought school credit for their work, although they diligently recorded the project on their college applications. Our guess is that they knew the value of what they had accomplished but saw no need to inform their high school of the work. Might there be something fishy about that behavior? We say more about that in a bit, but first, let us look at another story.

Late in 2010, 13-year-old Aidan Dwyer reported on a personal science experiment that caused quite a stir (Dwyer, 2011; Hollander, 2012). While walking in the Catskills with his parents, he observed the pattern of leaves as solar collectors, and from this observation he developed a highly efficient array of solar panels that won him a national science competition award and widespread recognition for his idea. That recognition prompted a closer examination of his reasoning and calculations by the scientific community, which found that he had measured the wrong thing, rendering his findings incorrect.

What followed this discovery of error was telling. The Internet exploded with chatter commenting—sometimes roughly—on his mistake. Aidan, a true learner, returned to his research in order to understand the source of his errors and correct them. As we write, Aidan is still working on his design, trying out a few more strategies and seeking another solution. He was recently featured on a Time Warner Cable Digital TV show *It Ain't Rocket Science* (Business Wire, 2012).

In our Big Picture Learning schools (BPL) (www.bigpicturelearning.org), few students make headlines, but hundreds of them have extraordinary tales to tell about the research projects they do outside of school. Here is an example:

Hannah Brown is a mathematics whiz; it has always been her passion. She overcame verbal apraxia in elementary school but still appeared to be quiet and shy. She wanted to attend the San Diego Met High School—a Big Picture Learning school—because of its internships and access to college courses. Hannah's first major internship, in a corporate engineering firm, lasted a year. She learned AutoCAD and produced a PowerPoint presentation showing the process of designing a road as her internship project. During that time, she started taking college courses at Mesa Community College, where the San Diego Met High School is located.

Hannah then did two education-oriented internships, the first as a teacher's assistant in a Regional Occupational Program (ROP) high school engineering course, the second at San Diego State University in a Projected Geometry course. She learned she did not want to be a teacher, and she became interested in robotics because her ROP mentor asked her to learn a new robotics program for the engineering class and write an easy-to-use instruction manual as her internship project.

Her mother found a start-up robotics company by searching the Internet, and the San Diego Met's internship coordinator convinced that company to give Hannah an interview for an internship. Hannah is now a robotics intern, testing circuit boards used to automate the flight paths of hobby drones. "This is my favorite internship, and I plan to stay here my whole senior year," Hannah enthusiastically told her principal.

Hannah has earned a unit of elective high school credit each semester for her Met High internships. She expects to have 27 units of community college credit by the end of her junior year at the Met High School. She is considering LeTourneau University in Longview, Texas for college and wants to declare a double major of computer science and mathematics.

What distinguishes the work of students in Big Picture Learning schools from that done by Kate, Louisa, and Aidan is that BPL out-of-school projects are an integral part of their in-school work. Hannah's story shows how a school with the appropriate organizational structure, culture, and tools can create a contextualized learning environment where students earn academic and graduation credit, and how the school, outside organizations, and the family all work together to support the student in an integrated manner. (We say more about structure, culture, and tools later.)

These young people provide images of what we want for all students. They motivate us to think about what opportunities schools and afterschool and community programs are missing for engaging and preparing all their students to be tinkerer-scientists, not necessarily interested in a career in engineering or the sciences but competent and comfortable in using science, math, and technology tools and processes to address real-world challenges they discover in their lives, be they solar panel efficiency or knowing what you are eating.

Both of us have been involved in schools for over 40 years. About 17 years ago, we helped establish Big Picture Learning and have since started nearly 100 schools in the United States and around the world. Our deeper look at how the sciences and mathematics are taught in schools is informed and guided by the experiences and perspectives of young people in our Big Picture Learning schools and other schools in which we have worked.

And, based on our work, we want to make the case for focusing less on creating future scientists and engineers through a STEM "pipeline" into college and the workplace, and instead concentrate on helping all students become tinkerer-scientists. We describe the changes that are needed and how schools might make them.

What is on the Line?

Getting science education right is a high-stakes endeavor not merely because our country needs more scientists and engineers, but also because we need a much more capable citizenry with respect to empirical and mathematical reasoning. The overriding goal for teaching the sciences (including the social sciences as well as mathematics and technology applications) in the secondary school setting should be to develop in all young people the ability to think independently about any complex problem, consider the merits of any argument, and question the validity of a conclusion—their own or someone else's. We need and want young people who are problem finders, who are inquisitive, trolling their everyday world to observe, conjecture, and hypothesize, and thinking critically about real problems they encounter in their lives. Our concern is less about algebra and physics as currently construed by traditional schools, and more about creating future generations of makers and inventors across all disciplines and career areas.

This is an outcome schools and society should value just as highly as we value the development of individuals who will enter into highly specialized careers such as medicine, engineering, and biology. Scientific and technological literacy among the general population ultimately affords a positive impact on the lives of all members within society (e.g., advocating for better health care, better preventive medicine, safer buildings, healthier environments, more nutritious foods, and time-saving technologies). The development of the capacity for objective observation and critical reasoning as the goal of science education is an approach to science pedagogy that acknowledges that science is not the exclusive domain of those who enter the science-oriented professions or industries but should have a "real-world" impact. In order to graduate more high school students such as Hannah, Kate, Louisa, and Aidan, we need to redesign schools, programs, and curriculum in the entire K-12 school system.

Why Are They Not Biting?

Most students do not gravitate to the sciences in high school, and of those that do, many never develop a STEM career. Our own observations reveal that most high school students are disengaged from the STEM curriculum their schools provide.

We see three major barriers to graduating tinkerer-scientists from U.S. high schools. First, schools, perhaps responding to pressures to improve students' test performances, give little or no attention to creativity, exploration, tinkering, and invention in the elementary and secondary school curriculum. It is these competencies that are considered essential to developing future generations of STEM graduates (Kamenetz, 2011; Turckes & Kahl, 2011).

Second, the school curriculum employs cognitive-abstract teaching and paper-and-pencil assessment methods that shoulder out other ways of engaging and understanding the world. Hands-on learning out in the real world assessed through authentic performance demonstrations is rarely a part of what most students experience in school. Most of what is taught is addressed to low-level competencies, and minimum performance is expected and accepted.

Third, the only learning that counts in school is the learning accomplished in school. Students have few opportunities to bring what they learn and accomplish outside of school into the school and earn academic and graduation credit. Let us take a closer look at these three barriers.

No Head for Creativity and Invention

The evolution of Mr. Potato Head provides a fitting metaphor for what has and is happening to the development of creativity and invention in our schools. Mr. Potato Head was created by Brooklyn native George Lerner, who as a young boy used to take vegetables from the family garden and make them into dolls for his sisters. Spinach, carrots, peppers, broccoli were transformed into hair, eyes, ears, and noses. His Mr. Potato Head kits, sold to Hassenfeld Brothers (now Hasbro) in 1952, were an outgrowth of these playful childhood activities. The first kits provided 30 different plastic pieces—with the option to order 50 more—to stick into a real potato, fruit, or other vegetable, or the Styrofoam head that was included.

The devolution from real to fake began in due course, and opportunities for creativity diminished. In 1964, Hasbro included a plastic potato with each kit—no more need for the real-deal potato. Predrilled holes became flat slots to signal where the parts must go and in what direction. To the dismay of budding Picassos, no longer could you put an arm where the eye should go (was that not half the fun?). Mr. Potato Heads could no longer, as the commercial stated, "look different every time you make them" (Mrpotatohead.net, n.d.; Walsh, 2005).

The original Mr. Potato Head allowed children to use their hands, minds, and hearts to fashion and refashion an object they could animate and to build an open-ended narrative from their imaginations. Today's Mr. Potato Head kit is more useful for assembling and collecting than for imagining and experimenting.

We said there is a metaphor.

We read that our global competitiveness will not be ensured solely through higher literacy and numeracy, perhaps not even by producing more scientists and engineers. Only through creativity, invention, and innovation will we be able to, as renowned observer of organizations Peter Drucker advised, leapfrog our global competitors (Drucker, 1995). And, we might add, to revitalize our communities by encouraging creative problem-solving and social entrepreneurism in addressing challenges in our cities.

And so we look to the schools to prepare their graduates to bring important innovation competencies—creative problem-solving, invention, inquisitiveness, design thinking, and experimentation—to our communities and workplaces. The school curriculum, however, has gone the way of Mr. Potato Head. Educators have distilled out of the curriculum practically any attention to creativity and inventiveness. No messing around or tinkering is tolerated. Important innovation competencies are neither taught nor assessed in most schools. These competencies are not part of the national focus on the Common Core State Standards. While society and the business community extol the virtues of having highly creative and inventive students, few complain when schools fail to teach and assess these competencies.

It is a No-Brainer

An over-reliance on cognitive-abstract methods of teaching and learning, particularly in math and the sciences, results in high levels of student disengagement (Eisner, 1985). Often, this approach is coupled with low-level instruction focused on learning for the test, with no time to go deep, and little attention to practice to achieve even competence (Coyle, 2009).

Many scholars, such as Elliot Eisner and Howard Gardner, remind us that other forms of knowing are equally, if not more, valuable to individuals and to society (Eisner, 1985; Gardner, 1999). Sir Ken Robinson (2001) argues that the current cognitive-abstract curriculum is designed to produce college professors. Arts, crafts, and technical skills are largely ignored. Yet it is these multiple ways of knowing that serve as the sources of many an invention or solution to a challenge or problem.

Kyna Leski (2012), dean of architecture at the Rhode Island School of Design, states that creativity is not in knowledge itself but in exploiting those multiple ways of knowing. Discovery and invention are not about arriving somewhere expected but deliberately moving outside what is known. Students need to employ such skills and dispositions in making their way in the world.

In attempting to ensure that every student masters a "common core" of content and skills, schools are completely overlooking the talents of their students and making them think they are not smart. In his book *Developing Talent in Young People*, Benjamin Bloom (1985) found that schools are not adept at spotting or developing talent. Examining how talent across many fields was developed, Bloom studied young people who excelled in the arts, sciences, sports, and games and found that they had an interest and some talent they wanted to pursue. A mentor of some kind told them and their parents early on that they had some talent. The child made the decision to pursue these talents and, as they improved, they attracted better mentors and coaches. Lauren Sosniak (Anderson & Sosniak, 1994), Bloom's researcher colleague, observed that there is no way to exploit such a talent development model within the traditional school design, with its inflexible organization, traditional curriculum, and narrow assessments. Many young people, consciously or unconsciously, would agree with Sosniak.

There are different ways of being smart. Recall Homer "Sonny" Hickam, Jr., the "rocket boy" in the movie *October Sky* (Johnston, 1999). His passion for rocketry motivated him and his friends to learn high-level math, but when they brought that learning into school, they were accused of cheating. The school had no way of paying attention to their out-of-school learning.

It was not until they proved to the principal they could do the math embedded in their out-of-school project that these students received credit. Thoroughly disengaged from their in-school math, they were deeply engaged with the math in their real-world projects.

Gone Fishing: You Cannot Do That in School

While everyone admires and celebrates the learning and work that enterprising students do outside of school, most schools are not willing to teach the sciences or math in the ways that these students learned. The tightly scripted curriculum focuses on preparation for high-stakes tests and leaves little or no room for science or math as tinkerer-scientists employ them outside of school. The way most schools are currently structured, it is not easy to bring students' outside learning and work into schools.

Notice how Aidan's project is very different from what goes on in school. The way he generated the question by walking in the woods with his parents, the fact that it is accomplished outside of school, the fact that it takes lots of time that is not tightly scheduled, and the fact that assessment is so different from a standardized test are just a few of the differences that make a difference. Appreciating those differences, you realize that such a project would fit poorly within the existing structure and culture of most schools, where the norm is scope and sequence of content curriculum in segmented disciplines. Aidan's project prompts the questions of why not do such learning in schools and how might it be accomplished.

Our observations indicate that schools are myopic about what constitutes productive learning and how such programs should be designed and implemented. Schools have blind spots that prevent them from looking out at the world outside of schools and thinking about what young people— all young people—might do. Schools fail to see the potential of learning outside of school. The kind of science that Kate, Louisa, and Aidan did does not fit that neatly into the way that science and math are taught in most high schools.

HOW MIGHT WE ADDRESS THESE PROBLEMS?

We see several major changes that would make a significant difference in addressing these problems.

Feel the Line

Experienced fishermen understand that "the tug is the drug." The fish have got their attention, and the fishermen are ever alert to the "messages" the fish will send along the line. Schools need to emulate veteran fishermen by being more attentive to their students' needs and expectations—their "tugs on the line" as they nibble the bait. Schools need to overcome their own "attention deficit disorders" by understanding and responding to students' expectations of their schools by focusing on students' interests, particularly potential career interests, and by paying close attention to the questions that students have about their world and how it works.

Young people have high hopes and expectations for themselves, and they also have high expectations of their schools and teachers. Based on our work in our schools and in others, we have identified ten such expectations, which might be stated as questions:

> *Relationships*: Do my teachers, and others who might serve as my teachers, know about me and my interests and talents?
> *Relevance*: Do I find what the school is teaching to be relevant to my interests?
> *Authenticity*: Is the learning and work I do regarded as significant outside of school by experts, my family, community members, and employers?
> *Application*: Do I have opportunities to apply what I am learning in real-world settings and contexts?
> *Choice*: Do I have real choices about what, when, and how I will learn and demonstrate my competence?
> *Challenge*: Do I feel appropriately challenged in my learning and work?
> *Play*: Do I have opportunities to explore and to make mistakes, and learn from them, without being branded as a failure?
> *Practice*: Do I have opportunities to engage in deep and sustained practice of those skills I need to learn?
> *Time*: Do I have sufficient time to learn at my own pace?
> *Timing*: Can I pursue my learning out of the standard sequence?

Learning flourishes when there are deep connections between the student, his or her emerging interests in given areas, and the complex learning challenges that define those areas. Note that Kate, Louisa, and Aidan came up with their own questions. They sought and received help from parents and other adults outside of school.

Schools need to pay attention to their students' questions about the world—even stimulate their developing such questions. Schools need to award credit not merely for answers, but also for interesting questions, promising heuristics (simple, practical problem-solving strategies), for smart mistakes, and for what are often called "soft" skills such as collaboration and networking, building social capital, design thinking, and entrepreneurism (Bornstein, 2011; Dyson, 2011; Symonds, Schwartz, & Ferguson, 2011).

Learning is not about delivering answers, but about the process of framing questions for oneself and then devising methods to answer them. The questions are important because the students own them. Research and our own experience tell us that without such ownership, students have little or no engagement in productive learning (Willms, Friesen, & Milton, 2009).

Focus on Productive Learning

Once schools have their students' attention by addressing their expectations, they can engage them in productive learning. We use the term *productive learning* to emphasize our goal, which is inspired by the definition that Seymour Sarason gave in his 2004 book entitled *And What do YOU Mean by Learning?* "By *productive*," wrote Sarason (2004), "I mean that the learning process is one which engenders and reinforces wanting to learn more" (p. x) (italics in original). We embrace that definition and add elements that are consistent with Sarason's focus on the generative aspects of productive learning. Such learning is marked by rigorous student work that focuses on demonstrations of competence and leads students to seek higher levels of accomplishment through craftsmanship, mastery, and artistry.

While educational leaders are vociferously advocating for "higher expectations," they attend primarily to what they can measure easily—mostly lower-order factual knowledge. Many experts and practitioners have lamented this lowered expectation that many current educational reformers, including bureaucrats, business people, and politicians, are promoting. Having all students able to read and compute proficiently is *not* a higher standard when the world we are coming into—no, the world we are already living in—requires creativity, inventiveness, design thinking, and alternative ways of thinking, learning, and performing.

Three strategies will contribute to an increased attention to productive learning.

Expand and improve the quality of projects. Projects—small and large, individual and group—are a staple of productive learning. We have identified several criteria for high-quality projects:

- Projects are built around students' group and individual interests.
- Projects originate in mysteries, as complex and messy problems identified by students. Pre-packaged, formulaic projects will not do.
- Projects are situated in authentic contexts and settings.
- Projects draw on multiple disciplines, including design and the arts.
- Time for project work is variable, allowing for opportunities to go deep—even double back and pursue related problems (more mysteries) as the need arises.
- Projects require deliberate application of multiple problem-solving strategies (heuristics).
- Projects are evaluated using real-world standards, often applied by adults doing similar work in businesses and in the community.

- Projects incorporate appropriate applications of appropriate technologies.

Increase attention to heuristics. Schools need to challenge students to discover mysteries (think Kate and Louisa's sushi) and unknowns—all the while picking up new information and cracking codes that turn magic into the known, crafting strategies for understanding and solving those mysteries, and developing procedures for addressing similar problems. Such an approach provides students with experience in heuristic thinking: creating, inventing, discovering, and applying rules of engagement in problem spaces (think Aidan's leaves as solar collectors). But these outcomes can be achieved only by devoting less time to memorizing algorithms and devoting more time to creating or discovering their own.

A focus on algorithms may work well with learning/using the alphabet or the multiplication table, but such a focus is minimally helpful in working through real-world problems and projects that require complex thinking. Competence in merely using algorithms is likely not good enough to negotiate life's problems or to obtain a high-wage job, while creating and understanding the use of algorithms and addressing multiple variables are highly valued.

Competence and beyond. Even competence may not be enough, since the best jobs will require high levels of craftsmanship in employing sophisticated heuristics to address challenging mysteries such as those Aidan Dwyer encountered. Craftsmanship involves the body as well as the mind, the hand as well as the heart, resulting in what Ron Berger (2003) calls beautiful work, "building craftsmanship in work and thought" (p. 65).

TINKERING AND MAKING

Tinkering and making are making a comeback. A cornucopia of fabrication and technology labs, public and private, is sprouting throughout the country. Fab labs—also called "makerspaces"—provide tinkerers with easy access to powerful and expensive technology tools in a community of like-minded minds. Maker Faires (http://makerfaire.com)—sprawling outdoor extravaganzas that combine the atmosphere of a medieval fair with old lo-tech and new hi-tech garages—are gathering makers of all ages to share their work and their learning. These new manifestations of "thinkering" bring wizened tinkerers and tech-savvy youth together in playful competitions that range from the serious and sublime—a solar car, for example—to the deliberately frivolous and outrageous—a gas-powered bicycle.

Making with hands and minds stimulates young people to develop their imaginative, creative, entrepreneurial, and scientific chops. Sociologist

Richard Sennett (2008), in *The Craftsman*, writes that "all skills, even the most abstract, begin as bodily practices; second, that technical understanding develops through the powers of imagination" (p. 10).

Making develops an alternative and powerful way of knowing and of thinking things through that contrasts with mere abstract analysis. Thus, making is typically antithetical to what traditional schools are all about. That is why the communities of practice that come together at Maker Faires and fab labs usually—some would say *thankfully*—flourish outside of schools.

Making provides opportunities for young people to use their hands *and* their heads. Sadly, most young people do not experience making in their schools or in their lives. Research reveals that the vast majority are not into making at all and instead are frittering away their time with a variety of wasteful and unproductive learning activities (Hanway, 2003; Lyons, 2005).

As a nation, we are ignoring the benefits of learning and working with our hands. Frank Wilson, neurologist and author of *The Hand*, reminds us, the hand has a mind of its own, as well as being at one with our minds (Wilson, 1998). To engage the hand is to engage the mind. Schools, therefore, must provide for all students a hand-mind approach to the essential academics. The hand-to-mind pathway is a way to engage all students and deepen their learning, to understand what quality looks like, and through practice and tinkering to apply discipline-based skills. Working the mind without the hands, and without a practice community of adults and young people, produces abstract learners who have difficulty applying what they know to the world around them.

We know that Uno Cygnaeus (Archambault, 1964), father of the Finnish public school system, influenced Sarason, John Dewey (Archambault, 1964), and other thought leaders in education around the world. In Finland, schools do not teach reading until the second grade. Instead, the early school years are devoted to play and making things. Cygnaeus was also the inventor of *sloyd* (from the Swedish *slöjd* for "handiwork," or manual training), a practical hand-mind philosophy that is still in use today in Finland. Although manual, this training is nevertheless decidedly intellectual and academic (Anderson, 2011; Hancock, 2011).

All innovators, from Edison to Einstein, tell us that mistakes made through play are powerful ways of learning. Mihaly Csikszentmihalyi (1996, 1997) writes that flow—a highly productive psychological state—is achieved when work looks like play. Play requires dealing with challenges, but the risks are low and the opportunities for recovery are many.

The most successful companies strive to increase purposeful, and even not-so-purposeful, play into their organizations and culture in order to spark creativity and invention. Stories abound about the most successful and admired companies that offer play, exploration, and interest-focused learning and work as a means of keeping and growing their employees and thereby growing their bottom lines. Through its Time Off program, Google encourages its engineers to spend 20% of their work time on projects that interest them. Some of Google's newer services, such as Gmail, Google News, and AdSense, were developed from this program.

Tinkering is a powerful form of play, and Mark Thompson, a colleague from Australia, provides an excellent description of its connection to productive learning (Big Picture Education Australia, 2011). He describes tinkering as a minor risk-taking activity without any great consequence; it is not goal-directed, nor is there a defined outcome. There are no key performance indicators for tinkering; it is research without a known outcome. Tinkering also allows for failure, an essential component of any process of evolution. Tinkering gives tinkerers a powerful sense of the possibility of things, which surely must be a wellspring of creativity.

The best teachers use play to develop higher-order thinking and tinkering. Their learning opportunities are full of what *ifs* and *why nots*. They provide a bit of serendipity in their work with students and focus on exploration, thinking differently, and "how-might-we" problem-solving. Students can play with materials or an idea.

Use the Real World

The world outside of schools provides abundant settings and contexts in which students can apply what they know. It is through such applications that students understand the messiness and uncertainty of making things work in the real world. Such opportunities allow students to develop tacit understandings and heuristics. There are few substitutes for the learning that results from delivering a product or service that others value.

Schools must take down the walls that separate the learning that students do, and could do, inside of school from the learning they do, and could do, outside. The learning in both settings and contexts must be seamlessly integrated. We call such learning "leaving to learn."

Here is how one of our Big Picture Learning students used the real world to stimulate and support her interests in science:

> Ruth's senior thesis project focused on Haiti. Her mother is Haitian, but Ruth had never been to Haiti to meet her family. After the 2010 earthquake, Ruth connected with a physician who ran a faith-based clinic in Haiti and supported a combination orphanage-school as well. Ruth raised the money for her plane ticket and accompanied Dr. Tom and his group of volunteer physicians to work in the clinic. She went twice and produced a documentary about her trips: about the clinic, the aftermath of the earthquake, and her finding and meeting her family for the first time. Ruth is now on full scholarship in a college premed program.

Her ambition is to become a missionary doctor, like Albert Schweitzer and her friend Dr. Tom.

Schools must provide students with opportunities to learn and work on projects that are nested in the real world of businesses, organizations, and communities. Such projects are not prepackaged around simple problems, but reflect the dynamic complexity of those settings. At one of our Big Picture Learning schools in New York City, several students each semester do internships at the American Museum of Natural History around their interests. The students earn elective and core science credits in subjects like marine biology, ecology, and geology, and some have earned health credits for their work there. The students exhibit their projects, presented as books, graphics, research papers, dioramas, and similar products, all produced at and for the museum and the school. There is always an extensive Q&A session with students, faculty, and museum staff at the end of the semester. Their mentor, the head of the museum's education department, always attends the exhibitions.

These experiences tend to be transformational for students because they have access to knowledge and opportunities usually reserved for undergraduate or graduate students. Aside from conducting their own project work, the students become experts at their exhibits, leading school tours, helping visitors, and categorizing documents used by professionals in the field.

One student decided that working in the Ocean Life hall wasn't enough. She wanted to study marine biology and to work with real ocean life, not just an exhibit. She secured an internship at the Norwalk, Connecticut, aquarium. Rising two days a week at 4.00 a.m., she endured a three-hour round trip train ride to learn more about marine biology and to work alongside experts in the field. She is currently enrolled at Stony Brook University studying marine biology.

Learning in the real world provides opportunities for bringing life to text and text to life, where students are exposed to new forms of visual, graphic, audio, and textual information and to the tactile, hands-on experience that is often part of the world outside of school. Out-of-school experiences move the schools walls further out into the community and render them permeable.

Teachers can encourage students to examine their real-life surroundings together in their community. Students can approach this cooperative examination of nature (or society) by examining the needs perceived by the community, asking open-ended questions about how science is affecting things already, and how empirical and quantitative reasoning might be used to develop initiatives to change the present situation. Small insights at this cooperative level of investigation can lead students to realize how they might seriously change their place (and world) for the better. Such deep and sustained interactions with people and places outside of school helps students develop the understanding and empathy essential for employing the sciences to improve the world.

Link Inside and Outside Learning

It's a struggle for schools to recognize and credit learning that takes place outside of school and outside the curriculum taught in school. For example, we would have liked to report that Aidan did all his research as part of his school-based learning, but we could find no evidence that the school played much of a role—from the identification of the question all the way through to his "solution." We would like to know if Aidan was able to bring his project into school as part of his schoolwork and whether he was able to earn academic credit for his work.

Lest you see these circumstances as anomalies, we checked on the other award winners and found that few did their work as part of their school studies. No surprise there. Typically, schools do not see the work that students do out of school as their responsibility. They see no need to document, assess, or award academic and graduation credit for learning and work that students do outside of school.

How might the school assess the learning and accomplishments? How, for example, would the school take into consideration all those "evaluations" of Aidan's math calculations that came in from every corner of the Internet? Would his work be given a failing grade because he got the wrong answer? Would he be given any credit for identifying the question? For seeing the problem? For thinking creatively about solutions? For taking lots of time to delve into the work? For connecting with others to help him figure things out?

Should not their high school, upon learning what Kate and Louisa accomplished, have "posthumously" awarded them some special credit for observing carefully what so many had overlooked? For designing the study and appropriately using cutting-edge technology? We know that these students eventually formally presented and received recognition for their work elsewhere (Rockefeller University, 2010; Stoeckle & Strauss, 2010).

And what about all those non-science competencies that Aidan needed to master? Many of those were not even academic—his persistence in the face of criticism, his creativity and inventiveness, his self-management of his learning and work, his passion for solving a problem that makes the world a better place. Would school have even noticed those competencies, much less considered them? Yet, these competencies—a blend of knowledge, skills, and dispositions—are at the heart of the scientific process.

CREATE A NEW LEARNING ENVIRONMENT

The recommendations we have made for markedly different learning opportunities cannot realistically be implemented within the existing organizational structure and culture of most schools. Schools need to create a new enabling environment for the learning opportunities we propose. This will require changes in the organization of time, space, faculty, and other human resources.

These major changes would go a long way toward enabling the kind of learning we have described:

- Treat the disciplines as the valuable resources they are but not as the defining organizational structure. Consider, for example, organizing schedules around various types of learning, such as projects, workshops, and lectures.
- Eliminate bells. Provide large chunks of time that can be flexibly arranged at the level of each class.
- Have teachers play a variety of roles in school, and even in the learning and work that students do outside of school.
- Schools must let the inside out and the outside in. They must embrace the expertise that exists in the community.
- Create spaces in schools where students can tinker and make, perhaps even alongside expert practitioners from the community.

Based on our work with creating new out-of-school learning environments, we have identified five essential components for making such learning work well: plans, protocols, people, places, and portfolios:

> *Plans* include a comprehensive student learning plan addressing important academic, social-emotional, and career competencies, a detailed specification of tasks to be accomplished, and a plan for documenting learning. These plans should guide in-school and out-of-school learning and be open to ongoing adjustments.
> *Protocols* include a delineation of the "rules of the road" for learning and work done out of school. There are both school-level and student-specific rules. These need to address such issues as student safety and privacy, logistics, transportation, communication, assessment, and accreditation. Protocols should specify expectations regarding student behavior in the workplace—those soft skills once again.
> *People* include the adults the students will be working with outside of school. Learners must be able to tap into a diverse network of experts, expert practitioners, and peers with and from whom they can learn both offline and online.
> *Places* include the specific organizations and contexts that will serve as the learning sites. These may include a community organization, a workplace, a college, or an online learning platform.

Portfolios include the diverse ways in which student learning and accomplishments will be organized, validated, and communicated. Students must be able to provide evidence—artifacts, logs, journals, and performances—that they have achieved specific academic and career competencies.

HOW MIGHT WE SEE DIFFERENTLY?

These recommendations for programs and practices are derived from a design framework consisting of design questions, design principles, and design requirements. Educators can use the framework for designing and implementing whole new programs or for reconstituting those in place.

Design Questions

Questions such as these can expand thinking about redesigning students' learning opportunities:

- In what ways can students see the science they do as emerging from their lived experience, their needs, and their interests?
- In what ways can students perceive the science they do as reflecting their daily realities (culture, race, home life, community life, etc.)?
- In what ways can students see themselves as users and producers of science?
- In what ways can students intentionally link the science they do with their perceived individual needs? With community needs?
- In what ways can students use science to identify societal and real-life problems and the needs of the local community?

Design Principles

These principles guide our approach to helping all young people develop as tinkerer-scientists:

- Science sometimes asks epistemological questions: How do we know what we think we know? How do we test our assumptions about natural and/or social realities?
- One goal of science instruction should be the creation of active tinkerer-scientists who can leverage their understanding of science to guide future actions and decisions. Simply being able to memorize science facts hardly compares to this ideal.
- The world is the classroom: Doing science requires bringing a life-to-text orientation to science education, complementing the traditional text-to-life approach.

- Science and math knowledge should help students understand and change the world rather than simply personally advance in the world.

Design Requirements

Given this vision and our understanding of the problem, described above, we suggest a set of design requirements that will make a difference without diminishing the pathways for STEM careers, and might even enhance both the quantity and the quality of such pathways.

- Use individual interest and project-based learning as the instructional strategy in all modules, projects, and workshops, as appropriate.
- Employ multidisciplinary approaches to addressing problems and challenges, particularly drawing on the arts and design.
- Provide flexible time structures and allocations so that students have sufficient time for deep practice that enables proficiency on essential learning standards.
- Provide focused learning opportunities to apply creativity and innovation skills in all modules, projects, and workshops, as appropriate.
- Provide multiple ways for students to demonstrate competence, including particularly performances that demonstrate both skill and understanding.
- Provide multiple opportunities for students to get out of school into industry and postsecondary settings and contexts in order to work with adults doing work the students wish to do.
- Provide opportunities for students to use a wide variety of general and specialized technology tools (both hi- and lo-tech) to support their learning and work.
- Provide opportunities to investigate authentic, real-world, real-lived experiences/realities.
- Encourage and support students in thinking and acting entrepreneurially in addressing personal and community needs and challenges.

LET US END WITH A FISH STORY

The movie *Dolphin Tale* (Smith, 2011) provides yet another image of the graduate we want from our K-12 schools. This time a fictional hero, Sawyer, is introduced to science by an encounter with an injured dolphin that blossoms into all-consuming learning and work. Sawyer, an indifferent student who must complete summer school just to move ahead, becomes a serious scientist devoted to obtaining a prosthetic tail for the dolphin.

This work expands to include taking a leadership role in the community on behalf of the local aquarium hospital threatened with closure.

Sawyer's mom initially sides with the school in requiring Sawyer's attendance in summer school, but she comes to understand what the science project has become for Sawyer and allows him to work in the hospital rather than continue on with summer school work. Only after Sawyer's work is recognized by professionals and by the community does the school relent and give Sawyer academic credit for his out of schoolwork. The school probably needed to break a few of its rules to award that credit.

Schools need to use these stories of young learners to guide their design of learning opportunities and learning environments. We have no doubt that if schools can support young people in their interests, our economy and society will have an abundance of scientists and engineers. More importantly, we will have an abundance of citizens who are deeply inquisitive learners who will contribute more generally to their communities and their workplaces.

Aye! And that's no fish story.

REFERENCES

Anderson, J. (2011, December 12). From Finland, an intriguing school-reform model. *New York Times*. Retrieved from: www.nytimes.com/2011/12/13/education/from-finland-an-intriguing-school-reform-model.html?pagewanted=all. Accessed April 1, 2012.

Anderson, L. W., & Sosniak, L. A. (Eds.) (1994). *Bloom's Taxonomy: A forty-year retrospective*. Chicago, IL: National Society for the Study of Education.

Archambault, R. (Ed.) (1964). *John Dewey on education: Selected writings*. New York: The Modern Library.

Berger, R. (2003). *An ethic of excellence: Building a culture of craftsmanship with students*. Portsmouth, NH: Heinemann.

Big Picture Education Australia (2011). *Making it big—BPEA Conference 2011*. Retrieved from: www.bigpicture.org.au/making-it-big-bpea-conference-2011. Accessed March 19, 2012.

Bloom, B. (1985). *Developing talent in young people*. New York: Ballantine Books.

Bornstein, D. (2011). Training youths in the ways of the workplace. *New York Times*. Retrieved from: http://opinionator.blogs.nytimes.com/2011/01/24/an-education-in-the-ways-of-the-workplace/. Accessed April 30, 2012.

Business Wire (2012, February 24). *Time Warner Cable's Connect a Million Minds premieres third episode of It Ain't Rocket Science on NY1 on Saturday, February 25th [press release]*. Retrieved from: www.marketwatch.com/story/time-warner-cables-connect-a-million-minds-premieres-third-episode-of-it-aint-rocket-science-on-ny1-on-saturday-february-2 5th-2012-02-24. Accessed March 13, 2012.

Coyle, D. (2009). *The talent code: Greatness isn't born. It's grown. Here's how*. New York: Bantam Books.

Csikszentmihalyi, M. (1996). *Creativity: Flow and the psychology of discovery and invention*. New York: HarperCollins Publishers.

Csikszentmihalyi, M. (1997). *Finding flow: The psychology of engagement with everyday life.* New York: HarperCollins Publishers.

Drucker, P. F. (1995). *Managing in a time of great change.* New York: Truman Talley Books.

Dwyer, A. (2011). *Aidan: The secret of the Fibonacci sequence in trees [2011 Young Naturalist Award].* Retrieved from: www.amnh.org/nationalcenter/youngnaturalistawards/2011/aidan.html. Accessed March 10, 2012.

Dyson, J. (2011). The missing link between STEM education and jobs of the future. *The Atlantic.* Retrieved from: www.theatlantic.com/technology/archive/2011/06/the-missing-link-between-stem-education-and-jobs-of-the-future/239978. Accessed April 30, 2012.

Eisner, E. (Ed.) (1985). *Learning and teaching the ways of knowing.* Chicago, IL: The National Society for the Study of Education.

Gardner, H. (1999). *The disciplined mind: What all students should understand.* New York: Simon & Schuster.

Hancock, L. (2011). Why are Finland's schools successful? *Smithsonian Magazine, 2012.* Retrieved from: www.smithsonianmag.com/people-places/Why-Are-Finlands-Schools-Successful.html. Accessed April 1, 2012.

Hanway, S. (2003, December 23). *How do teens unwind?* Retrieved from: www.gallup.com/poll/10222/How-Teens-Unwind.aspx. Accessed July 1, 2010.

Hollander, S. (2012, January 5). *A youngster's bright idea is something new under the sun.* Retrieved from: http://online.wsj.com/article/SB10001424052970203550304577138511287470508.html. Accessed January 24, 2012.

Johnston, J. (Writer) (1999). *October sky* [Motion Picture]. C. Gordon, L. J. Franco, M. Sternberg & P. Cramer (Producers). United States: Universal Pictures.

Kamenetz, A. (2011). Why education without creativity isn't enough. *Fast Company.* Retrieved from: www.fastcompany.com/magazine/159/indian-engineers-education. Accessed March 14, 2012.

Leski, K. (2012). *Design intelligences: Kyna Leski's thoughts on navigating the creative process.* Retrieved from: http://designintelligences.wordpress.com/. Accessed May 17, 2012.

Lyons, L. (2005, April 19). *What are teens doing after school?* Retrieved from: www.gallup.com/poll/15943/What-Teens-Doing-After-School.aspx. Accessed July 1, 2010.

Mrpotatohead.net. (n.d.). *Mr. Potato Head on TV and movies.* Retrieved from: www.mrpotatohead.net/tv/tv.htm. Accessed March 13, 2012.

Robinson, K. (2001). *Out of our minds: Learning to be creative.* West Sussex, UK: Capstone Publishing.

Rockefeller University (2010, February 20). *Program for the human environment: Archives for February 20, 2010.* Retrieved from: http://phe.rockefeller.edu/news/archives/1112. Accessed March 13, 2012.

Sarason, S. (2004). *And what do you mean by learning?* Portsmouth, NH: Heinemann.

Schwartz, J. (2008). Fish tale has DNA hook: Students find bad labels. *New York Times,* p. A1. Retrieved from: www.nytimes.com/2008/08/22/science/22fish.html. Accessed April 1, 2012.

Sennett, R. (2008). *The craftsman.* New Haven, CT: Yale University Press.

Smith, C. M. (Writer) (2011). *Dolphin tale* [Motion Picture]. R. Ingber, B. Johnson, & A. A. Kosove (Producers). United States: Warner Brothers.

Stoeckle, K., & Strauss, L. (2010, April 9). *Fish story.* Retrieved from: http://phe.rockefeller.edu/news/wp-content/uploads/2010/02/kate-stoeckle-aaas-feb-2010-v6.pdf. Accessed March 13, 2012.

Symonds, W. C., Schwartz, R. B., & Ferguson, R. (2011). *Pathways to prosperity: Meeting the challenge of preparing young Americans for the 21st century.* Boston, MA: Pathways to Prosperity Project, Harvard Graduate School of Education.

Turckes, S., & Kahl, M. (2011). *What schools can learn from Google, IDEO, and Pixar.* FastCo.DESIGN. Retrieved from: www.fastcodesign.com/1664735/what-schools-can-learn-from-google-ideo-and-pixar. Accessed March 16, 2012.

Walsh, T. (2005). *Timeless toys: Class toys and the playmakers who created them.* Kansas City, KS: Andrews McMeel Publishing.

Willms, J. D., Friesen, S., & Milton, P. (2009). *What did you do in school today? Transforming classrooms through social, academic and intellectual engagement.* Toronto, Ontario: Canadian Education Association.

Wilson, F. R. (1998). *The hand: How its use shapes the brain, language, and human culture.* New York: Pantheon Books.

CHAPTER 13

MANOR NEW TECHNOLOGY HIGH SCHOOL

The New Wave of STEM-Focused Schools

STEVEN ZIPKES

Manor New Technology High School (MNTH) was designed to unlock the hidden talents of underserved students and to inspire them to go to college. The immediate challenge was to get students excited about attending a science, technology, engineering, and math (STEM) campus. The longer-term challenge was to inspire these students to even contemplate college, and then to enable them to attend the college of their choice. That included closing the achievement gap for students coming from low-performing middle and high schools, increasing the high school graduation rate, and finally, getting the students enrolled in college.

In 2006 Manor ISD's high school and middle school were rated Academically Unacceptable by the Texas Education Agency. Today, 84% of MNTH graduates are in college and moving forward.

Until recently, Manor, Texas, about 14 miles northeast of downtown Austin, was a traditional farming community. With a diverse student population that includes 80% economically disadvantaged, 32% limited English proficient, 52% Hispanic, and 24% African American, Manor Independent School District (ISD) faces unique challenges; these include excessive mobility, teachers inadequately prepared to teach this heterogeneous student population, and high staff turnover. With its schools rated unacceptable by the state, the district was urgently aware that it needed to improve its teaching and learning.

Through a partnership with the Texas High School Project, the Texas Governor's Office, and Samsung Semi-Conductor, Manor Independent School District was awarded a $4 million Texas Science, Technology,

Engineering, and Math (T-STEM) grant to open a T-STEM high school: Manor New Tech High, aka MNTH. The target was Manor's underserved youth. The purpose was to create a more diverse college-going population of students interested in the STEM fields.

I was given the charge of designing and implementing MNTH. I had full autonomy to develop not only the curriculum and schedule, but also the graduation requirements. I also had unrestricted freedom to select the staff. I had a proven track record as a high school principal (I had led two Texas high schools to their first-ever Exemplary Rating by the Texas Education Agency), but the Manor opportunity was both uniquely promising and rather frightening.

I began by choosing Andrew Kim, MISD Deputy Superintendent of Schools, Victor Valdez, Director of Technology, and David Greiner, MNTH Dean of Student Services, to serve as my administrative team. We all knew that good teachers are the key to student learning. We hired innovative teachers with passion who wanted to teach differently. We hired teachers who would be leaders in the design and functioning of the school, who would use their own creative ideas rather than textbooks to develop projects. We also wanted the teachers to be collaborators, willing to give and accept critical feedback to each other. The teachers also had to be willing to be friends with and role models for the students. Above all, in our innumerable discussions about how to build a utopian, inquiry-based STEM school, we made sure all staff had a say.

From the beginning, we knew we needed to create a unique school culture to attract and sustain the interest of the Manor high school population. Based on our collective experiences and ideals, we decided to shape all our efforts at this new academy in accord with a new three R's: relationships, relevance, and rigor.

Relationships are needed to get the targeted student population to believe in the school, the staff, and themselves. Relevance is essential for the students to be engaged; otherwise they tune out and turn off, especially when the content is math and science. Finally, rigor is embedded to ensure that students are college-ready and prepared to tackle the work of higher education.

The foundational R, however, is relationship. Many schools try to emphasize rigor first, but that way loses many students. If you do not have a relationship with the students—that is, if you do not know their individual interests, their strengths, their weaknesses, their fears and hopes—they are not going to do anything for you. Plus, they need to know it is safe for them to ask questions or seek advice, and not be belittled. When you work at relationships first, then relevance, and then rigor, you are going to reach all students.

PROJECT-BASED LEARNING

We knew we had to change the traditional delivery of instruction if Manor New Tech wanted to change these students' lives. During my years as a teacher and principal, I had observed that many students are not prepared for deeper levels of learning because they are not being engaged in the application of what they are taught. When students are taught to memorize and regurgitate facts on a standardized test, they respond by wanting only enough information to answer the questions and move on. Could they solve a real-life problem? Probably not.

Manor New Tech adopted project-based learning (PBL) as its primary mode of instruction and applied it to all subjects, from the sciences to language arts. The New Tech Network (NTN), a nonprofit organization based in Napa, California that helps implement innovative public high schools, helped us develop who we are today.

Using project-based learning, the teacher develops projects with students based on the students' particular interests as well as real-world situations. A student in rural Kentucky may have different enthusiasms from a student in Los Angeles, so why use a textbook or canned project that assumes all students are the same?

Project-based learning is a lot of work for both teacher and student. Students usually work in groups. Every project at Manor starts with teachers outlining the Texas state standards for each student and giving detailed assessment rubrics; every project's final assessment requires students to publicly demonstrate their mastery of the standards (through written pieces, oral presentations, dramatic performances, etc.). Besides the state standards, the project must also embed the 21st-century skills of collaboration, oral and written communication, critical thinking, work ethic, organization and time-management skills, effective use of technology, global and community engagement, and numeracy.

When building projects with different students, teachers can be really creative, but at the same time they need to scaffold the students' learning while continuously assessing their progress in a variety of ways throughout the project. The student's final grade is based on both mastery of content and a demonstration of 21st-century skills.

Why do we do all this? Because what project-based learning achieves is to shake students out of their extreme boredom with sit-and-get lectures, worksheets, and textbooks, and instead engage them in talking, interacting, being creative, and sharing stories they have researched and discovered with their peers and teachers—and sometimes the local public. In other words, PBL encourages students to learn the way most people do outside of a typical classroom—through collaboration, critical thinking, communication, and research, not in isolation at a desk by themselves. It is "authentic"—that is, based on real life issues and real-life ways of doing things.

With PBL, students have control over how they learn. They see how the knowledge they possess can be applied to real-world situations, and thus learning becomes relevant to them. PBL gives students the freedom and responsibility to research a subject and present what they have learned to others. The project outlines what they are to cover, but how they do that is up to them. To make sure they are on track and to keep improving, students often use a peer-review process with teachers and other students, called Critical Friends. Teachers, and sometimes peers, prompt them through questions (the process encourages using question in the form of "I like . . ." and "I wonder . . ."), or problems or references to real current or historical situations.

For example, an English teacher and a World History teacher wanted to leverage the extraordinary popularity of the dystopian *The Hunger Games* novels among young people. They decided to team-teach a three-week module called Controlling Factors that would address Texas state world history standards on the rise of totalitarianism and the origins of World War II as well as the English language arts standards of analyzing moral dilemmas in works of fiction.

First the teachers created a newsreel to introduce key vocabulary (e.g., "Mussolini," "totalitarianism," "World War II") to their students. The students created workshops on moral dilemmas based on history as well as on *The Hunger Games*. (One presentation was a student skit on how to treat an escaped prisoner: return him to the Germans, who would kill him, or take him to a medical facility to save his life, a choice that would deplete scarce local resources for the sake of a complete stranger.)

The students' final presentations for this included a multimedia presentation with audience participation about a moral dilemma faced by Nazi concentration camp survivors and a skit dramatizing the moral decisions made by world leaders leading up to the attack on Pearl Harbor (see Edutopia, 2012).

Another example of PBL at Manor New Tech is a multidisciplinary project based on the *Odyssey*. As students read the classic poem about Odysseus' journey home from Troy to Greece, they paralleled his experiences by journeying to a destroyed planet and researching its original state in order to salvage it. Students had to explain how different relationships between geographic regions affected their climate, their settlement patterns—where people settled and why—and the way cultures developed. That is, the students, just as Odysseus, needed to investigate the species, cultures, climates, and geography of a completely unknown territory.

In their public demonstrations, students presented visuals showing the planet's bodies of water and continents, with forests and mountain ranges; they explained and demonstrated how a region's weather is affected by distance from the equator and elevation above sea level.

The goal of this project, and indeed all MNTH projects, was for students to recognize the complex interrelationships among things of all sorts— human, environmental, geographical—and see how things began, changed, and have come to be what they are now.

What Else We Do at Manor New Tech

At Manor New Tech, we look at a STEM education as a way for our students to be successful and give them a path to college. In 2005, students in Texas had to take three years of math and three years of science to graduate. In 2006, when we were designing Manor New Tech, Texas increased the graduation requirements to include four years of math and four years of science. Up to this point, most STEM schools distinguished themselves by providing an additional year of math and science. Manor New Tech, in contrast, decided to provide cross-curricular content instead of teaching each subject in isolation.

For example, we integrated Principles of Engineering into a Fine Arts Theater Design class, so that students design sets and build them in the Theater Design class, and then produce a short play.

The Trimester Schedule

Instead of offering Advanced Placement courses, MNTH created a comprehensive, extensive set of graduation requirements that mandated five years of math, six years of science, and two years of engineering, within the span of four years of high school. To enable students to fulfill this seemingly impossible set of requirements, we had to step away from the known and move to the unknown of a trimester schedule.

Using a trimester schedule addressed two important needs: the graduation requirements and remediation. First, the trimester schedule accelerates the curriculum. Instead of running two 18-week semesters, Manor New Tech runs three 12-week trimesters. A year's worth of work is completed in two 12-week trimesters, leaving a third trimester for remediation if needed.

What happened next demonstrated the power of PBL. Because PBL is so engaging to the students, we quickly found that they were just not failing. Our students have been so successful that to this date, MNTH has not had enough students fail to even offer a remediation class.

A third benefit of the trimester schedule was allowing MNTH to offer more classes than a traditional school calendar year. Because of the trimester schedule, most students actually graduate with six years of math, six years of science, and three years of engineering—that is, more than the requirements stipulate.

Under the trimester schedule, students at Manor New Tech attend five different classes a day, two of which are team-taught, for a total of seven different content credits a day. Each class uses 100% PBL. This means each student always has five classes, and thus five projects at different stages of completion. He or she may be presenting in one class, launching a new project in another, and researching other projects with a group in three other classes. Each student at MNTH on average completes 50 to 65 projects a year, each project lasting an average of three to four weeks.

This schedule also means that each student gives 50 to 65 public speeches every year, or 200 by graduation. At the end of every project, student teams are required to present their product to a panel; the panel usually consists of experts in the project's field, parents, and community members. When students know from the beginning that they must make a presentation to an external panel, they find their projects inherently more rewarding; this requirement also sharpens their oral presentation skills.

Knowledge is not useful unless it can be communicated clearly to others. For MNTH students, the 21st-century skill of proficient oral communication offers several practical benefits. It helps level the college-admissions field for MNTH students: when a college admissions officer sees five math credits, six science credits, and two credits of engineering on the high school transcript of a student who lacks top SAT or ACT scores, that student usually gets an interview; when MNTH students get an interview, their oral communication skills are so good that most are admitted to the college of their choice. An added bonus is that the number of speeches MNTH requires effectively improves students' time-management skills.

The Engineering Business Model

PBL at Manor New Tech replicates an engineering business model in which students are accountable to each other to complete their project. Students work in collaborative groups unless they have been fired. They develop and sign contracts outlining each member's role and responsibilities, collaborate on the finished product, and must meet specific deadlines throughout. If a student does not abide by or fulfill the contract, the group must take corrective actions or begin the firing process, whereby group members document contract violations, their efforts to work with and turn around the violating student, and all email correspondence and face-to-face contacts. They submit all this evidence to the teacher for a teacher/violating student conference. If all these steps have been satisfied and the violating student shows no improvement, the group may fire the violator, who must complete the project alone, leaving any previous work with the group.

A client of a real-world engineering firm expects a project report by a specific date, and the firm expects and demands that the project be ready for presentation despite any individual differences within a project team. Because the school replicates practices from the real world, students develop an understanding of the relevance of timelines, the importance of collaboration, and the need for a strong work ethic, all real 21st-century skills.

Student Engagement in Learning

PBL, with its focus on relevant real-life problems, offers a natural framework for incorporating global and community issues into teaching and learning.

Further, our students are active participants in what is happening in today's world. Social media, instant access to information, and youth activism have led our students to be more aware of what is happening not only in their own backyards, but also across the globe. Our students are creating comic books, making movies, developing web pages, designing video games, and developing web or iPhone applications through their project designs. Some projects have authentic impact outside the school. For example, one MNTH student created a college scholarship, "Make DREAMs Reality" (named after the DREAM Act), for MNTH graduates whose parents are illegal immigrants. This sort of relevance has proven to be key to real engagement for our students.

Many NMTH students are continuously refining and improving their projects even after the projects have been completed and graded. When students post their products online or give them to interested parties, they no longer regard their project as an assignment, but rather as an extension of their student group and their creativity. This type of engagement is not generally seen in traditional classrooms.

Relationships with Others

Using PBL has helped the school develop business relationships and higher education partnerships as well as impact the community. It has also helped the students improve their personal relationships with their families and the community.

The numerous businesses that visit yearly have told us repeatedly that they are not necessarily looking to hire candidates who are able to regurgitate facts they learned in college. They tell us that they seek candidates who have knowledge about their field they acquired in college, but who are not experts. They tell us they can and will teach their employees what they want them to know within their company, but what they cannot teach is the ability to communicate orally and in writing, to collaborate, to think critically—and finally, they cannot develop someone's work ethic. As part of their hiring process, many of our business partners put candidates together in a room with a problem and watch them all day as they attempt to develop a solution. They are looking for the very 21st-century skills that are embedded and assessed in every project at NMTH.

Numerous businesses come through and engage with our students in ways they have never engaged in traditional schools. Our students are aware of their own learning process and able to tell visitors what they are working on and how it connects to larger issues; they have developed excellent presentation skills. As a result, businesses develop partnerships with us, offering internships to our students, opportunities for our students to make daylong visits to their locations, or professional outreach from their engineers.

We also have relationships with various universities. Professors from universities around the country come visit us to see what we are doing. The University of Texas UTeach teacher program offers a semester-long Project-Based Instruction course that uses MNTH as a professional development site for its student teachers. Professors in the Sam Houston State University College of Education have actually attended our PBL training.

MNTH has changed our students' relationships with others. For example, we require students to perform 50 hours of community service to graduate. Our students help run the community food bank, a homeless shelter; they man water stations for local 10k runs, work different stations at the Austin Trail of Lights (a mile-long holiday festival of music and lighted scenes). By graduation, most students perform well over 100 hours, impacting their community as well as improving their own self-awareness and sense of purpose.

In addition, PBL has significantly improved students' relationships with their families. Numerous accounts from parents and students validate this impact. Students report, for example, that PBL promotes their ability to solve family-relationship problems as well as to talk with their parents about their projects in detail instead of just casually brushing off what they learned in school that day. In addition, the oral communication component of PBL has significantly impacted students' ability to speak in public, at home with their parents and siblings, in church, and in the community.

The Students

MNTH was designed to be a small school with 400 students. Each incoming class would be 100 students, and we needed a system to admit a student body that reflected the demographics of the district while also ensuring that the target students in particular had the opportunity to enroll. We developed a blind lottery to select students for admission. Unlike many magnet and charter schools, or math and science academies, MNTH has only one admission requirement: the student must have been promoted to ninth grade (because MNTH offers no eighth-grade courses). Students fill out an application for the blind lottery that asks for their name and address, the middle school they attended, and whether they have any siblings attending MNTH. No other information is required. There are no grade requirements, no state test scores are looked at, nor is any norm-referenced information asked for. We accept applications for about three weeks; the time and date are written on each application at the time of submission. On the day of the lottery, the applications are separated into a box for girls and one for boys, then drawn alternately from each box. Once 100 applications are drawn, the remaining applications are put on a waitlist in the order of their submission by date and time. Thus, it benefits students to turn their applications in as soon as possible.

For school year 2009/10, two years after it opened, Manor New Tech received 180 applications, representing 40% of the entire eighth-grade cohort in Manor. This was significant, and, in recognition, the District designated Manor New Tech as a research-and-design facility, disseminating and implementing its best practices throughout its schools.

VALIDATION

A school's effectiveness is generally measured by the state assessment scores of its students, and our practices needed to be validated. Validity can take on many forms, and, depending on a school's demographics and target population, validity can be varied and structured in many ways. But in general, validation entails some measure of achievement or improvement. When Manor New Tech opened its doors in 2007/08, our students came from a low-performing middle school and a low-performing high school. What was unexpected was how fast MNTH took off and the impact it had not only on the students, but also on the district and community as a whole.

Student Attendance

By not offering any Advanced Placement courses, we chose to not target the usually higher-performing and motivated students. In our first years, our demographics were very representative of the district: 47% Hispanic, 24% African American, 29% white, and 1% Asian/Pacific Islander. Our student population was 54% economically disadvantaged, 5% English Language Learners, 11% special education, and 44% classified as at risk. Many had attendance issues, severe gaps in their learning, very poor state test scores, and discipline issues. Moreover, many had not passed the math state assessment since the third and fifth grades.

After Manor New Tech's first year, it became evident that project-based learning was making an impact. Our attendance rate for the year was 97%, a higher attendance rate than any other school in Manor ISD, including the seven elementary schools that have a captive audience since the students are dropped off by school bus and must wait for the bus to take them home. MNTH has made such an impact in the lives of the students that over the last five years we have maintained an attendance rate of over 96% each year. In fact, we have a difficult time getting students to go home after school. Even though school lets out at 3.35, so many students stay after school working on projects that we have to run a 5.00 bus to take students home. This is a very good problem to have and demonstrates the students' commitment to their projects.

Another measure of effectiveness is teacher retention. MNTH had three years of 100% teacher retention and had not lost one teacher. By our fifth year, we lost several teachers for a variety of personal reasons, but not one left for a regular classroom with traditional teaching from textbooks. It would be fair to say that once a teacher has been exposed to project-based learning, and the autonomy and ownership of creating projects, it would be extremely difficult to return to direct teaching voluntarily.

Student Achievement Scores

In education today, no criteria are more widely used to establish validity than students' academic achievements. Over the last four years, Manor New Tech has shown dramatic increases in students' assessment scores in math, science, English language arts, and social studies, the four areas currently tested in the state of Texas. In order to fully understand where our students are and the specific gains they have made, we measure our students in several ways. We graph our students' overall state-test scores against those of the state as a whole and the district's comprehensive high school, Manor High; and we chart our students in cohort groups of their eighth-grade state assessment scores upon entering Manor New Tech against the academic gains or losses shown by the time they take the exit exams in math, science, English language arts, and social studies in the 11th grade. In the first scenario, Manor New Tech students have outperformed the state and Manor High School's passing rates for "All Students" in the four consecutive years the students at Manor New Tech have tested.

Another measure used to identify a school's performance is to measure the growth or loss of academic achievement in its student subpopulations. This measure is a distinct disadvantage for schools with a diverse student population or a large economically disadvantaged population. Often, they are compared with schools with homogeneous student bodies or with a very small economically disadvantaged population. The true measure of a school's effectiveness is when the comparison is between the exit scores and entrance scores of the exact same students. Call it value-added or cohort scores, this type of measure gives a true and accurate measure of students' four-year academic gains or losses, because economic background and subpopulations become irrelevant when students are compared only with themselves. When examining Manor New Tech's cohort groups, the huge academic gains of the students from the time they entered Manor New Tech to the time they exited from their exams in the 11th grade are clearly identifiable and documented. Some cohorts have almost a 30% gain in their math and science scores. To date, there has been no educational loss for cohorts since the school's inception. These data show that incorporating 21st-century skills and allowing students opportunities for agency do not reduce rigor or fail to meet state standards if projects are designed correctly.

After High School: Graduation Rates and College Enrollment

Among the most crucial criteria for measuring the value of the school's design are the rates of student graduation, college readiness, and acceptance into or enrollment in college.

In 2009/10 Manor New Tech graduated its first class, with 100% of its senior class completion rate and a 0% dropout rate. Every one of the seniors was accepted into college, 84% into four-year colleges and universities, with 62% of all seniors considered first-generation college-bound. The following year, 2010/11, MNTH graduated its second class, and again 100% of the seniors completed high school with a 0% dropout rate. Of these, 97% were accepted into college, 80% into four-year colleges and universities. Like the graduates before them, 50% of these seniors were classified as first-generation college-bound. According to the National Student Clearinghouse, 84% of our students are still in college and moving forward.

External Reports and Honors

Another measure of effectiveness for Manor New Tech's design and practices is external validation. Since 2007, we have been the subject of a remarkable number of external studies whose findings validate our best practices, student academic gains, and as well as staff support and ownership.

Studies have been written on our PBL practices (e.g., Johnson, Smith, Smythe, & Varon, 2009; Yáñez, Schneider, & Leach, 2009). MNTH is currently participating in two case studies: an NSF-funded study by George Washington University on STEM-focused high schools, and a University of Texas study on teachers. We have been invited to make innumerable presentations at educational conferences around the country.

We have also been awarded great honors by institutions such as Harvard University and the U.S. Department of Education (in 2010, Secretary of Education Arne Duncan highlighted MNTH School as a model school for reaching underserved youth in his speech to the Association of American Publishers Annual Meeting). We have hosted several conferences for key associations.

And thus Manor New Tech has become a national STEM leader as well as a leader in school redesign.

Systemic Change

Ultimately, validity derives from the potential for systematic change. Can Manor New Technology be scaled up across the district for all students? In 2009, Manor New Tech designed and developed Think Forward: A Project-Based Learning Institute. Think Forward is a four-day institute where visiting teachers are embedded in the school for four days and our practitioners teach other practitioners the processes of developing projects from modules we wrote. Currently, MNTH's Think Forward has trained over 300 teachers in Manor ISD as well as over 300 teachers in seven states across the country and in Mexico. Importing the best practices and successes from MNTH, Manor Independent School District has converted one elementary campus, Decker Elementary School, into a project-based learning school, and one middle school campus, Decker Middle School, into one of eight New Tech middle schools in the country incorporating project-based learning and joining the New Tech Network. Manor ISD has revised its teacher hiring practices to reflect its new 21st-Century Teacher Hiring Protocol. The MISD Board adopted into the district's Graduate Profile the 21st-century skills of collaboration, critical thinking, communication, work ethic, and digital citizenship, and has declared that all students in Manor ISD will eventually be taught through project-based learning, a pedagogical shift for the entire district. And it all began with the start-up and success of Manor New Technology High School.

Does Manor New Tech face challenges? Of course! Some of ours are how to keep students excited about projects year after year; how to keep juniors and seniors from transferring to a different school with fewer graduation requirements in math, science, and engineering; how to prevent teacher burnout; how to create a blended learning model that incorporates project-based learning and challenge-based learning and maintain an environment of mobile learning consisting of anytime, anywhere, and anyplace learning.

As practitioners, we need to embrace mobile learning outside the classroom, such as content from iTunes University, and create an environment such that students want to come to school every day.

As educators, we need to keep working, but the results are worth it.

REFERENCES

Duncan, A. (2010). Using technology to transform schools—remarks by Secretary Arne Duncan at the Association of American Publishers Annual Meeting. Retrieved from: www2.ed.gov/news/speeches/2010/03/03032010.html . Accessed December 9, 2012.

Edutopia (2012). *Project-based learning: Success start to finish: Manor New Technology High School, Manor, TX.* Retrieved from: www.edutopia.org/stw-project-based-learning-best-practices and www.edutopia.org/stw-project-based-learning-best-practices-new-tech-video. Accessed December 9, 2012.

Johnson, L. F., Smith, R. S., Smythe, J. T., & Varon, R. K. (2009). *Challenge-based learning: An approach for our time.* Austin, TX: The New Media Consortium. Retrieved from: www.nmc.org/pdf/Challenge-Based-Learning.pdf. Accessed December 9, 2012.

Yañez, D., Schneider, C. L., & Leach, L. F. (2009). *Summary of selected findings from a case study of Manor New Technology High School.* Texas High School Project. Austin, TX: University of Texas, Charles A. Dana Center. Retrieved from: http://www.utdanacenter. org/downloads/products/manornewtech_casestudy.pdf. Accessed December 9, 2012.

INDEX